IN THE SHADOW
OF DEATH

IN THE SHADOW OF DEATH

The Story of a Medic on the Burma Railway 1942 – 1945

by

Idris James Barwick

Pen & Sword
MILITARY

First published in Great Britain in 2005 by
Pen & Sword Military
an imprint of
Pen & Sword Books Ltd
47 Church Street
Barnsley
South Yorkshire
S70 2AS

ISBN 1 84415 246 4

A CIP catalogue record for this book is
available from the British Library

Typeset in Sabon by
Phoenix Typesetting, Auldgirth, Dumfriesshire

Printed and bound in England by
CPI UK.

Pen & Sword Books Ltd incorporates the Imprints of Pen & Sword
Aviation, Pen & Sword Maritime, Pen & Sword Military, Wharncliffe
Local History, Pen & Sword Select, Pen & Sword Military Classics
and Leo Cooper.

For a complete list of Pen & Sword titles please contact
PEN & SWORD BOOKS LIMITED
47 Church Street, Barnsley, South Yorkshire, S70 2AS, England
E-mail: enquiries@pen-and-sword.co.uk
Website: www.pen-and-sword.co.uk

Dedication

My dear Mother

**The Best and Truest of My Many Friends
Who Died in the Jungle**
Padre John Foster Haig
Private Howell Griffiths
Driver Kenneth Scovell
Corporal Dick Richards
Driver 'Darky' Ross
Driver Bob Blanchard
Lance Corporal Matt Hellens

The Best of Pals Who Survived the Jungle Epic
Padre Noel Duckworth
Lieutenant William S. Mitchell
Staff Sergeant Gordon Davies
Corporal Gordon Gleeson
Sergeant Les Brand
Driver Gwyn Williams
Sergeant Jack Swales
Corporal Jim Payne
John Hawkins
Norman Brunkie (Australia)
Sidney Rodrigues (Malaya)

All Those Who Slaved on the Railway of Death

All Members, Past and Present, of the Far East Prisoners of War
Association, especially Douglas Skippen, who assisted in the
publication of this book.

Contents

Foreword

by

Alan Barnsley MRCS LRCP BA

I have read Mr Barwick's book with enjoyment and constant interest.

Those who slaved and suffered on the Burma – Siam Railway deserve to be remembered in just this simple way. There is not, I imagine, a man who served in any part of the recent World War who will not be stirred by the events which Mr Barwick records so sincerely and modestly in these pages.

It is fortunate that one of the survivors of that terrible experience should have been gifted with the patience and sensitivity necessary for the making of this record. For myself, I shall be glad to have his published work sitting, side by side with Sir Winston Churchill's *War Memoirs*, on my library shelf.

374 Loose Road
Maidstone
Kent

Prologue

Idris James Barwick was born on 25 March 1907 in Neath, Wales. He was one of twelve children born to William and Bessie Naish Barwick. The family was poor but very loving. Idris was a happy, impish young man who completed an elementary school education and then followed his father and brothers into the coal mines. While still in his twenties, he moved to London, where he became a bus driver and married his sweetheart, Ruby Jones.

They began their family in 1931, when Isobel was born. Anne and Bob soon followed. With the storm of war brewing in Europe, Idris joined the Territorial Army. He had been too young to fight in the First World War, as his father and brothers had; all, thanks be to God, returned unharmed. The Second World War would be Idris's war. At the age of thirty-two he was one of the first men to set foot in France to face the Germans, serving in the Ammunition Supply Company of the Royal Army Service Corps. Later, in the Far East, though through no choice of his, he would change his area of expertise from that of a driver to medicine. There were many men who would come to owe their survival on the Burma-Siam railway to his devoted and diligent care.

This book is his story.

His daughter Elizabeth has written:

These pages were written during the years following the Second World War by a gentle man trying to recover from a nightmare. He died in December 1975 and was not able to see his book published. To honour his memory, his family laboured to fulfil his dream – a task so willingly undertaken for one who we so dearly loved.

Reverie

Give me the woods with their leafy trees,
Bluebells and birds and bumble bees,
A quiet grove and a rippling brook,
Some Fern and moss, and a useful book.

Give me the sunbeams struggling through,
The leaves that gleam with morning dew,
Give me the thought of who doth give,
Yes, God in Heaven still doth live.

I see God's hand around me now,
In all the trees and every bough,
I hear His voice on the morning breeze,
Like music wafted through the trees.

I see the beauty of simple things,
The butterfly with painted wings,
It flits and flutters and passes by,
So short its life and soon to die.

The spider's web appeals to me,
The greatest marvel there could be,
A thought and a lesson it doth give,
That all must work and plan to live.

The bees, the wasps, with silver wings,
They're interesting, but mind their stings,
All have a purpose here on Earth,
Which we must study to know their worth.

So let us use the sense of sight,
And reason out the wrong and right,
Of many things that we detest,
God is the maker, and He knows best.

William Barwick

Introduction

This book is the personal narrative of an Other Rank serving with the Royal Army Service Corps as Regimental Nursing Orderly and taken prisoner by the Japanese in February 1942.

I have written of my experiences – of what I have seen, what I have heard, the things that I have done and of my reaction to a very tragic adventure.

Much of what I have written may sound ridiculous or fantastic and, in many cases, exaggerated. What I have said is true.

In order to keep as closely as possible to that truth, essentially, I have described my own experiences in order to compare them with those of the others who suffered on the 'Jungle March' and so to portray a true picture of the endurance of my fellow prisoners.

Wherever possible, I checked the stories of other men's experiences which were related to me and I am prepared to believe them.

I have given some gruesome details of men who died in the jungle because I wanted to give the true facts as I saw them, with my own eyes. In doing so, I apologize to any relative to whom anything I have described may cause pain. I have felt it was essential to give this true account of the living hell under which we existed in the hope that it may aid the unfortunate survivors who are now suffering from the effects of their lives as prisoners of war in Japanese hands and enlist help and understanding from those authorities who might otherwise be unsympathetic.

If what I have written will do some good, I will have achieved my purpose.

SOLILOQUY

When sweet thoughts bring sad ones to the mind

William Wordsworth

Have you ever felt on top of the world – really glad to be alive? Have you ever walked through a wood in spring when the air is sweet with the scent of pine trees? If you have, then you will have some idea of how I am feeling on this warm May morning in 1946 as I walk leisurely through the woods of Wye, one of the beauty spots of Kent.

I will not go through the details of the beauty around me. It is sufficient to say that the shadows, the rabbits that scuttle through the undergrowth as I approach, and the thousand and one things that fascinate the lover of the countryside, now bring a lump to my throat.

Why should I have that lump in my throat? A moment ago I was enjoying myself, then I was reminded by pain in my legs of captivity and its unpleasantness. The pain gnaws away maddeningly. It is something from which I can get very little relief. During my climb up the slight incline to the woods, I puffed and blew and my head swam. For a little while, I was quite dizzy. Of course my ill-health is a legacy of my life as a prisoner of war. It reminds me very clearly of things I'd like to forget. Those memories make me so bitter and melancholy. How can I get rid of them? It is not easy, especially when I get such painful reminders.

I sit down and, from where I sit on the summit of the hill in Wye, just above the crown, I can see for miles. Little hamlets, cattle grazing, traffic entering and leaving Ashford on the Maidstone-Folkstone road, a train steaming lazily away from a village halt. Near and around me the long grass swaying in the breeze. Everything is so peaceful. I close my eyes, the quiet beauty of this spot is really overpowering and I doze. I jerk back to wakefulness and reach up and slap my neck. I am bitten by an insect, nothing serious, but it made me jump and I am back in the jungle again. I feel I must do something about these wandering thoughts. I wonder, what if I go over the whole experience again? In short, if I tell my story and get the whole thing off my chest. I wonder if it will help? I have got quite a lot of time on my hands, as I am convalescing. My employers have given me light employment and I find that I am free at Wye from 8 a.m. to 5 p.m. for five days a week – time to roam the hills, walk along the stream and, at leisure, time to write my story.

I. J. B.

Glossary of Terms and Abbreviations

AA or Ack Ack	Anti-aircraft
Bully	Tinned corned beef
Chink	A Chinese
CO	Commanding Officer (normally a Lieutenant Colonel)
CSM	Company Sergeant Major
Division (going to)	Colloquialism for 'going to Divisional Headquarters'
GOC	General Officer Commanding a Division or equivalent
GOC-in-C	General Officer Commanding-in-Chief (Normally a Lieutenant General's appointment)
Gula Malacca	Palm sugar
Gunners	See RA
MI Room,	Medical Inspection Room – the MO's surgery
MO	Medical Officer

Mossies	Mosquitoes
Nip	Soldiers' slang for Japanese
OC	Officer Commanding (of a Company-sized unit)
OR	Other Rank (a soldier below the rank of Sergeant)
Ordnance	Royal Army Ordnance Corps (Note 2)
Padre	Army Chaplain
Provost	Military Police
Railway of Death	The Burma-Siam Railway, built by the Japanese using mainly POW labour
RA	Royal Artillery, known colloquially as 'the Gunners'
RAF	Royal Air Force
RAOC	See Note 2
RAMC	Royal Army Medical Corps
RASC	See Note 1
Rations	Soldiers' food
RE	Royal Engineers, known colloquially as 'the Sappers'
RNO	Regimental Nursing Orderly
Rookie	Recruit
Sappers	See RE
Speedo	Japanese exhortation to hurry
Supply Point	See Note 1
Thailand	The Kingdom of Siam, long the homeland of the Thais, became Thailand in 1939. However, the old name lingered on in daily conversation for some years.
Yasumi	POW were on the march.

Notes

1. The Royal Army Service Corps (RASC) was responsible for the organization of Supplies and Transport throughout the Army. Within the Division a Commander RASC had command of the Divisional Column RASC and was the adviser to the GOC on Supply and Transport. The Corps was concerned with consumable items – ammunition, food and petroleum products. Some of its transport companies were specialized e.g. 55 (Ammunition) Company, the Divisional Troops Company provided support for those units of the Division which were not brigaded and also contained some specialized elements such as the Field Bakery. When the Division was on operations, the RASC would establish Supply Points from which the brigades could draw. At times the RASC would deliver right forward to units to save time in emergency and to save double handling of stocks.

2. The Royal Army Ordnance Corps (RAOC), usually referred to as Ordnance, was responsible for all aspects of technical support – the issue and repair of vehicles and weapons, the provision of spare parts and 'non consumables' such as uniform and hardware. As the war progressed the newly-formed Royal Electrical and Mechanical Engineers took over the repair function but at the time of the fall of Singapore it was still an Ordnance responsibility.

IN THE SHADOW
OF DEATH

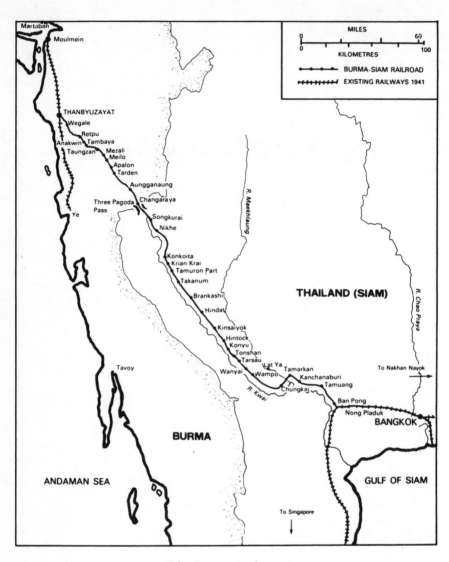

The Burma Railway

Part One

From Gourock to Changi

Chapter One

A Voyage to Disaster

*Did you think life would be all credit? Did you think you would
escape the bearing of a Cross? Did you hope for easy paths and
roses all the way? Did you dream that every dawn would bring
a perfect day?*

*Life is not like that at all. We were not meant to be safe and
happy all the time, just living peacefully, never being made to
think or to fight. If the darkness never came, we'd never see the
light.*

Patience Strong

The fighting in France and the evacuation from Dunkirk had given
me my first taste of war and the heartbreak of losing my pals in
action, an experience that would be repeated a thousandfold in
the years to come. Yet it never seemed to lose its intensity.

On Tuesday 29 October 1941, as a member of 18 Divisional
Troops Company Royal Army Service Corps, and in company
with some 2,600 other troops, I sailed from Gourock in the Polish
Motor Ship *Sobieski* for an unknown destination.

As part of a well-escorted convoy, we crossed the Atlantic to
Halifax, Nova Scotia. On the evening of 7 November, as we
approached our destination, our ship's Captain spoke to us all
over the intercom. He said that we would soon be leaving his ship
to start upon the second stage of a very mysterious adventure.
Where we would end up, he could not say. He wished us
Godspeed and good luck. His words gave rise to much comment

3

and conjecture. Much was to happen to us and there would be terrible hardship and suffering in the years that followed before we would see him again.

On arrival in Halifax, we were transferred to a former American luxury liner of 36,000 tons, the USS *Mount Vernon*, which had been converted to trooping. Of course we did not know then that, on that very day, the Japanese had attacked the American naval base in the Pacific, Pearl Harbor, and that, within a matter of hours, the United States would have come into the war, having declared war on both Japan and Germany. So, naturally, we were very surprised to find ourselves on an American ship. However, she proved more comfortable than the *Sobieski* and the crew were friendly, so we quickly settled ourselves in to enjoy our voyage into the unknown. Sailing down the American eastern seaboard, we came to Trinidad and thence across the South Atlantic to Cape Town, where we were greeted with overwhelming kindness and hospitality. While there, we learned not only the news about Pearl Harbor but also that two important British ships, the *Prince of Wales* and the *Repulse* had been sunk by the Japanese off the Malayan Peninsula. So now we knew that we too might find ourselves fighting the Japanese, although our own destination remained a mystery – from Cape Town we might have gone to the Middle East, India or the Far East. During an oppressively hot and sticky Christmas in Mombasa, the secret was broken. We learned from the crew of a cruiser alongside us, that we were heading for Singapore and they would be escorting us. Following a wandering course across the Indian Ocean, with a refuelling stop in the Maldive islands, which gave us our first glimpse of the beauties of the tropics, we finally arrived at Singapore on 13 January 1942 – an unlucky 13th if ever there was one.

During the voyage, I was appointed batman to Lieutenant Mitchell. As our Company had only been formed just fourteen days before we left England, we had to be sorted out and formed into platoons during the voyage. One day, Mr Mitchell said to me, 'I see from your pay book that you've done a first aid course. The Company Commander has decided that you are to be the Regimental Nursing Orderly for our Company.' I objected, for I had had no practical experience of first aid. However, Mr Mitchell insisted and, since orders are made to be obeyed, I became a Regimental Nursing Orderly. Little did I guess what a milestone in my life that appointment was going to prove.

Singapore

As we approached the island, we could hear the air raid sirens being sounded; that wailing sound we had come to know so well in Britain. I heard an officer say, 'Now we're in for it'. Twenty-seven planes could be seen approaching from the north with ack-ack puffs appearing all around them. Just then it began to rain. It came down in torrents. I had never seen tropical showers. This one was a real snorter. In a few minutes, vision had been reduced to a few yards, but that rain was our saviour since the Japs couldn't see us. So we sailed safely into the dock.

On our way in, I had glimpses (through the rain) of the Island. It looked very colourful. The buildings appeared very costly, with coloured roofs, of green or red tiles and cream or white supporting pillars. The coconut palms, banana trees, and tropical flowers in the gardens all adding up to the brilliant scene in front of us, and offering a promise of pleasant times on this tropical island fortress. However, at that moment we were getting very wet and we disembarked in torrential rain. We were rushed onto waiting lorries. The one I got on was covered with tarpaulin so I kept reasonably dry. The lorry that followed was open and on it was Old Bob Blanchard, the Officers' Mess cook and a great character. He was having the soaking of his life but roaring, happily, with laughter. He shouted at us, 'I'll be all right when I can have a bath!'

We soon arrived at Tanglin Barracks, which we had been told were the most luxurious barracks in the world. We found this to be true – for the officers, at least.

Meanwhile, some of our infantry units were immediately sent up north, to help stem the advance of the Japs. Our Company was to remain in Singapore to collect and then deliver supplies to the forward units in northern Malaya.

We had barely started to settle into our new quarters when we heard our first air raid warning. Twenty-seven Japanese aircraft dropped bombs on the Island and cleared off. We saw six Brewster Buffalo fighters of the Royal Air Force bravely taking to the air to drive them off but, in truth, they could do little for they were hopelessly antiquated and under-armed and so no match for the modern machines flown by the enemy. When I explained to some lads from the Manchester Regiment, who had been out in the Far East pretty well from the outset of the war and knew nothing about the Blitz or the Battle of Britain at first hand, that some Hurricanes had arrived in our convoy and would soon be able to compete with the Japs, they were quite bucked to think that, at least, the tables might be turned on 'the little yellow bastards'. However, having seen two Hurricanes streaking across the sky, about three days later, cheered by us all on the ground, we were then bitterly disappointed that we saw no more of them. The Japs had been tipped-off and had destroyed all the Hurricanes on the ground. A severe blow. *No only a few come in Crates had to Be Put togethr*

Singapore seemed to be a hive of activity. Everyone hurried about full of importance, and all were draped in some kind of uniform. Had I met a Jap I'm sure I would not have known him as such. While in Singapore City after an air raid, I noticed that the native quarter had been bombed badly, and that gangs were out clearing up the debris. Lorries were being loaded with bodies of men, women and children. They were being picked up by the shoulders and feet and flung into the lorries where they flopped like animal carcasses, some with heads missing. Most were just lumps of bloody mangled flesh and bone. It was a dreadful sight and it made me feel quite sick. I thought to myself, 'What if I, as a Medical Orderly, get men smashed like this to attend to?' I offered a silent prayer that such would not be the case, and if it was, that I would have the guts to deal with it.

During the ten days we spent in Tanglin I divided my time between the Officers' Mess, working for my officer, Mr Mitchell, and the Medical Inspection Room working under our Medical Officer (MO) Captain Grant and his orderly, Lance Corporal Matt Hellens. The MI Room frightened me, with its shelves of bottles, containing drugs, medicines, disinfectants and antiseptics and the MO's instruments. Matt had quite a good knowledge of all this stuff and I at once set about learning about the contents of the bottles, their uses and dosages. My motivation was the fear of a court martial for killing someone by giving them poison by mistake.

Matt was a good lad and helped me quite a lot. What I learned from him was to stand me in very good stead when I was left to cope on my own. I was scared stiff that I would have a casualty to deal with who would die because of my inefficiency or lack of knowledge.

The Officers' Mess was where the British officers had spent their leisure hours during peacetime, living much like the idle rich and, so I was told, much more snobbish. The Mess overlooked a small golf course. One day, as I looked out from the upper veranda, I was reminded of Drake and his game of bowls. There were three officers playing golf. The Japs were reported to be advancing down Malaya and the air raid warning had sounded. However, our gallant officers were finishing their game and 'be blowed to the Japs'. Then a few bombs dropped a mile or so away, grabbing our gallant officers' attention; they promptly did credit to the fastest milers of our day. I learned later that these officers were from one of the infantry battalions defending and holding positions in Malaya, but they had somehow found time to visit Singapore for a game of golf and an evening in the city, despite the Japs, who were advancing down the peninsula. This was one of the many incidents we saw of indifference being shown by people in authority. One choice remark I overheard, when an officer was ridiculing the Japs was, 'Before too many days we will have the little bastards' guts for boot laces'.

One of our Lieutenants in charge of a convoy was detailed to pick up vital stores for delivery somewhere in Malaya. When he arrived at the warehouse on a Saturday afternoon, he found the place locked up. It took some time to find the Colonel in charge of the warehouse, who was most annoyed at being disturbed on his weekend off. He stated this in very choice language pointing out that it was Saturday and didn't everyone know that the warehouse closed early on Saturdays for the weekend. Our Lieutenant explained that the stores were urgently needed for our troops in action up north. The Colonel then explained that his coolies had gone home for the weekend so he couldn't do anything about it. The Lieutenant volunteered to find loaders but was told that there would be trouble with the coolies. He offered to try to persuade them to work on Sunday morning. He then made certain remarks for which he was told he would be reported for insubordination.

Next morning the convoy returned at 7 a.m. but there were no Colonel or coolies. Our Lieutenant burst open the doors, directed the loading and delivered the goods twenty-four hours late.

Troops continued to arrive in town from the fighting area. They had tragic tales to tell of retreat down the peninsula, and of how our men were dying by the hundreds in marshes and swamps in the jungle. Some of these men who drifted into Singapore had lost touch with their units, or in some cases they were deserters.

But my company was quite comfortably installed in Tanglin and I considered that I was having a reasonably good time, despite the fact that the Japanese were only a few hundred miles away and advancing rapidly on Singapore. Our chief worry at this time was the air raids and at night a real dread of anything that crawled. I had been told that there were plenty of scorpions, tarantulas, centipedes and snakes. At the thought of these, a chill ran up and down my spine. Every night before retiring, I folded my clothes carefully and put them under my bedding, the bedding first being well shaken. Then my boots would be wrapped in paper and tucked under the bottom of my mattress. Then I would get into bed and tuck my mosquito net well under the mattress. I was taking no chances. During the night I would be hot and sweat profusely, but the warning buzz of the mosquitoes and the dread of crawlers and creepers kept me rolling and turning under my net.

During my short stay at Tanglin I had had very few patients to attend to, just the usual little troubles; cut fingers, scratches and headaches, and a few temperatures and pulses to record. But I was gaining some experience. Matt and I were kept very busy packing for the move. What a big job it was, packing away the bottles, since we were taking everything we could with us.

Chapter Two

With Our Backs to the Sea

At 2 p.m. on 23 January, our little convoy of lorries pulled out on our way to the new location, Holland Village. When we arrived there we were very indignant to find that our campsite was in a rubber plantation and that the underbrush and grass was, in some places, three feet high. We ran our lorries in off the road and proceeded to cut the underbrush, which was alive with all kinds of queer looking insects. We had to fix tents, dig latrines and, since fresh water came from the main water pipe about 500 yards away, we had quite a time of it carrying water and getting through all the other odd jobs.

It was well after dark by the time we had our tents pitched and a meal prepared, a difficult job during blackout. Anyway, the job was accomplished and when the platoon convoys came in, a hot meal was ready for them. There was many a curse when the men saw the campsite and found that they had to pitch their own tents before they could settle down for the night. Many just made a temporary job of it and spread their groundsheets on the under-brush. During the night, we had another tropical rainstorm and many men awoke to find their tents collapsed on them and streams running about them.

Next morning, while Matt and I started our unpacking, Jim Payne and Gwyn Williams came over early for treatment. They had been bitten all over, as was the case with most of the men. We had men lining up before breakfast with insect bites to be treated. The bites were like large red pimples and, in some cases, there were punctures and blood. Some of the men were in great pain. The only antiseptic we had available was white spirit, and this was applied to the considerate discomfort of many. A number of the men suffered from these bites for up to nine months. They often turned septic. Nevertheless, the lads kept doing their job on convoy despite suffering severely.

During the first night in our rubber plantation I heard a queer sound under my groundsheet. I struck a match but failed to see anything. In the morning I discovered thousands of red ants, about half an inch in size. They were pulling, pushing and carrying lumps of coconut about the size of a half-crown from under my bed. The ants had marched in an orderly fashion over my feet to get at the coconut. I was amazed to see lumps of coconut moving along the ground with the ants all around them.

I found Old Bob in his new cookhouse preparing the officers' breakfast. He called me over and said, 'Get outside quick if you'd like some fried bread and kidneys'. I grabbed it in case he changed his mind. He said, 'Take what you want while you can before the ants get it all'. Sure enough, the ants were carrying small slices of bacon and other bits of food off the table, down the legs, along the ground, up the tent rope to the tree. I had never seen anything like it, and asked Old Bob why he didn't put the food out of the way of the ants. 'Oh,' he exclaimed, 'while they have that to take away, they will leave me alone.'

As the days passed, our men returned from journeys in Malaya with news of the Japanese advance. This was so rapid that, in many cases, our men were being overrun and finding themselves encircled. The lads brought in many kinds of fresh fruit, and many cans of various fruits. They also had numerous articles of value which they had purloined from the dock area. The docks, they said, were being evacuated. Amongst the loot were many bottles of spirit. I was given the bottles of rum and brandy for use in the MI room.

At about this time the Jap Air Force was making things very unhealthy for us and we had to spend quite a lot of our time under cover. Our CSM rather got on our nerves. At the first sign of approaching aircraft he would shout at the top of his voice, 'Under cover everyone!' and set us all a wonderful example by sprinting to the nearest trench. From that position he would yell abuse at all who straggled behind.

During the day, we didn't have many men in camp since most were away on convoy duty.

There were quite a number of coconut palms near our camp but they were too high for us to climb to get the nuts. A little Chinese boy about eight years old came along while we were looking at the nuts and said 'Coconut?' I replied, 'Yes' and nodded my head. To my astonishment, he then skimmed up the tree and, in a few minutes, dropped us about six nuts. When he came down again, he demanded five cents a nut, which I willingly gave. I was very amused at the business head on that young body.

On about the first of February we were shaken by some violent explosions at the back of our camp, and having been in the Royal Artillery, I recognized the sound at once. Some of the men made for the trenches. I said to my officer, 'Our guns are firing' but he couldn't understand it. Salvo after salvo was being fired and the shells came whistling overhead. When our men came in that night they looked very gloomy for they brought news that the Japs were now in Jahore State and our troops were retreating across the causeway. The RA moved a few more guns nearer to our camp and kept firing at short intervals.

Paya Lebar

On 3 February, we had orders to make a quick move. In a few hours we had struck and were on the road in convoy heading for Paya Lebar rubber plantation. It was very like Holland Village Camp, but as infantry had been there before us, we found trenches and dugouts already prepared. Matt and I selected a large dugout and erected our tent near it. We obtained permission to reserve it for casualties.

Our Company shared this plantation with an RAF supply unit. The RAF occupied the east end with a well set up camp and NAAFI. Many of the RAF personnel visited us, to make use of our trenches and dugouts when things got a bit lively.

On the second day, just as we felt we were settling in, Matt received instructions to move to headquarters Rascal Division. So I helped him pack up again and then travelled with him to assist him to rig up his tent. While doing this, it started to rain and I found myself covered in black spots. It was raining black, dirty

11

raindrops. The whole island was covered by a cloud of black smoke from the burning oil tanks at the docks. As the rain fell through the smoke, it picked up soot particles and deposited the mess onto everything. I returned to camp feeling very dirty and looking very black. Now very much on my own, I no longer had Matt to turn to for advice. Any emergency that came along would be my responsibility to treat and give the casualties first aid myself. Matt had been ordered to take away all the medical stores but, knowing how I was fixed, he left me a few necessities. I had depended on Matt to help me with emergency cases and I now wondered if I could really cope with the injured should there be casualties. I felt that I dare not show the men how shaky I was about things. I felt that I had to keep their confidence or I was sunk. So I went about dealing with the various cases and tried to appear as if I was quite used to it. It was quite amazing to see how much confidence and respect I won from the men.

My first serious case was when I called to see a sick man in his tent. I found him rolled in his blanket and very feverish. His temperature was 103.2 and his pulse 88. When the MO arrived the next morning, he introduced me to Lieutenant Emery and explained that he was taking over as MO from then on and that he himself would be leaving to take up duties as a surgeon at the Military Hospital. I was instructed to show Doc Emery the ropes, since he was a rookie as far as Army procedure was concerned. I told him about the patient I had visited the night before and that I had given the patient Dover Tablets and had seen that he was kept warm. After an examination, the Doc ordered the patient to the hospital and told me that it was likely that my prompt attention had possibly averted pneumonia. I was very pleased at his encouraging words. He did much to build up my self confidence.

The Japs were now in Jahore Bahru and our troops were fighting a rearguard action to hold them long enough for our men to cross the causeway which linked Jahore to Singapore. This causeway was to be blown up and those left on the mainland would be doomed to capture. This was very depressing news and, while I was doing my rounds, I heard an explosion not many hundred yards away. I knew from experience that it was a shell burst. Many more followed and seemed to be getting nearer. The men in our camp didn't seem to be taking much notice so I shouted, 'Take cover'. Our Major rushed out and wanted to know what the fuss was about. I told him that enemy shells were exploding quite near and were getting nearer. Just then there was a whistle, followed by another explosion. The Major, fixing his eyeglass in position, remarked quite casually, 'Damn it, I think you're right' and ducked as another one whistled overhead and then said, 'Damn it, I KNOW you're right!'

From that day on, we had very little rest. Jap guns were blasting away in the distance and the shells came shrieking over, exploding as they struck nearby trees and sprayed shrapnel. We seemed to be continuously throwing ourselves to the ground. First we would hear the distant batteries firing. It would sound like a very quiet pop-pop, like a child's cork-firing gun, then we would count ten and down we'd go again. On one occasion a shell arrived a little earlier that the usual ten seconds, probably through the Jap artillery moving nearer, and caught us all by surprise. The whine of the shell made everyone duck. After the explosion a few seconds elapsed and I was just getting my breath back when I heard someone shouting for the Medical Orderly. The voice came from the direction of the RAF camp. I jumped up, grabbing my emergency bag, which I always kept ready at hand and which I had filled with what I considered necessary for the first aid in the field. I also grabbed a stretcher. As I ran in the direction of the cries, I shouted for help and for men to follow me. I was able to run about twenty paces in between each shell burst. They kept coming over, but gave plenty of warning.

In a few minutes I was with the injured man, having covered about 300 yards, ducking and running. The casualty was an airman. He was lying on his stomach and bleeding profusely. I tore off his shorts and exposed a badly lacerated buttock with a large lump of flesh missing. In a flash I realized that the man would bleed to death if I didn't do something about the bleeding immediately. There was no stop I knew of for this kind of injury other than blocking, plugging or packing to congeal the blood. I decided on a thick pack and tore open two shell dressings and placed them on the open wound. The man yelled out in pain but I soon had him bandaged and looked around for help. Everyone but my patient and I were below ground.

Reaction was taking effect and I knew it would only take one carefully fired shell and we would both be casualties. I got panicky and began shouting for assistance. One of our men popped his head up and seeing my plight came to my aid. But two of us weren't going to do it. I wanted to get the casualty under cover, so I got the man to start a lorry and help me lift up the airman, who was in terrible pain. My helper drove the lorry to my dugout and I dashed over to get someone to give us a hand with the stretcher. When I arrived there I found it full of men taking cover from exploding shells. I don't think I have ever let go as I did then and I'm sure the names I called them lingered in their ears for quite some time. Captain Wadesley heard my blaspheming and ran over to see what it was all about. He saw in a moment what was going on and ordered the men out, detailing four to carry the stretcher into the dugout. I then took another look at the injured man. He was rather weak from shock and loss of blood. I wanted to get him to a dressing station, so I asked if some men could be detailed to get him there. Captain Wadesley then took over and the patient was soon on his way to the Advanced Field Dressing Station. I never saw the patient again but I heard that he was evacuated on the last hospital ship to leave the island.

When I returned to my tent, I found several rips in the canvas and pieces of shrapnel embedded in the wooden table top. All of a sudden I got wobbly about the knees and felt that I wanted to be sick. I suppose that, until that moment, I had been running on adrenalin – but no more. I sat down very hard and tried to get my breath. The OC then walked in and said he had watched the incident throughout and told me never to expose myself like that again. But before he left, he turned to me and said, 'Good job, man'.

That evening an officer told me that the causeway had been blown up by retreating troops and that we were now besieged. We were fighting to keep the island fortress from the Japs. I saw the futility in the officer's eyes and had visions of Dunkirk. Hard times were upon us.

Next morning, Doc Emery came by at about 10 a.m. I had the sick parade waiting for him and produced the sick forms. To my surprise he didn't know how to complete them, so I had to fill them in for him, and sick parade progressed.

After the parade, the new MO dropped his bombshell. He told me that he too was leaving, for an unknown destination, and that he might not be able to see me again for quite some time. 'You will have to do your best without me' he said, so I enquired, 'What am I to do in the event of bad casualties?' He replied, 'You must do your best, you cannot do more. If you lose a man, and you have done your best for him, well, you have nothing to worry about. I will contact you as soon as I possibly can, but for now, you must make do. Cheerio, my friend and good luck.'

I was stunned. I had almost run out of medical kit, the MO had gone and I was left with the responsibility of caring for over 300 men at a time when we could expect many casualties. I sat down and thought things over. I requested an interview with my OC and told him how I was fixed and asked if he would allow a dispatch rider to be sent out to locate the shortest route to the Advanced Field Dressing Station and Advanced Clearing Station so that we could transfer casualties there in an emergency. I also got leave to go and scrounge around to see if I could get hold of some medical supplies. I was told not to go too far. The DR was detailed immediately after my interview and I went off on my scrounge to the RAF camp.

To my surprise, when I got there, I found them all packing up. I asked their CO if they could let me have any medical kit. He pointed cheerily to their MI Room and Dispensary and told me to 'help myself'. 'Take the lot,' he said. 'We're being evacuated today!' I was stunned. If the RAF were leaving, things were indeed in a bad way. Taking him at his word, I had soon filled an ambulance with what I needed and drove it back to our own camp. When the OC saw me, he was delighted. 'Take good care of that ambulance;' he said, 'we may soon be needing it.'

I went back on a further scrounge that afternoon, only to find the place being ransacked by the locals. To my disgust, I found that the RAF had even left their rifles – an unforgivable crime. However, a couple of shots in the air and a menacing wave of a loaded rifle soon had the natives running for their lives!

However, it was not the locals only who were looting, for I found three lusty lads from our Company busily cracking the NAAFI safe!

Next day we had great difficulty in moving our transport due to heavy shelling and bombing. One of our platoon convoys had had a strafing and one of our corporals was missing. In the early hours of the following morning we were all called to move out and form a defensive line behind the camp. The Japs had landed on the island and had advanced in our direction. We had been RASC up to now, but from now on we were to combine infantry duty with our own. The order was for every able-bodied man to fight. The alarm had been sounded and we took up our positions in the cold morning, shivering. We were informed that the camp was now empty of our men so, if we saw any movement, we were to fire. We were all on our toes with excitement but, as the hours drew on and nothing happened, except for the noise of the battle going on a few miles away, the flashes of bursting shells and the roar of artillery fire, we began to feel the cold more. Mr Mitchell dropped into my 'better-ole' on his tour of inspection and asked me how I was faring. I told him that 'Apart from lost sleep, the cold and the noise, also the blooming "mossies" and ants, things aren't too bad'.

On about 9 January, I had a most pleasant surprise. My old OC from 55 Company, Major Kennon, with whom I had served in France, drove into our camp. I dashed across to have a word with him. After asking me how I was faring, he told me that 55 Company was not far away, fighting as infantry in the front line. I had a great regard for that officer. I could never forget how I saw him from HMS *Vimy*, as I sailed away from Dunkirk. He was standing on the quayside, pistol in hand, as he directed and regulated our men into the waiting boats. Casualties were mounting as bombs and shells fell all around. The din from our AA guns and field artillery was deafening. There he stayed for thirty-six hours until the last of his soldiers was safely away. Now, here he was again, as serene and regimental as ever. Just to see him and have those few words with him was a tonic.

My sick list had increased considerably and I was getting concerned. It was rather a responsibility taking a sick parade of men suffering from so many and such varied complaints. I wanted advice and was most conscious of my own amateurish efforts at treatment and diagnosis. With no promise of an MO in the near future, I made enquiries in the hope that perhaps there would be Medical Officers with units nearby. I discovered that a company of Royal Engineers was billeted in the woods a short distance away. I went over and asked for the MO. Luckily, he was there and, after I explained my problems, he agreed to see my patients that day. I rushed back to camp, informed my OC who rapidly agreed for me to take the men over. I then rounded up the sick and we made our way to the RE's camp. Some of the men were limping, one had to be carried. On our arrival the MO (Captain Rolston, RAMC) examined them, ordered our man to hospital and advised me about the others. He said he would see them again the next morning. This certainly eased my concern and the burden of my responsibility, but it was short-lived. When I took my sick parade over, as arranged, I found the camp deserted. The Engineers had moved in the night.

On my return to camp, I found that we too were going to move, and I was instructed to pack up as quickly as possible. In a very short time everyone was busy packing and rushing about. There was an air of urgency in the camp. Some men were detailed to visit the RAF camp and destroy everything that might be of use to the Japs. In our own camp we were taking the same action. Petrol and stores which we couldn't take with us were dumped into one of the large trenches and set on fire. The officers' kit was packed into the ambulance. One of the officers said, 'It will be safe there for I know the ambulance will be looked after.' He obviously gave no thought to the fact that the ambulance might be wanted for casualties. Old Bob came over from the officers' cookhouse and placed a large wooden case in the ambulance. Knowing how I felt about loading and seeing me eye him up and down he said, 'You can't refuse to take this – it is medicine. Officers' medicine.'

After he had gone, I had a look inside the case and discovered several bottles of whisky and gin. I was just thinking of throwing the case off when Bob came back with a cup and said, 'Here, drink this coffee.' I took the cup and found that it was more rum than coffee and Bob, seeing the look on my face, explained that the coffee had been pretty strong so he had thinned it out with rum. I couldn't throw his case out after that!

We were soon ordered to take up our places in the convoy. I was to follow the leading car in my ambulance. As we started to move, a Jap observation balloon went up not far away and our guns opened up on it, with the Japs returning fire. The officer in

17

the leading car, who had never shown much love for shellfire, took off like a rocket. Fast as my ambulance was, I could not keep up with him and very soon lost sight of him.

The rest of our section of the convoy caught up with me and we decided to get off the road under the trees, for cover. We could see that the small road junction just ahead had been heavily bombed and shelled and the occasional shell was still whistling overhead to burst just beyond it.

A group of Malay and Chinese refugees came past and, as best I could, I asked them for news. Looking very frightened, they said, '*Nippon Marri Le Kas*', meaning 'Japanese coming quick'. This was the first time I had heard the name 'Nippon'. From then on, all Japs were 'Nips' to me!

We decided to follow the refugees and very soon came to a crossroads on the far side of a village where a military policeman told me that our car had gone off to the left. He added that we were damned lucky, as the village through which we had just passed was already overrun by the Japs, who were being plastered by our own guns.

As he spoke, the small car appeared. They had taken the wrong road and narrowly escaped capture. However, they had then scouted around and discovered the location of our next park, on a racecourse. The place and the route to it were both under fire and we would have to make a dash for it, one vehicle at a time. As my ambulance was still the leading vehicle, I was to be the first away. I noticed that the shells arrived at about thirty second intervals. So, as soon as the next salvo arrived I was off, heading flat out for the racecourse.

As I reached the end of a long, narrow stretch of road, I saw that the monsoon drain on my left was manned by a cheerful-looking bunch of Gurkhas, who were clearly treating the whole business as a huge joke – especially the fact that the road I had come down ran between them and the enemy. Despite that, the rest of our convoy soon arrived behind me. All of a sudden, we heard the voice of our Company Sergeant Major, calling us to fall in at a point about 500 yards away. There he ordered us to get into the back of an open truck, abandoning all our own kit and vehicles, including my precious ambulance and medical stores, despite my vigorous protests.

After about an hour of dodging shells and bombs, we arrived at a place called Chancery Lane and were shown a house that was to be our quarters. I was very angry about the loss of my medical kit and wondered how on earth I would now be able to cope. For me, this was Dunkirk all over again – when I had had to help destroy 55 Company's vehicles.

An NCO told me that we could now retreat no further. We had our backs to the sea. This was to be the site of our last stand.

One or two of our platoon convoys were missing and I was told that some of our men had been killed. There were many disheartening rumours and our little party was very miserable indeed. It was now dark except for the terrific detonations and flashes from explosions all around us. We were cold and yet perspiring, hungry with no visible signs of a meal, and very worried about our future. We had been waiting about for two hours when I heard the remainder of the Company moving in. The cooks came up to our house and started getting things fixed to provide a meal. It wasn't long before there was a shout above the din of explosions, 'Come and get it!' So over I went where the cook gave me a bully sandwich which, as one of the men described it, looked like a horse between two bread vans. To wash it down we had a cup of lukewarm tea, which had been stewing in the big flasks all day. But it tasted good and we felt very much better after it.

Hearing that the OC's driver intended to try and get to the race-course with food for the men who had been sent back as pickets, I asked to be allowed to go with him so that I could at least try to get the ambulance. I was told I could take the chance if I wanted to, so off I went with Lance Corporal Welsh driving and Captain Poulter and myself as passengers.

Chancery Lane

Chancery Lane was barely wide enough to allow two vehicles to pass but, nevertheless, it was chock-a-block with traffic going both ways – guns trying to get into position and our lorries trying to get through with ammunition. The air was thick with angry shouts and abuse as everybody tried to force their way through.

Suddenly, we could see a line of shell bursts moving up the road

19

towards us. When one round landed only about ten yards from us, I leaped out of the car into the monsoon ditch, calling Lance Corporal Welsh to take cover also. When he saw that that shell had made a gap in the traffic, Welsh jumped up into the car and, before I could join him, he had shot off down the road, leaving me stranded.

When I had landed in the ditch, I had felt a sharp pain but had not paid much attention to it. Now, I suddenly realized that I was bleeding and that I must have been hit by a piece of shrapnel in the face, although I had felt nothing.

I found that I had a nasty cut under the eye. I grabbed a bit of sterilized cotton wool, and held it over the wound until it stuck and then started back, wondering how I could find the house. After wandering down the road for about an hour, I saw a lorry parked on the roadside and recognized it as one of our Company vehicles. A little farther on I found the Company house, which showed little signs of life. I found the lads taking what rest they could behind hurriedly built barricades, their only protection from the shrapnel.

After a pretty miserable night, deafened by a battery firing almost non-stop nearby and by the incoming shells and bombs, with only a concrete floor upon which to sleep, I awoke to the roar of intensified gunfire and bombing. When it all quietened, I was able to take my first look at our new surroundings. Although we were in what had been the house of a prosperous Eurasian, the sight was depressing. However, the cooks had got their petrol burners going and three steaming dixies promised tea.

Needless to say, the officers were pretty well fixed up upstairs. I slipped up to find Old Bob. There he was, opening a tin of bacon. After the usual exchange of banter, and fortified by a mug of his 'special' coffee and a bacon sandwich, I quickly made myself scarce before one of the officers caught me.

I went in search of my officer, Mr Mitchell, and found him looking for shaving water. So, back to Bob, who gave me some from his dixie.

Just as I got back to Mr Mitchell's room, a shell burst close by and the window blew in. As I got to my feet, I saw that Mr Mitchell was standing there quite calmly and unmoved. He looked at me and said, 'Damned close that' and smiled. I honestly believe he was getting a kick out of all this. Both he and Captain Wadesley gained my very deep respect and esteem for their coolness under fire. Their example certainly had a great impact upon the men's morale.

My officer attended to, I now established my MI Room in a small outhouse, placing a large red cross on the door. I was still fretting about that ambulance and all my medical kit. So out came the car and we were off to the racecourse again. Despite the heavy shelling, we got there in about an hour. The place was a shambles, looking as if there had been a fierce battle there during the night. Our Company vehicles lay irreparably damaged all around. Three were still burning. But, wonder of wonders, my ambulance was only slightly damaged and started at first touch. Without further ado, I crashed my way through, and sometimes over, the wreckage and drove hot-foot for Chancery Lane. Apart from an inevitable Jap air raid, of some fifty aircraft, which had me face down in an unspeakable Singapore gutter and left me stinking to high heaven, and three more similar incidents, I reached the billet safely, parking the ambulance in the trees across the road.

While I had been away, the lads had got on with a good deal of sandbagging between the pillars of the ground floor, which supported the house, and dug a number of trenches out at the back. Fortunately, the house backed onto a steep hill which gave good protection. Most of the shelling came from that side and whistled straight over our heads.

Our men seemed to be taking things very well and casualties were very light. The firing seemed to be in spasms. Our artillery would open up, then the Nips would return the fire, which rose from a seemingly friendly exchange of fire and increased to a maddening inferno of continuous explosions, easing off to an occasional shot again. During the short time of quiet between each barrage, the most amazing thing would happen. The birds would come out and burst forth into song. It was the most beautiful sound in the world and it made me think of the madness I was involved in. Why couldn't we all live as happily and contented as the birds who seemed to be satisfied, with so little being everything to them? We humans have so much in life and yet we must be doing all we can to destroy each other in all this terrible nerve-racking noise, whilst the bird just sits and patiently waits for it all to end so that he can sing. Oh, beautiful bird, with your glorious song! What an example you are to us humans!

I came back to earth again, and wondered if I would ever get out of this inferno. But it was no use dreaming, so I set to and began to prepare my little room for casualties. While I was doing this, in came Old Bob with a cut finger. 'Had to do it' he said. 'Had to have something to flavour the stew.' I laughed and, while I bandaged him up, he whispered, 'Could you do with a cup of tea?' He fixed me up with a cup well flavoured with the Major's 'medicine'. It warmed me up from top to bottom and from then on I didn't care for all the Nips in Nippon!

When I returned to my room I found everything all over the place. Cotton wool was scattered everywhere. I turned and, in the corner, I saw a little head looking back at me and blinking with wide eyes. It was 'Jack' the monkey, whom one of our fellows had brought in. I tried to shoo him out but he took offence and showed me his teeth. So I walked around behind him and he made for the door, grabbing handfuls of cotton wool as he went, stuffing them into his mouth. At the door he turned and, as if in defiance, he screamed at me. I threw a boot at him and he disappeared, making an awful noise which, I am sure, meant nothing complimentary, had he been able to speak.

Most of our men were now out on patrols or entrenched not far away. One of them, Fred Crane, on returning from a patrol, came to me and said that if I wanted medical supplies he knew where there were plenty. I said that I needed all I could get and, grabbing a large basket, followed him up over the bank at the back of our billet where I discovered that there was a lane running along the top of the bank between an avenue of trees. Lining the other side of the lane were two houses. My guide made for one of these. When we arrived there, I was surprised to find that it was a private maternity hospital. There was plenty of evidence of a very hurried departure by the occupants as the front porch was piled with trunks and cases which, though packed, had had to be left behind. From an open air ward crammed tight with beds, it seemed that there must have been wounded there recently because some of the beds were saturated with blood. I was about to pass through the hospital when I was challenged by an unseen sentry. I explained what I was doing and was told to carry on, but to hurry, as the

Nips were expected at any moment and I might be caught in the crossfire. Fred and I hurriedly grabbed everything that we thought might be useful and cautiously returned to our billet. Back in my little MI Room I checked the spoils. There were two stethoscopes, half a dozen thermometers, Spencer-Wells forceps, scalpels, tweezers, scissors, kidney bowls, bedpans, a quart bottle of spirit, a box containing 500 phials of morphia, hypodermic syringes and many drugs of which I knew nothing. There were also RAF medical bags containing a little of everything useful for first aid. I decided that I would keep one of these untouched, in case of an emergency. There were the most useful medical bags I have ever seen. Every little mystery phial and all the other articles were clearly explained on a little card. I learned quite a lot from that little card and the bag became a treasure to me. In fact, I have never parted with it to this day. Its contents helped to save lives and brought comfort to many, as I will explain later.

A little later in the day, two men brought in some more sheets from the hospital, so now I was stocked with a bale of white sheets, hundreds of bandages, ointments, antiseptics and numerous other things. I didn't know what to do with them all, but thought they might come in useful later on to someone, if not to me. How true this proved to be in the months ahead.

That night became a nightmare. It seemed as though we were right in the front line. The continuous roar of the guns went on all night long, with shrapnel whizzing about and ricocheting all over the place. I was glad when at last there were signs of daylight. We all considered it was going to be an unlucky day, as it was Friday the 13th, so we had many misgivings as the day dawned with an increased barrage from both sides.

'What is in store for us today?' we all wondered. To start with, there was no tea for breakfast and only hard tack issued. Our cooks could not use the stoves due to the blackout. After breakfast the men left, some going on patrol, others to relieve the guards. As they left, they had to rush for cover as things were warming up. At that stage the continuous explosions seemed to be having an effect on me, though I tried to keep myself occupied doing things all the time. A few of our men were showing signs of strain also. I sorted them out and told their NCOs quietly. There were some that had been on patrol all night and who were trying to sleep. One of them jumped up after a particularly heavy explosion quite near and started to scream. I rushed over to him. I could see the panic on the faces of the men around him, so I gave him a violent shake by the shoulders and shouted at him to pull himself together. He steadied up a bit, though he was still trembling pretty badly. I gave them all cotton wool and told them to stuff it into their ears. This they did and, with the help of some tea, which had just been made, some of them got to sleep.

I visited Old Bob in his little cookhouse and asked him if I looked like an officer. He answered 'Definitely not, but you can have some of what's going. Help yourself!' So I dived in. Just then, over came the Nips again and all hell seemed to break loose. I ran through the back door and dived into a trench outside where there were several more of our men and everyone seemed to be trying to push themselves to the bottom of the trench. We remained there for about half an hour as the planes returned and bombed all around us. It seemed they were trying to find the battery that was quite near our billet. However, although the bombs dropped by the dozen, that battery still kept firing. When the attack eased off I was amazed to see Old Bob open the cookhouse door and shout 'Come on you lads, there's tea here for those who want it, also a roll of toilet paper hanging on the wall.' We all laughed; we couldn't help ourselves. Old Bob had been working all through the attack. He said 'They will get me when it's meant for me to be got.' He was a fatalist, and a brave one at that. I could imagine him wisecracking even if he knew he was going to die, though, thank God, he couldn't look into his future and see his end.

All this time there was a continuous din of shellfire, and over would come the Nip Air Force for some more strafing. It was after a particularly heavy bombing attack that I was called to attend a badly wounded man. I had great difficulty in getting near the position where he lay, because of flying shrapnel. When I was about fifty yards away I met one of our men, Harry Hutchinson, who told me that there wasn't a thing I could do for the poor fellow as he had died a few minutes before. Shrapnel had severed the jugular vein and in a few minutes he was dead. I was very upset about this, as he was my first fatal casualty. His name was Smith. I had earlier treated him for 'Singapore ear'.

I returned to my little room where I found a fellow waiting for me with a few minor injuries to be attended to. As I completed the dressing Mr Mitchell came along looking deathly white, with tears in his eyes. I asked, 'What on earth is the matter, Sir?' He seemed to be in great distress and quietly said, 'I have just buried Smith. It was awful and I never want a job like that again!' I suggested a bracer and he went along to his room to get one. Mr Mitchell was a man who wouldn't flinch even in the heaviest bombardment, yet the death of one of his men brought him to tears. I was quite impressed by this. He was soon himself again and was back directing operations within a few minutes.

The birds had had no chance to sing during that day for the Nips didn't give us a minute's respite. As the daylight faded and the darkness came on, the firing eased off a little and I was very relieved. Our convoys had not returned and it was rumoured that they had been ambushed. Morale was very low. There were few men to do the guard, so I volunteered to take the beat on the drive in front of the house. I took up my post at 8 p.m. and at 9 p.m. I was joined by Fred Crane. The order had been given that the guard was to be doubled. Old Bob sent word, as we passed his door on our patrol, that we were to knock. This I did and, on my return, a mug was handed out with hot coffee (Bob's special). My mate and I got a mug every half hour and by 11 p.m. were feeling like taking on the whole Nip Army. I remember taking a little rest on the bank of the drive only to discover that insects, especially ants, were crawling all over me. It struck me as funny that, only a few days ago, I had lived in dread of those things. Now I was saying, 'Let them all come!'

Fred came up to tell me that a conference of the officers was being held. Clearly something was afoot. Shortly after, a group of officers led by the Major, all carrying tommy guns, came past. The OC called me over and said that we must be on our toes as the Nips might arrive at any moment now.

When they had gone, Old Bob came out to refill our mugs and told us that there was something doing of the utmost gravity. He had been told that one of our sections in the convoy had been surrounded and that the officers had gone to see if anything could be done about getting them out.

At this time the countryside around us was lit up with continuous flashes and explosions and I wondered how our men were faring. They had been coming in each night at all hours and were up and away again before daybreak, red-eyed and weary. They were doing a good job delivering ammunition, petrol and food to the fighting men with the very few lorries we had left. They had been loading up in one of our dumps when the Nips arrived, and got away as our shells started dropping on the dump to destroy it. They were involved in many similar incidents.

At 1 a.m. I came off guard. Something was certainly going on in the house and various key men of the Company had been called in for a conference. It was rumoured that our officers were going to try to escape and leave us, which I did not believe. Dead tired, I managed to doze off with a feeling of 'Let come what may and let tomorrow look after itself.'

Up and about at 5 a.m., I found Bob getting things ready for breakfast. He turned to me and said, 'Well, a few less to prepare breakfast for this morning, less work for me.' I said 'What's up Bob?' and he replied that the Major had taken a party to attempt an escape from the island. After I had helped Bob to dispose of a mug of coffee, I went down to see what I could find out about it and learned that the Major had taken at least six men with him on an official escape party. I think that each company on the island had sent a similar party of key men to escape when it was realized that our case was hopeless. The party had left in the early hours and made for the docks in the hope that they would find a boat of some kind to take them away.

I was very relieved to find that the other officers of our Company were still with us. Of course, I had had very little time to get to know them all, and what I had seen of some of them didn't give me much faith, except for a few who had proved – and were still proving – themselves worthy of our respect.

I went to visit the house next door where 'B' Platoon was billeted for there were a few men lying there. There was a man who was suffering from shell shock and was in a terrible state. I told him to pull himself together, but he became hysterical and I could think of no other way of helping him than by hitting him, but I didn't feel up to that, and didn't. Then he screamed out and another man began to babble. Finally, I started to see red and socked him on the chin. The screaming stopped immediately and he laid back on the floor sobbing. I had to leave them or I think I would have sobbed too.

I returned to my little room feeling quite upset. One of the Lieutenants came by to ask if I was all right. He told me that General Wavell had visited the island a day or so before and had left instructions that we were to hold out at all costs and fight to the last man. Having given these orders, he had then left the island by plane. I told the Lieutenant that if we had many more days like we were having, the men would give way under the strain. He replied that things would get much worse. That left me very depressed and I began to worry again over my responsibilities.

I was making emergency tourniquets when I heard Bob cursing, swearing and shouting at someone. He was running and coming towards me. I ran out to investigate and nearly collided with the monkey, who dashed past me and into my room. Bob followed with a long stick but the monkey was now up in the rafters of my room, making faces at Bob and screaming. Bob began to laugh and said that the monkey had tipped over one of his dixies and he would have to cook the entire dinner over again. The monkey was becoming a nuisance and a danger to us as he was getting very excited and frightened.

It was decided that he must be shot. I heard two shots and a scream and one of the lads appeared carrying out the dead monkey by the tail, poor little bugger. We were all sorry for the monkey but consoled ourselves that we had done the right thing. Bob said 'This calls for a cup of my special' to which we all readily agreed!

After we had dispersed I was called on by a man who wanted his dressing attended to. He had been out on patrol and said that the situation was very serious, for the Nips weren't far away. Just then, a couple of mortar shells burst outside the house. Shrapnel flew everywhere but luckily no one was hit. I thought we might get a bit of fighting around the house and would require stretchers. I had one in my little room and I knew there were four more in the ambulance so I asked for volunteers to help get them. I had great difficulty getting volunteers and Jock Campbell, fired by the stimulus of Old Bob's medicine, came out calling everyone cowards. He set an example himself by offering to go and went dashing off. I tore after him and made him take cover. Two other fellows, seeing us go, followed. We reached the ambulance safely and were about to return with the stretchers when three Nip planes flew over very low. Dozens of ack-ack guns opened up and we dashed for cover as the planes passed over the house where 'B' platoon was billeted. The men opened fire with their Bren gun and got one of the planes. I saw him wobble and then dive down into the trees. The gunners were cheering and dancing at their success when the Nips came back for revenge. After they had dropped several more bombs and cleared off again, I noticed that one of the field guns that had been firing was now strangely quiet. I was told later that the crew and gun had been blown to pieces.

We got our stretchers up to my room and then all hell let loose again. As the shells came over I noticed that there were many duds and as many as one in three failed to explode. The same thing happened when the bombers came over. Many of their bombs failed to explode. I mentioned this to Mr Mitchell and he suggested sabotage. Towards evening shots were fired in front of the house and then in the back. Every man was called out for action, so I grabbed my rifle and took up my position in the garden hedge. The firing continued and one of our men near me said there were snipers about. We all began firing at everything that moved and in some instances fired at each other. There was movement on the other side of a hedge about 100 yards away, so we all opened fire. Then the hedge seemed to bristle with rifle fire. I thought 'Now, we're in for it. They are Nips all right.' But after about ten minutes of continuous rifle fire a very weak voice began shouting 'Cease fire, cease fire! I'll shoot the next man that fires a shot!' I could see one of the Captains. He had been in his specially built shelter most of the time. He was trembling very badly and waving his revolver about, shouting abuse at the men. One of the officers led him away and shouted for everyone to cease fire, for the men behind the hedge were Indians. Finally some semblance of order was restored. We then discovered that what we had thought were shots and had started the trouble, weren't shots at all but rather a very clever trick played by the Nips. What we had thought were dud shells and bombs turned out to be delayed action firecrackers. These, when exploded, sounded like rifle fire making us think the Nips were behind us. This ruse had succeeded in Malaya and made our troops fall back thinking the Nips had got in behind them.

Later in the day there came another scare. We were ordered to fill all pans, pots, pails or anything that could hold water, as our water supply would be cut off at any moment. As it was, the water was unfit to drink, due to the bodies contaminating the small reservoir on the island. In consequence, our water was chlorinated, making it abominable to drink. In the terrible heat, we had such a thirst.

I was told that our ammunition and petrol dumps had all been blown up by our people and it was just a matter of time before we would be out of ammunition and petrol. It would be very difficult to obtain food through lack of transport. We were in a very bad way. Before lying down that night, I visited Old Bob and, while drinking a cup of his special, listened to the news on his radio set. I believe it was the Empire programme relayed from Delhi. The announcer was saying that Singapore was sorely pressed but the men were determined to fight to the last man, with their backs to the sea. It looked pretty desperate for us and, when I returned to my billet, I offered up a silent prayer for the safety of our little force.

All through the night and late into Sunday the Nips gave us all they'd got – shells, mortars and bombs. It was almost unbearable. During the morning of that ill-fated day, Sunday, 15 February 1942, we could not move out from under cover. The cooks had been ordered to put out the stoves, as they were making too much noise and our officers wanted to be able to hear all that was going on around us.

It was nearly 11 a.m. when the Nips increased their mortar fire, and many bombs burst in the backyard of our billet. I was down on the floor, taking what cover I could, when above the din, I heard the voice of Captain Wadesley yelling for me. I grabbed my bag and made a dash for the door, but quickly ducked as some mortar bombs dropped with terrific explosions. I waited for the next salvo and, as soon as that had arrived, I dashed across the yard to where Captain Wadesley and one of our men were carrying a casualty into a shelter. I dived in just as I heard more approaching mortar bombs and found two men, Sergeant Kennerley, who had fainted, and Lance Corporal Hawkins, who was bleeding freely from a wound behind the left ear. I swabbed the wound with Eusol and applied a field dressing. While I was doing this, a Captain pushed his way over to me and started giving me instructions. He kept it up whilst I was doing the job, then, turning round, I asked him if he would give the patient a drink of water. He was livid and was about to tell me off, so I asked him if he could save it until I had finished with the other casualty. I walked over to where Sergeant Kennerley lay. When I got to him, his clothes had been taken off to expose a flesh wound to the left shoulder. I cleaned and dressed it and, after he had recovered sufficiently, I turned to leave, asking Captain Wadesley if the casualties could remain in the safety of the shelter. The other Captain said they would have to be moved but Captain Wadesley told me to leave them for the time being. They were still there that evening, so Captain Wadesley must have had his way.

We were taking a terrible pounding and I felt sometimes that the top of my head was lifting off. The roar of the guns and the general din was nerve shattering. We noticed that another gun, which had been firing almost continually, had now stopped. We all thought that the crew must have been injured or killed, so some of the men crawled over to the gun position to investigate. They returned to say that the crew was all right but had run out of ammunition. One lad said that there was a lorry in a ditch about half a mile away fully loaded with 18-pounder rounds, so off went a gang to find the lorry. Just over an hour later, the gun started firing again. We gave a cheer and some more men volunteered to carry the ammunition to the gun. That gun seemed then to have new life and kept firing away all that morning.

Ceasefire

At 3 p.m. I was told to parade with the rest of the men under the house. When we got there I found everyone crowded around a Captain who had tears in his eyes. He was holding a paper in his hand and trembling badly. He said in a very quiet voice filled with emotion which he was trying to control, 'I have called you all here to give you a message from our OC. He wishes to thank you all for the very fine way in which you have all carried out your duty against terrific odds. He said that he couldn't have wished for a better Company of men and that he is proud of us. He very much regretted having to leave us as he did but, like us, he had to obey orders and so left with an official escape party. He wishes us all the best of luck and hopes to meet us soon again under more pleasant circumstances. It is now my very unpleasant duty to pass on to you the information I have just received.'

He then read out an official message from the General Officer Commanding, Lieutenant General Percival in which he explained that within a few days we would be out of petrol and food and that there was already a shortage of many types of ammunition. The water supply, upon which the vast civil population and many of the troops depended, was threatening to fail. Without the sinews of war, we could not fight on. He had therefore to order us to lay down our arms and surrender. The ceasefire would become effective at 4 p.m. He ended by thanking all ranks for their efforts in the campaign.

A message from Major General Simmonds, our Area Commander then followed:

To: All Units From: H.Q. Southern Area

After weeks of anxious and steadfast watching you have taken your turn in the fighting on Singapore Island. Some of you have done your part most gallantly on the Mainland. Throughout the operation on Singapore Island I can only thank you for your gallant effort to stem the attack. You have had little support from the air, you have been outnumbered and out-gunned.

Notwithstanding this you have borne yourselves magnificently. Remember this, in your hour of trial – you have done your part, your best, and have no need to blame yourselves.

Keep your spirits up – Good times will come again.

(Signed) F. Keith Simmonds Major General – Commander Southern Area. 15/2/42

By this time the Captain was crying and I felt a lump rise in my throat. Several of the men collapsed and many were sobbing. I had never seen such misery. The reaction was awful.

The Captain then left us to our misery. I tried to console a few of the men who seemed to be sobbing uncontrollably but they were beyond consoling so I left them to it. It was strange to see men who a short time ago had a dogged look on their faces and, though tired out, seemed as though they would be prepared to fight on indefinitely. Now they were just like children.

The shells kept coming over and the planes kept up their visits of hate. I was very relieved when my watch showed 4 p.m. and then all at once everything eased off and became deadly quiet and still. The silence was eery and seemed so much worse than the noise of a few seconds before.

I lay down on the floor of my little room and closed my eyes. My head seemed to be on fire and my thoughts were of my loved ones at home – my wife, my children and Mother and Father. How would they take the news? How would the telegram read? I thought it might read something like this:

> Regret to inform you that your husband is reported missing, believed taken prisoner of war.

At this thought, I felt my head would burst and the awful quiet was more than any human could stand. I got up and walked about. I met Mr Mitchell who told me to destroy anything I had that might be of use to the Japanese. He also told me that some of our men had left to attempt an escape.

Some of the men were burying their belongings. There were rumours that if the Nips found any man with a sharp weapon they would use it on the owner. So I buried an ornamental knife I had bought while in Mombasa. I had bought my son a double-barrelled airgun in France and had had to destroy it before the evacuation at Dunkirk and now I had to destroy the knife. But I was consoled by the thought that as our troops would quickly retake Singapore I might retrieve the knife later on, so I wrapped it in a waterproof cloth and buried it with my diary which was a treasured possession.

It was about 6 p.m. when the cooks shouted 'Come and get it' and though there were many hungry men, very few answered the call for tinned M & V (meat and vegetable) stew, tea and Army biscuits. I went into the cookhouse for a cup of tea and one of the cooks told me that he had just been listening to the news on the radio. Churchill had said that we were still holding out, and that Singapore would not fall. I thought that Churchill must be keeping the news of our capitulation from the people.

I then went over to see how Old Bob was getting on. He was just the same as ever and said that he was preparing a good meal for us as it might be the last for a long time once the little yellow bastards came for us. When Bob had the meal ready, I joined him and later, when he brought out the bottle from its secret hiding place, I joined him in wishing the Japs to damnation.

At 7 p.m. I heard someone shouting for me, and my MO appeared in the doorway. I was pleased to see him again and told him so. He told me that there had been many casualties in the other Companies and asked me how I was faring. I told him about Smith and the other minor casualties and took him to see my patients. He ordered the wounded to the hospital. I then took him to 'B' Platoon billet to see the shell-shock cases. Martindale was sent to the hospital and Bolter, who had long been suffering from alcoholic poisoning, was still very ill and was sent with him. Bolter was never heard of again, and as far as I know, he was admitted to the Alexandra Hospital and I assume that he died there. The others eventually returned to our Company. The MO told me that he didn't know what was taking place as the Nips would not be taking over until the next day – Monday.

The silence of the ceasefire was blissful. That night I slept as I had never slept before. Though the smell all around was sickening and getting worse every day, it didn't bother me that night. When I got up the next morning feeling quite refreshed, I was surprised that the Nips hadn't yet arrived. I dressed, washed and shaved (the first shave for two or three days) and then began to think of the day with great foreboding. Some of the men who had left the day before to escape had now returned with the news that the docks were a shambles and there wasn't a boat anywhere. The lorries and guns were all wrecked and had been driven into the sea. Singapore was in a very bad state.

Chapter Three

Prisoners of War

One of our officers came to tell us that one of the conditions of surrender was that all arms would be handed over undamaged and he advised us to put all our arms on a pile. This we did but not before making an effort to render them unserviceable.

At about 8:30 a.m. we were all very surprised to see our Major coming up the drive. He hadn't shaved for days and his clothes seemed much the worse for wear. He looked all in. He told us that all the others of his party had got away. He had left them in a small sailing boat for only a few minutes, but when he returned they had gone, so he decided to return to us. We were all very pleased to see him again and he would now be with us to the end. At about 9 a.m. Mr Mitchell came to me and asked if I would attempt an escape with him. He had found a man who could handle a sailing boat. We could make our way to the docks and see if we could bribe the natives to let us have one of their fishing boats. I told him I was game and packed my bag with the barest necessities and made my way to the road while Mr Mitchell was taking his leave of our Major. As I waited at the gate of our drive, I saw a car pull up near one of the Sergeants and a Nip officer stepped out and took the Sergeant's weapons. I dodged back up the drive and told Mr Mitchell that the Nips had arrived, so we decided to abandon the escape and remain to take our chances with the others.

Everything was in a bad state – rifles, tommy guns, machine guns and ammunition were all thrown into untidy heaps. There were old trunks, suitcases and clothes strewn everywhere. Worst of all, the smell hanging from the drains and lavatory was shocking. I felt I would be very glad to leave that place and soon.

Men were lying around, making up for the very strenuous time they had had recently. I started packing my things in case the Nips decided to move us. While I was packing, I heard a voice coming from the direction of the trees which lined the bank at the back of our billet. I went to investigate and the voice continued from the trees repeating an urgent 'Coo-ra, Coo-ra'. I stared in the direction of the voice but could not see who was shouting. As the voice seemed to be excited I thought I had better do something about it, so I shouted for an officer. He came with several of our men and then I saw a movement in the trees and out stepped a Nip soldier, pointing his rifle in our direction. He was about 4 feet 6 inches in height, his face daubed with mud and the net on his helmet held leaves. His uniform was greenish brown and he wore light rubber boots. His camouflage was excellent. If he hadn't moved, I wouldn't have seen him. He motioned with his rifle for us to climb up the bank. I grabbed my medical bag and small pack and followed the others onto the lane, where we formed into threes. The Nip kept on shouting the word 'Coo-ra'. He pointed at a man's small pack and we thought he meant us to open them for inspection. We all tipped the contents of our packs into the roadway and were then hustled away, marching down the lane to a small field where there were quite a lot of our men sitting and lying about looking very dejected. We made ourselves as comfortable as we could and waited through the heat of the day for instructions from the Nips.

There were a few sentries patrolling around the field and there was a machine gun mounted on a bank directly behind us. During the day, many more of our men were brought into the field from various places.

Two Nips, obviously looking for a bit of fun at our expense, began to drive a captured lorry round and round our crowded field. Faster and faster they went and we feared they were drunk. Having kept us all dashing out of the way as they drove straight at us, they suddenly drove at the hedge, where the vehicle stuck and they climbed out.

Fortunately, nobody had been hurt but, as they crossed the field towards us, we feared that they might now be up to some other form of devilry. But no, they were wreathed in smiles and wanted to try a few words of English on us. I could understand them enough to gather that they were saying that they were mighty soldiers and would conquer the world. They were going to conclude their conquest quickly since they had been away from home for many years with the Japanese Imperial Army and now wanted to return. Apparently, their families were paid nothing by the Government but had to fend for themselves while their men were away fighting. They became quite friendly and offered us cigarettes, which smoked like burning straw and tasted like cow dung. Many of our men had come to me for dressings that day so I started a 'free for all' dressing station of my own and was kept busy most of that afternoon, but my little emergency bag was soon empty and I was unable to carry on. I suggested to Mr Mitchell that we ask these seemingly friendly Nips if we could return to our billet for medical supplies. He tried to make the Nips understand what we wanted by pointing to my red cross, then to my empty bag and the sore arm of one of the men. When I picked up my bag and started in the direction of our billet, the Nips merely grinned and made no effort to stop me. I was within a few yards of the billet when a Nip soldier jumped out of the hedge and pointed his bayonet at me, babbling away in his own language. I was badly shaken by the suddenness of this action and tried to explain. I showed him my empty bag and pointed to the red cross on my arm but when I moved to pass him he raised his rifle and tried to strike me with the butt. I jumped aside and backed away and as he didn't follow, I kept going.

On my way back to the field I saw Nips looting everywhere. I passed the spot where I had to turn my pack out and I had a look for my belongings. My luck held good and I found them almost immediately, although many things were missing. Nips had taken everything they thought might be of value to them. I found my photographs, the only ones I had of my family. I was putting them into my pocket when I heard a grunt. I looked up and standing close to me was a little Nip. He was filthy dirty and smelled foul. He grunted again and pushed me aside with the butt of his rifle, motioning to me to empty my pockets. He pointed to his wrist and showed me his watch. I was thankful that I had taken the precaution of removing mine and hiding it in a small pocket in my shorts. As I pulled out my photographs, I showed him one of my little son dressed in my Dunkirk equipment. I thought it might soften him a bit. But no! He knocked it out of my hand. I had quite a job to control myself, as I could have murdered him for that, but there were other Nips about and they had the whip hand.

I had to put up with the humiliation of being half stripped by this Nip, who was half my size but who, I knew, would bayonet me at the slightest excuse. He searched everywhere, except the pocket with my watch in it. He looked through my wallet and took $110 and a few £1 notes (the dollars had been given to me by Mr Mitchell, as he thought we would soon be parted). He then gave me a backhander across my face and moved away. I had had enough of this so I snatched up the photo of my little boy and hurriedly returned to the field.

When I got back to the field I told Mr Mitchell of my experience and he cautioned me not to go anywhere alone in future. We then saw a Nip officer enter the field. Mr Mitchell said 'We must get some food here from the billet. If I get permission to go for it, you can come with me for your medics.' He then went over to the Nip officer and in a few minutes returned saying, 'Come on, and bring three or four men with you.' I quickly got together a few of my pals and off we went down the road.

When we arrived at the front of our billet, we found that there were a few lorries in the field where we had buried Smith. These lorries had been knocked around a bit by bombs and shells. Two of them were leaning over and would fall on their sides at the slightest touch. They had been loaded with quartermaster's stores, and had been looted, the stores being strewn all over the field including tinned foods of all kinds. Some of the fruit tins had been jabbed with bayonets and the juice consumed. Then the tins were thrown away, bully tins, fish tins, all opened and thrown away with millions of flies feasting on the remains.

I said to Mr Mitchell, 'How about getting one of these lorries righted and use it to take back the food?'

He said, 'We can try it'. So we tinkered around a bit with a Bedford and got the engine running, but it took the best part of an hour to get it righted and out of the ditch. Anyhow, we managed it and I left the loading of it to my pals while I went to the billet for medical supplies. As I approached the billet I thought about my ambulance and looked to where I had left it. It was still there but rather the worse for wear, as shrapnel had torn it to ribbons.

The billet had been overrun by Nips, who had been looting and throwing everything about. My MI room was in great disorder but I sorted out a few things and packed two large wooden boxes as tight as I could with all the most useful things. I had just completed packing when the lorry arrived and on went the boxes. Then I went up to Mr Mitchell's room, got his two trunks out and put them on as well and away we went.

I gave one last look at the house where I had spent the most intense days of my life. I was leaving it behind having survived five days of hellish, intense bombardment where we had all suffered agony of mind and body from death and defeat. And now where were we going? To what new life was this lorry taking us? We were humiliated, defeated and prisoners; prisoners to a race of people whom we knew were almost inhuman.

The outlook for the future was not very good. We had survived the fight of our lives and were full of life and vitality, and though the times ahead might be tough for us, it wouldn't be for long. Churchill wouldn't rest until Singapore was recaptured and then we'd see the grins wiped off the faces of the little yellow rats. We would show them. They had us at a disadvantage now, but our turn would come. These were the thoughts which each man openly voiced and I didn't hear a man suggest anything but hope for the near future. This was the same spirit which remained through the years of starvation, torture, sickness, disease and death, which lay ahead. When I returned to the field I found that many more of our men had drifted in, some having been directed by the Nips, others being brought in by Nip soldiers at gun point. Our officers had congregated in one corner and, as more officers arrived, they joined the others, keeping apart from the men. When new men arrived, they were told to make themselves comfortable anywhere in the field except in the officers' corner.

Many of the officers were disliked by the men, and during my short stay in that field, among men from many units, I heard endless tales of bad behaviour by the officers: of how they were good at shouting orders and abuse but very slow, if ever at all, at setting an example. It was always 'Get on and do it', rarely

'Follow me'. But I also heard tales of bravery, where officers had given their lives in brave and daring deeds, and in every case the men stated that they would have followed those officers through hell. I honestly believe this, because it is an inspiring sight to see an officer leading his men in action. I have seen it many times and I never saw a man waver. Where the officer would go – even in the worst kind of danger – the men would follow him. However, if an officer gave orders from under cover or from behind, I always found the men muttering, hesitating, and, in the most cases, bewildered.

As the afternoon wore on, the feelings of resentment over the attitude of the officers grew. Had they only moved about amongst the men and chatted to them and shown some sort of spirit of comradeship in adversity, all would, I am sure, have been forgiven. Those officers who did so only highlighted the shortcomings of the rest. We knew that, as prisoners of war, our officers would soon be separated from us and we should have felt sorry that this would be so. However, so strong were the men's feelings that some were openly saying that the sooner we saw the back of them, the better.

We had been able to grab a large number of stretchers from the garden of a nearby hospital. Bloodstained and smelly though they were, they offered a much better chance of sleep than the bare earth. The field soon became one mass of stretchers and it was difficult to find a spot at which to bed down. This nearly gave rise to a very ugly incident when one officer was foolish enough to kick a man out of his stretcher because it was too close to the officer's camp bed. This gave rise to a loud chorus of boos and angry shouting. But for the actions of some more level-headed officers, who tried to restore calm, the situation might well have degenerated to blows. The appearance of a group of Nips with fixed bayonets finally led to the restoration of quiet.

We spent a very restless night and, as I lay on my stretcher, I asked myself what was going to happen to us all. We were in a strange land and had not even had time to find our way about. It was just over a month since we had disembarked and now we were prisoners about 10,000 miles from home and facing a very uncertain future. It was enough to dishearten any man. Small wonder that men had cried when we capitulated.

39

There were, of course, no latrines and throughout the night there had been curses on every side from those who were being tripped over or trampled on by men making their way to the edges of the field. When morning came and the sun blazed down on us mercilessly, the conveniences of the night became a massive inconvenience of the day, with countless flies adding to the dreadful smell. Men were given permission to fetch our water trucks, and the cooks started breakfast – three biscuits and a cup of tea were issued. At about 11 a.m. we got the order to be prepared to leave by 2 p.m. and we were told we would have to march fifteen miles. We couldn't overload ourselves and each company would be allowed to take one lorry for cooking gear and stores. I was rather concerned about my boxes of medics so I took the matter to Sergeant Kennerley and he said 'I'll fix that'. Officers had given the order, 'Only cooking gear and food on the lorry,' but I saw some of them wangle their trunks aboard. The Sergeant grabbed my boxes saying 'If their bloody trunks are going, so are these' and on they went, regardless of the protesting cooks, one of whom reported the matter to an officer who chose to ignore the complaint (his trunk having been tucked away on the lorry).

The lorry was now loaded to capacity, and Old Bob had found a place to sit on the top of the load. I had some bandages and other medical stuff in a little box and a few white sheets, so I asked Bob 'What about it?' He said 'Yes, I'll find room for them'. Mr Mitchell's trunk was to be left behind, and was on the grass nearby, so I put the medical kit in the trunk with his kit, and put the trunk on the lorry, then Old Bob made a seat of it.

Destination – Changi

Waiting was difficult. We were almost melting in the sun and there was no shade. We lay there, using our packs as pillows, waiting for the order to move. As I waited, I saw many Indian troops being marched past our field. There must have been thousands of them. At about 3:15 p.m. the order came for us to get ready to move and at 3:30 p.m. we were on our way. Our destination was Changi. I hadn't heard of the place before, but I was destined to know it only too well. Changi is a little village on the north-eastern tip of the island.

It was a long time since we had done any marching or even taken much strenuous exercise. As we now plodded along under the blazing sun, we soon began to pay the penalties of our inactivity. We poured with sweat under our heavy packs and had to make constant stops to adjust our shoulder straps, which were chafing our shoulders. It was not long before our feet started to swell and blister.

Our route lay through areas of seemingly endless destruction, the smoking ruins of the native kampongs being searched by a veritable army of looters, who seemed indifferent to the mass of putrefying bodies of men, women and children that lay on every side. The smell was overpowering and we were utterly sickened by all we saw.

Whilst many of the local people who watched us pass seemed genuinely sorry at our predicament, there were many too who openly jeered at us, grinning evilly. I was surprised at the number of houses flying Japanese flags, a clear confirmation of the stories about fifth columnists abounding.

Suddenly I realized that we were no longer under guard. We had just been left to get on with it. No wonder really for there was little prospect of escape.

Two incidents during that march touched me very much. A Tamil family were ferrying water in petrol cans from a nearby well to the roadside where the father was ladling it out in a dirty-looking coconut shell to the men as we passed. We filled our water bottles gratefully. That kindly Tamil, too poor to possess a glass or a jug, was risking not only his own life by helping us, but also those of his family. Their compassion was deeply moving. Sadly, I have little doubt that the Nips dealt with him later. A bit further on, we came across a rather stout Chinese woman standing outside a little hut to give the lads water from a little jug. As she did so, the tears were pouring down her face and she was saying, 'OK. Soon more British come', in an attempt to give us courage in our plight. Doubtless, she too was made to pay for her brave and kindly gesture.

Later, as we rested by the roadside, a passing lorry broke down a few yards up the road. An officer from the truck asked if we had anyone who knew anything about lorries and who might take a look at the engine. Our fitters offered to help and, in no time, the lorry was ready to move off again. Our kit was put on the lorry and the officer had instructions from our Major where to dump it for us. This was a great relief and made the remainder of the march much more bearable.

We reached Changi, at last, at about 10 p.m. The whole place was in darkness and we had no idea where to go. Fortunately, we found an officer who was directing parties as they arrived and he told us how to find Captain Wadesley of B Platoon, who told us where our kit was and to get into any hut for the night. All would be sorted out in the morning. Gwyn, my mate, and I made for the nearest hut where, to the accompaniment of loud snoring and the chirping of crickets, we tried to find a spot where we could settle down. After being roundly cursed by several men over whom we inadvertently stumbled, we found a corner and lay down on the hard boards, using our small packs as pillows. We soon found that we were resting against an enormous ants' nest. No sooner had Gwyn ingeniously got rid of them by opening a tin of 'Bully' which he had in his pack, for which they at once made a bee-line, than an enormous spider dropped on Gwyn from the roof and then landed on me. Gwyn cautiously struck a match to reveal what some chap said was a tarantula and deadly poisonous. Without further ado, I crushed the brute with one of my boots. Taking off those boots earlier had been a difficult and painful business. When daylight came and we started to move about, I found my feet had swollen so much that I could not get my boots on again. Every muscle in my body was aching.

Chapter Four

Changi

While remaining in a reclining position I was able to look about. The hut was quite open. It had an atap roof, much like our thatched roofs, the sides had been knocked out for air circulation, I think, leaving just the supporting wooden pillars. I was in No. 4 hut and could see the recreation field and officers' quarters, a fine big white building made of concrete. Next to it was St George's Church on the right and another white block on the left.

Inside my hut I looked for the spider and discovered little trace of him. The ants had taken him to pieces during the night and carried him off. The timber which was piled up to one side consisted of parts of wooden beds, so I helped myself and soon had a passable bed. But I had disturbed the ants again and there were thousands of them. A tin of creosote was found and used with good effect and soon we had our bed space reasonably tidy. The next thought was food. I was hungry. Our cooks had got started and rigged themselves up a few boilers, collected together some firewood, and the water was now boiling away merrily – but what to cook? There was no food anywhere. We asked about the food that had been brought up by the lorry and were told we would have that in good time. Tea was brought in, some tinned milk and a little sugar, and each man was given three army biscuits. I didn't know that army biscuits could taste so good, but it was the tea that I really wanted. I had developed an unquenchable thirst, which lasted for many days.

The first morning passed very quietly. We were quite content to be left alone to rest. At about midday, I was asked if I could do a few dressings, so I asked Sergeant Kennerley if he would fix me up with a place that had a little privacy where I could work. This he did and two men were detailed to carry my box from where it had been dumped. I felt very touched by the way the men offered to help me with everything. Several were asked to give up their bed spaces so that I could work and attend to the sick. There was no hesitation. Up they got, found another place and helped me to move my things in and then took their places in the queue for treatment. I made full use of the hot water at the cookhouse, and as bowls became available, got each man to wash the infected or injured parts before I treated them. After I had unpacked and placed my bottles and dressings on the shelves in the corner, I rigged up a seat outside and dealt with four patients at a time. After they had washed their feet, all I had to do was apply a dressing with antiseptic, poultice or healing ointment, and give advice.

My main job that afternoon was attending to chafed, blistered, and sore feet. I was very glad of the unlimited supply of hot water, because although the men washed themselves before being attended to, their sweaty feet gave off a very unpleasant smell and after attending to about 200 of such cases I felt quite sick. On one occasion there was a queue about 200 yards long. It had apparently got around that they could have their ailments tended to. Gwyn Williams and Jim Payne gave me a hand cutting dressings, but we had to work until it became too dark to do any more. What food was going was brought to me and I had my meal with the smell of sweaty feet to destroy my appetite. That night I was utterly weary again and very glad of the bed that I had rigged up.

The next day I was up early and found men already queuing up for treatment, so I had to start straight away. I found there were many strangers among the men as they were coming from all over the place; Gunners, infantry, Ordnance, and so on. There was no other dressing station operating that I knew of for a population of thousands which was increasing by the hour. As I worked, I found that, instead of the queue decreasing it grew longer. Finally, I just couldn't cope with them. I sent out a call for the Regimental Nursing Orderlies (RNOs) of the other companies to come and give a hand but none came forward. I told my Sergeant that I couldn't carry on like this for long and asked him if he could do

44

something about it. He said he would have a look around, and a little later came back with my MO. Was I glad! I sat down with a sigh and told him what a welcome person he was. He answered with some very complimentary remarks about the work I was doing and asked, 'But where did you get all this?' pointing to a box of medical gear and the coloured bottles on the shelf. I told him how I had brought it up on the lorry and he said, 'Thank God. Do you know that what you have here are probably the only medical supplies in the camp?' He said I would have to stop giving treatment, except to the very bad cases, as my little store would have to be distributed equally to the other units, so that everybody could have a little of what I had for the treatment of their own men. He told the men to go back to their respective units as medical supplies would get to them as soon as possible, and told the worst cases to come forward. We had about fifty, which were soon dealt with. I then packed my things away with a heavy sigh of relief.

That evening, I was instructed to take my equipment to the Post Office building, as it was being used as a temporary hospital. When I reported there, the officer who seemed to be in charge met me at the door. When he saw what I had, his eyes nearly popped out of his head. He wanted to know where the hell I had got the stuff. Instead of being pleased with what I had for him, he was questioning me as though I was a thief and selfishly keeping it to myself. I told him I had pinched it from an evacuated hospital and had carried it all the way from Singapore, knowing it would be needed. I then saluted and walked out. I have often wondered if he had to have medical attention himself after I left, as his face looked as though he was about to have a fit!

The next day I was sent for to assist at an MI room that had been opened on Quarry Road. When I got there I recognized the medicines as the supplies I had handed into the temporary hospital at the Post Office. I worked there from early morning to late at night and all day long men queued outside in the hot sun. It was nothing unusual to have a dozen or more men fainting while they waited.

I didn't see much of outdoor life during the first month or so at Changi. I was kept so busy at the MI room, but I heard all about what was going on from our boys when I returned each night to my hut.

We were in India lines at Changi. It was a very healthy spot being near the sea. The hut we were now in had been occupied by Indians, who had left their pets to keep us company – bugs, thousands of them. I could smell them before entering the hut.

The Nips decided that the camp would be run by the POWs themselves as a military unit. Major General Beckwith-Smith, the GOC 18 Division, was in charge and responsible to the Nips for its administration and our good order and discipline. He issued orders that we were still on active service and that the camp would be run on that basis, units being kept together and run by their own officers. After various officers' conferences had been held to decide on responsibilities and the system under which the camp would run, duties based upon units 'normal military' roles were laid down. For example, the RASC would take charge of supplies and the Royal Engineers responsibility for the repair of roads and buildings. All spare gear was also looked after by them and held in an RE yard from which ultimately, it became possible to get almost any material, given an officer's permission. Similarly, the RAOC had control over quite a collection of spares, tools, engines, oil and petrol and so forth.

While the administration was being sorted out, the Nips ordered working parties to build a wire entanglement around the whole camp which was then divided into five areas for the various national or service groups. Then, apart from the patrolling of the wire by their own soldiers, the Nips stayed away from the camp except for visits on Tuesday, Thursday and Saturday evenings to take a roll call.

The five areas were also wired and barricades placed on the roadways. Our own Military Police then controlled all movement through the barriers.

The five camp areas were run independently although certain activities were run centrally. For example, everybody drew rations from the RASC Supply Depot on the car park. Similarly, forestry parties were sent out daily to cut down rubber trees for fuel. As no lorries were allowed to be used for either rations or fuel, our lads stripped down a number of lorries, which were around the camp, to their chassis. These we called 'trailers'. Each unit was allocated a number of them according to its ration strength and unit teams were formed to pull them.

The issue of rations to the Supply Depot was made by the Nips, who called for working parties each Tuesday, Thursday and Saturday. These were transported down to the docks in lorries to collect supplies from large refrigerators in a warehouse on the dockside.

Unit ration parties assembled on the car park with their ration indents and their trailers. The NCO in charge then drew his ration of meat and rice or, sometimes, fish or vegetables. Then off the laden trailers would go, the half-naked teams sweating and straining at the uphill pull. The Australians were fortunate enough to have a downhill route and would tear down the camp roads, crowded on top of their loads and yelling to everyone to get out of their way as they charged at a dangerously high speed back to their area.

It was, of course, some weeks before this very well organized system became effective.

One aspect of life in Changi angered me very much – the enforcement of discipline. Whilst I well understood the need for discipline to be maintained and that we had a number of unruly men who needed little encouragement to break the rules, I could never find any excuse for the tyrannical methods by which it was maintained by the officers responsible for the administration of our camp at that time.

There were, of course, many reasons why men living under conditions of stress and hardship should sometimes feel disinclined to maintain the traditional standards of military discipline. For the same reasons that all men were entitled to be treated with humanity and understanding, two characteristics which seemed to be sadly lacking in the Military Police and their officers, who were responsible to the GOC for the administration of discipline in the camp.

They ran a military prison or detention centre on Temple Hill. In my opinion, it was a disgrace to those who ran it and to the British Army. At night screams could be heard coming from the prison. Men who I spoke to who had served a spell in it described the prison as 'a hell run by evil monsters'. Punishment by a diet of rice and water was commonplace for men who were already seriously undernourished, beatings took place and stubborn offenders were strung up by the wrist so that they were standing on tiptoe and left in that position for many hours.

We came to look upon our MPs as men to be avoided. They had become the agents of tyrants and snooped round the camp like a form of Gestapo. Punishments were handed out for the most trivial offences, such as a failure to salute, making the lives of many already miserable men almost unbearable. To many of us it seemed as if we were living under the very regime which the Allies were fighting so hard to destroy.

As the months rolled by, we settled down to a daily routine and much was achieved to ameliorate the misery of our situation. The areas were being efficiently run and we were like a lost legion, making our own little world and starting a new life. The companies pooled their entertainers and we had some excellent concerts, plays, revues and musical evenings. For recreation we had in our area two sports fields. On one we held cricket matches and sports and on the little one in front of our officers' quarters we had football and hockey. We had matches arranged between our own platoons, then inter-company matches and a league, and later, inter-area matches.

Clubs were formed. I started the idea going and eventually helped to organize a Welsh Society, which was followed by a Cockney Society and so on. Classes started and we even had a small university for the more advanced. There were a great many subjects to choose from and anyone could take up as many subjects as he wished. We were taught by experts, in some cases, college professors. Evening lectures were arranged and there was something on almost every day or night of the week.

News from the outside was available. We had a well concealed wireless, operated by a team of men picked for the job. They would monitor the broadcasts and every Sunday morning one of the journalists from the team would give us a summarized account of the news of the week. He would also give us his views on the development of the war on the different fronts and would finish up with Saturday's football results.

We posted sentries around the hut. If a Nip approached, our sentry would shout 'Red light' and the journalist would then immediately change his subject and talk about something commonplace. The aerial of the wireless set always had clothes

48

hung on it during the day, making a good deception as a clothes line. The wireless was never discovered.

In our camp, everybody had a job to do. A party of gardeners was formed and soon made headway. We gave the Nips money and they bought seed for us. After a few months, our garden produced its first vegetables which, for the most part, went to the hospital for our sick men. We also bought a few pigs, which provided pork for some of the sick at Christmas. In addition, many men started breeding chickens. They built chicken houses with any material they could find and then, through the canteen, they bought chicks at twenty-five cents each.

Coconut trees were strictly out of bounds. The coconuts were picked by an organized party of men who would go around every week and, using a long bamboo pole with a curved knife tied on the end, would lop off coconuts. They were then taken to the RASC for distribution to the many units. Coconuts, when grated up and toasted, went very well with the rice.

Our forestry party went out each day of the week except Sunday, which was a rest day for everybody. The wood was brought in from the forestry site by trailers and dumped at the RASC Supply Depot and was then distributed on a scale of one pound per head to every unit. When the wood eventually arrived at the cookhouses, teams of men would be anxiously waiting for it. Their job was to cut it up into convenient sizes for the boilers and they were kept busy all day with saws, sledges, wedges and axes. The rubber trees made poor fuel but our cooks soon got used to it and managed to keep reasonable fires going.

Many commodities were purchased for sale through our canteen. With an escorting sentry, we were allowed to take about six trailers in convoy once a week for purchases at nearby villages. This was a grand thing and meant an outing for the lucky ones. If we had a reasonably decent Nip with us, he might let us buy cigarettes, hot coffee and peanut toffee at the villages, but the main thing was provisions for the canteen and a trip outside the camp. And when the Nips started paying us a wage (ten cents a day), our canteens began to flourish. The men were noticeably happier. The ten cents was indeed little enough, but it provided the men with enough money every ten days for a smoke or something extra to eat.

Houses of worship were built by volunteers of the various denominations and where bomb damaged huts had been, beautiful little churches appeared. They contained little organs, pulpits, and many other things that make up the inside of a church. They were collected from the wrecked churches in Changi. As our gardens began to thrive, altar bouquets appeared, adding a lovely atmosphere to the churches.

We had a Church of England, a Free church and a Roman Catholic church. They were a credit to the Padres and the men who assisted them. We could go to any of the churches daily until 10 p.m. Our RSM started compulsory Church parades. However, after one or two Padres had stated that they preferred volunteers, the parades ceased.

Theatres were also built. Many were very rough with seating accommodations in the sand. Most of them were in the open and the stages were built as near as possible in pattern to those we have in our theatres at home, but what we lost on the appearance we gained in the performances.

When concerts and plays got going properly, arrangements were made with the Nips for parties to visit the different areas to see the shows. Many were the different types and forms of entertainment given in the respective theatres and budding producers found fame, if not fortune, among their fellow prisoners.

I have given a brief résumé of how, after becoming prisoners of war, about 75,000 men were settled into a small area which became a concentration camp. This area had been ravaged and blasted by the action of war. We were left under our own administration. Although we met with many irksome situations and trying difficulties, we surmounted them and, out of the ruins and chaotic conditions, a well organized and efficiently run camp materialized.

Chapter Five

Prison Life

I will now attempt to describe my experiences, feelings and opinions on things in general that occurred while I was at Changi during the fourteen months from February 1942 to April 1943.

After our capitulation, I heard many tales of the horror brought about by the Japanese occupation of Singapore. Of how the Nips executed innocent people without any trial, by cutting off their heads with swords. I also heard tales of how the Chinese and natives were tortured in an attempt to gain information, but one of the most dastardly things I partly witnessed was on about the 24 February.

I noticed many lorries loaded with Chinese men travelling through our camp in the direction of the Southern Area. I wondered if they were working parties, but my thoughts soon changed for each time I saw these truck loads go by, I would hear machine-gun fire a short time later. I learned in the months to follow that the Nips had picked up these men in Singapore city. They had toured the city with the lorries and when they saw a Chink, they grabbed him and put him on the lorry. When the lorries were full, they were driven to Southern Area. The Chinks were tied with rope into groups of six or more (like a bundle of skittles), they were taken out to sea, about 500 yards, and thrown overboard. As the men struggled in the water they were machine-gunned. This was no doubt a warning to the people of Singapore of what treatment they could expect at the hands of the Japanese Imperial Army.

Other things cropped up to occupy our minds at this time; one thought, persistent day and night, was of food. My empty stomach was continually gnawing at me, and I would long for a good feed of any of the food I had been used to. But now, when the meals were served, it would be rice for breakfast, lunch and dinner, and not much of that.

The change over from a European to an Eastern diet caused much suffering. Rice, being the staple food of the East, was our main issue. It was sent to us by the Nips and boiled and issued by our cooks – three quarters of a pint of steamed rice with a spoonful of watered jam for flavour (one pound tin of jam to two gallons of water). I had great difficulty in eating the rice as sometimes it would be sour or musty, and always contained maggots and weevils. After taking a few mouthfuls, I sometimes vomited and many times had to leave my meal untouched.

Many of the men were suffering as I was. We wondered if we would ever get used to that rice. This went on for months, and consequently more and more men went down with dysentery and other ailments. I had drawn my belt in eight inches during that short time. Then I got my first dose of dysentery.

I had been up practically all night, running to the latrine where I often found a queue waiting. When I started work in the morning I felt really ill. One day, after a few hours in the terrific heat, I must have fainted, no doubt due to weakness brought on by lack of food, the heat and sleepless nights. I came to on a stretcher with the MO leaning over me. I took the water he gave me and he told me to rest for a while. He came back and asked me some questions about myself, after which he prescribed a good dose of castor oil. For days after that I dared not move far from the latrine and felt light-headed and really ill, but rather than lie about in the hut, I carried on working as best I could. It was very exhausting, but I think I did the best thing. By working, I kept my mind active and off my illness and I gradually came around to eating the rice again and picked up strength.

At the MI room we now worked in teams of four. Four men working from 8 a.m. to 2 p.m., and four from 2 p.m. to 8 p.m. The team I worked with decided to work according to a system. One man would do the dispensing, two would do the dressings, and one would attend to skin diseases and the sterilizing of instruments. I was particularly interested in the skin diseases and, as the others didn't care for the job, I took over attending to the skin patients. I tended many interesting cases of scabies, prickly heat rash, tropical ringworm, fungi rot, impetigo, dermatitis, foot rot and athlete's foot.

I now began to acquire a lot of very valuable experience in dealing with these skin diseases, most of which were much more virulent in form than they would be in a milder climate and under less horrific living conditions. Our resources for treatment were very limited and, unfortunately, what we had were often very painful. For example, the treatment for impetigo was such that my patients would sit gripping the bench on which they sat, gritting their teeth and, often, with tears in their eyes. However, after about three weeks of intense suffering, manfully borne, there would be a complete cure.

I admired those men for the way they took the treatment. They not only suffered while being treated but continued to suffer agonies until they came next day for more. I made some very good friends from amongst them. They all seemed so very grateful for what little I did for them.

Our medical supplies by now were running low, so our issue was very small. We were given three small rolls of bandage, a square of gauze for dressing and very little, if any, of other necessities for an MI room. This daily issue would be for the treatment of about 400 men. Appeals were made for dressings, and it was amazing to see the load of bandages and dressings that were handed in. Our MI room became too small to cope with the number of men who became sick each day so we moved to a small building which was between the officers' block and the RE block. More RNOs were brought in to help us, so we were able to get our work done in less time and were able to arrange time off. During my time off I was able to give more attention to the sick of my own Company.

Very queer things were happening to our men. Some who, to all outward appearances, were strong and healthy, would collapse. Others would have blackouts and dozens of other ailments, suffered by men who had rarely had a day's illness in their lives. The rice diet had a lot to do with it, and the climate didn't improve matters. The bouts of dysentery weakened the men until very soon they became mere shadows of their former selves. I was being called out almost every night to treat someone. If I was called to anyone who was really ill and I was uncertain, or didn't know what the trouble was, I would always send for an MO. We had three on call each night: Doc Emery, Doc Sillman, and Doc Rolston (when the latter saw me for the first time at Changi, he recognized me as the orderly who had brought the sick parade to him at Paya Lebar).

These call-outs were often to men who were suffering from stress and had, perhaps, been bitten by one of the thousands of centipedes which abounded throughout the camp. Their bite was very painful for a few hours. Such a bite can lead a man under stress to panic and imagine all sorts of things. I soon worked out a technique for dealing with such cases. Although I did not like bluffing, I knew that, in many cases, it was the discreet thing to do. The man would calm down and by morning would have quite recovered.

We had a very beautiful little cemetery, run by a Major who had volunteered for the job having, tragically, lost his son, a Lieutenant, in the camp and was determined that our dead should be given a decent burial place. Our military funerals were carried out with great care and dignity and I witnessed many touching and impressive services there. The Major was assisted by a group of men with experience in that sort of work. I suppose that in a gathering of 75,000 men, there can have been few skills that could not be found somewhere amongst us.

I can never forget the funeral of our first death in Changi – Trevor Smith of our Company. He had come to me complaining of a sore throat and feeling very shaky. I looked at his throat and at once saw what I was certain were the first signs of diphtheria. Very alarmed, I quickly took him to the MO, who confirmed my suspicions and rushed Trevor into hospital, where he died. There had been no anti-toxin available and his heart could not stand the strain. He had a long history of illness and, like the rest of us, was suffering from the effects of the disastrous camp diet. When I told the Major's driver, Co Welsh, of my fears for Trevor, Co exclaimed, 'Hell, I only hope I shall never get that'. Poor Co. Within a matter of months, he too would have died from that deadly disease.

Trevor's funeral cortège was led by Major Kennon for, like me, Trevor had been a member of 55 Ammunition Company in France. As we marched, I mused that there we were about to bury a good comrade. I thought of everything I had known about him: he was a fine boy, had joined in all our fun and games, and our tricks. In fact, he had truly been one of us. He had told me of how, before leaving England, he had applied for forty-eight hours leave to see his brother who was home on leave from the Navy. He hadn't seen him for two years and felt he would like to see him before going abroad, but his application had been refused. A week or so later he got information that his brother had gone down with HMS *Hood*. Trevor had been very depressed about that and no doubt it had had a lot to do with his illnesses. But he had become quite cheerful again when he mixed with the men.

Two things about that funeral are etched in my memory. The first was the violent storm which struck even as the Padre began to read the service. There was a sharp clap of thunder and a wind bent the palm trees almost double. The rain fell in torrents and soaked us to the skin as we stood grouped round the grave. As the trumpeter began to sound the Last Post I looked up and there, to my astonishment, was a lorry full of Nip soldiers which had pulled up outside the cemetery. Every one of them was standing at the British salute in honour of a fallen soldier. As the last notes died away, the lorry moved on.

The problems of sickness in every imaginable form, mounted daily. In addition to my fixed hours in the MI Room, I was in demand throughout the twenty-four hours. Captain Wadesley, who well understood the pressure under which I worked, allotted me a little room of my own with a lock and key. I lived there for eight months.

I worked and worked, treating men for skin diseases, boils, cuts, bruises, indigestion, whitlows, ingrowing toenails and many other complaints. Deficiency diseases were on the increase and dermatitis would give us much trouble. Our problems were, of course, greatly increased by the lack of medical supplies but I found that it was possible to do much to alleviate suffering by using certain treatments which I had evolved from past experience. Many of them were initially rather drastic when applied but became surprisingly effective and the help I was able to give was greatly appreciated by my suffering patients.

It was now that I saw tropical ulcers for the first time. The men being in such a low state of health were easy prey for any infection. If they sustained the smallest scratch, it invariably turned septic and into a bad sore, later developing into an ulcer. We tried everything for them, we had been using dressings soaked in Mag Sulf, Eusol, and saline. A solution of Mag Sulf crystals seemed to heal them very slowly, so our MO ordered that they should be applied in crystal form. The first patient to whom I did this said he would never forgive me, until later, when he saw the result. I made a pack of crystals and bandaged it onto the ulcer: the man walked about in agonizing pain for hours afterwards, but he didn't disturb the dressing. Next day when I removed the dressing I found the ulcer free from pus and inflammation, and looking pink and healthy. Zinc ointment was then applied and, in a week, the patient was discharged.

While visiting the hospital, I made a friend of the pharmacist with the result that when we could not get medical supplies through the Nips, I got most of the requirements for my own little MI room with little difficulty.

Mornings and evenings I still had long queues to contend with. As food continued bad and meagre so sickness of all kinds increased. We were hard put to cope with the work. There were many cases of dry beriberi. The men would have maddening rheumaticky pains in the legs, chiefly in the feet and ankles, and could be seen walking about during the night unable to sleep owing to the pain. I started massaging feet, ankles and legs, and the men found that after being rubbed down they would get relief for about two hours, so I decided to do the job just before lights out so that they could get some sleep. I had a queue each night at 10 p.m. waiting for this treatment.

It has only been possible to touch upon the scale and scope of my medical work, which was so completely filling my life. Little did I realize at the time how invaluable the experience and knowledge of tropical diseases and health hazards that I was gaining all the time would prove, under terrible circumstances, in a few months.

Men from other units soon got to hear of my work or had met

me in the MI Room and came to me with their problems. From several of them I heard the most dreadful stories of Nip brutality, the worst being that of the massacre in the Alexander Military Hospital in Singapore on the day before the capitulation on 15 February 1942. As the attacking Nip troops arrived in the area, medical staff and patients were bayoneted or treated in the most brutal fashion. Not until the Japanese equivalent of our own Deputy Director of Medical Services arrived and put a stop to the savagery and set a guard on the hospital, could any sort of order be restored. A measure of the seriousness with which that terrible affair was regarded by the Nip High Command was shown by a visit to the hospital by General Yamaguchi himself, who apologized to the CO and promised him that they would have nothing to fear in the future. That horror story and the others I had heard made me realize how lucky we had been ourselves – so far.

Meanwhile, the outbreaks of diphtheria had become an epidemic. The Nips' adamant refusal to provide us with the anti-toxin meant that many men died, including Co Welsh, a loss that was a sad blow to us all and cast a gloom over our part of the camp. As the epidemic mounted and assumed very serious proportions, the order was given for the complete isolation of all diphtheritic cases.

At about this time, I developed acute pains in the bottom of my abdomen. I noticed it while stretching and, upon examination, I discovered two egg-like swellings and thought I must have a double hernia. I couldn't think of anything I had done to cause such strain, but later I remembered the sharp pain I had had when diving for cover the night I attempted to get my ambulance back from Chancery Lane. I was told that I wasn't to do any heavy work, or anything that might cause a further strain. It was surprising how this injury affected my future and was possibly the means of my eventual survival.

The Cymrodorians

As I have already mentioned earlier, at my suggestion, we formed a Welsh Society. We called ourselves 'The Cymrodorians'. It was a great success and before long, men who had come to our meetings from other areas were setting up their own branches of the society.

As for me, thanks to that society, I made many wonderful friends in the camp including: Padre John Foster Haig, Staff Sergeant Gordon Davies, Corporal Gordon Gleeson, Howell Griffiths, a carpenter and a special pal, Sergeant Bob Evans and many others. Only those who have experienced the stresses and strains of life as a prisoner of war can really know how deep, lasting and important such friendships become and what an immense part they play in enabling individuals to survive.

My medical duties, which took up so much of my time, day and night, made it impossible for me to do more for the society than become its assistant secretary. Nevertheless, I gave it every moment that I could and it was a source of great pleasure and interest to me.

I set up a register of all the Welshmen who were members of the society and made this freely available to anyone who wished to locate a friend or relative.

We held our meetings each fortnight on Sunday afternoons and, to make it interesting, it was arranged for someone to give a talk or lecture. During the week, we organized concerts and singing parties. It made a very pleasant way of passing the time. At each meeting I had my register handy for everyone to examine. A man came to me one day, just after the arrival of the Welsh Regiment, and asked if he could see the register. Afterwards, he shouted excitedly for me and wanted to know where he could find the man whose name he pointed to. The name was recorded as 'Fine – Cardiff – S.A.' (the name was Fine, he came from Cardiff and he was then in the Southern Area). The man told me that this was his brother and asked if I could arrange for them to meet. I sent a note to Padre Headly, a Welsh Padre in the Southern Area and, next morning, the Padre arrived in our area with the brother. It was a very happy reunion, for neither of the brothers had known that the other was out East. That was only one case. There were many similar instances of friends or relations meeting in this way.

One of the parties to arrive from Java brought someone I knew from my home town in Wales. Phillips was his name and we became firm pals. He used to come to my little room each night and we would chat about people we knew at home and events. If there was anything to eat, we always shared it. During the day we often looked round for waste vegetables which had been thrown away and, from the little that was edible, we cut them up and had a good 'boil up', inviting a few friends to join in.

Unfortunately, Phil didn't stay long at our camp as he had to move on with his party – destination unknown. We gave him a good send-off and held a little farewell party the night before he left. Little did we know, or guess, of the future, and the dreadful experiences we would both have during the next few years, which, in his case, ended in his death in New Guinea.

Padre John Foster Haig became president of our society. He was very popular and had a wonderful tenor voice. He used to work from morn to dark on his ministerial duties and entertaining. He would be seen during the day in hospital wards singing and cheering the sick and usually had with him his little party of musicians and singers; Aubrey King, George Wall, Reginald Renison and Dennis East. This party became very well known for their high class musical entertainment. They were a great team and did much to make life more bearable in our prison camps.

The Padre had sung professionally as 'John Foster' and would sometimes spare some of his valuable time to come to our meetings, where he would tell us of his experiences as a singer. In a talk he gave, entitled 'Singers I have known' he kept us keenly interested for over an hour, and told us about his great friend Paul Robeson. He once shared a programme with Paul and, not being very well known, he had not expected much of a reception from the audience. When the announcer introduced Paul Robeson as the event of the evening, Paul pushed John Foster forward from the wings to take the applause, and then stepped forward himself. On one occasion our Padre had filled in for Richard Tauber when Tauber was ill, and John did the whole concert at short notice. He had met practically all the singing celebrities during his career, and when he spoke of each one, he played a record of that person's favourite song. He had kept and preserved these records all through the action and they became a real treasure to us.

I grew very attached to the Padre. Through being assistant secretary of the 'Changi Cymrodorians', a member of his church choir, and later a member of his male voice choir, I was with him for a short time almost every day. I have sat for many quiet hours, talking to him in his billet, where we would discuss news, our future, Christianity and the society. Regarding the latter, I told him that there were quite a number of Welshmen who had died or been killed in Singapore, and I would like it if he would arrange a memorial service. He consented and, at the society's next meeting, it was discussed and a programme decided upon.

The Padre made it possible for me to have access to the camp records and there, in company with my two Welsh pals, Staff Sergeant Gordon Davies and Corporal Gordon Gleeson, I spent many hours looking through registers for Welshmen. I found about 700 names of which about thirty-five were those of men who had died in action. These names were carved on a wooden plaque in preparation for the service. (The plaque was later presented to a little chapel in Cardiff.)

We rehearsed daily for our orchestral and male voice choir concerts, and it was during one of these rehearsals that our Padre broke down from overwork and lack of food. He had to take a rest and another very dear friend of mine, Kenneth Scovell, took charge of the choir. Ken was responsible for the scores for the orchestra and the arrangement and composition of the music. He was a teacher of music and a brilliant conductor.

The Japanese Honour the Allied Dead

The Nips sent in an order that a party of men were to be ready to move away from Changi to Singapore City to assist in clearing up the place. Many of my old friends of 55 Company went with that party, leaving at about the end of March 1942. We heard later that many of these were employed in building a memorial on Bukit Timor, the highest point on Singapore Island, to honour those Allied soldiers who had fallen during the Japanese invasion.

More Working Parties and Rumours of a Railway

I often thought about the extraordinary paradox between the erection of that memorial and the tribute paid to Trevor Smith's funeral by the Nips in the lorry and the terrible stories of such atrocities as the massacre in the hospital and the slaughter of the unfortunate Chinese in the sea.

A second working party was demanded in June and many were

the wild rumours regarding its destination. There were stories of a railway to be built in Thailand (or Siam as we knew it), or that the party might go to Japan.

When the men for the party had been detailed, those who remained at Changi were ordered to hand in their surplus clothing so that the men going away could have reasonably decent clothes to wear. Mr Mitchell came to tell me that he would be leaving with this party. I told him that I would like to go with him. He was pleased with the idea but was concerned about my condition as I had lost a lot of weight since going down with dysentery. He took me to the MO who refused to let me go, saying that the party might have heavy work to do, and he would not be responsible for sending me. So that was that. After a few days Mr Mitchell and I were wishing each other farewell – he was going to an unknown destination and I was to remain at Changi. I helped him pack his kit and load it on the lorry. After promising a reunion after the war and arranging that whoever should get home first would write to the other one's relatives, we wished each other the best of good luck. It seemed that most of my friends were going away. It was very depressing. The fact that we couldn't get any word to our people at home – and, worse still, couldn't get a word from them – didn't help matters.

After the party had left, the Nips told us that there were likely to be many such working parties and that Changi would be used as a transit camp. Prisoners of war from outlying islands would be brought to Changi and from there would be drafted to the various working camps. Each working party to leave would be recorded as a force, so the first party was 'A Force', the second party 'B Force' and so on.

We had taken it for granted that our officers would remain with us. Despite the hatred we often felt towards them for their selfish ways and their failure to make the least effort to share the hardships of prison life with us, they dealt on the black market for decent food, for which, unlike us, they had the money to pay and which was so desperately needed by so many sick men. Men who were dying daily from malnutrition and their inability to fight against the terrible tropical diseases from which they were suffering. We did not want the officers to be taken away. Their selfishness and seeming indifference to our suffering and hardships made us pretty sore. Nevertheless, there was a certain feeling of security whilst they were there. Consequently, when the news came that all officers above the rank of Lieutenant Colonel were to go to Japan, it came as a bit of a blow.

Generals Percival and Beckwith-Smith left Changi towards the end of February 1943.

Unlike so many of his subordinate officers, General Beckwith-Smith was admired and respected by us all. He seemed to have quite a bit of influence with the Nips and had got us many little things which we would otherwise never have had. We were sorry to see him go. Lieutenant Colonel Harris RASC took over command after the party had left.

Before he went, General Beckwith-Smith issued a Special Order of the Day of farewell to his Division, of which we were part. I have taken this extract from it, for it shows just what a fine man he was and how much the Division meant to him:

No Commander has led a more happy and loyal team into battle. The Division was sent into a theatre of War for which it was neither trained nor equipped, to fight a clever and cunning enemy who was on the crest of a wave. It was sent to fight a battle already lost and, had to pass through troops whose morale had been badly shaken. It had to endure long periods of hardship without food or rest, yet it fought with great courage and intensity, inflicting heavy losses on the enemy. Every man may rightly hold his head high knowing that he has upheld the best traditions of the British Army.

In his closing paragraph, the General undertook to devote the rest of his life 'to help' in any way, the officers, WOs and men of the 18th Division! Sadly, we later learned, he died of diphtheria on the ship taking him to Japan, so could never fulfil that under-taking.

The Selarang Incident

Until the end of August 1943, we had had little direct contact with the Nips, apart from the thrice-weekly roll call and various admin-istrative working parties for such things as the collection of rations and wood cutting. Essentially, our General and his staff had stood between us and our captors.

On 28 August we were paraded in a field near Selarang along with some 20,000 other prisoners of war. After waiting for nearly two hours in the blazing heat, we were subjected to a harangue by General Shimpei Fukhei, who had arrived from Japan to assume responsibility for all POW camps in Malaya, Sumatra and Java. His closing words were to the effect that if we were good, he would be kind to us 'I think'. That he was shot in 1946 for war crimes says it all!

On 3 August we were called on parade before our CO. He told us that General Shimpei Fukhei had sent in forms which he wanted each man to sign. They stated that we would promise not to escape. The Colonel said that it was entirely up to us. We could do just as we liked about signing. He asked for a show of hands of those who didn't want to sign, and every hand went up. Then he told us that that was also the decision of the officers.

On 1 September, we were told that General Shimpei Fukhei now ordered us to sign the forms. If we disobeyed, he threatened heavy punishments. We still refused to sign and the forms were sent back.

That same night, our Command received orders to prepare everyone to move. At 7 a.m. on 2 September, we got our orders. We were to pack up everything we could carry, food, clothes and stores and be clear of the camp by 6 p.m. to move into Selarang Barrack Square.

We started the four mile journey, men loaded with their packs and carrying pails, cooking pots and tins, some would carry their belongings on a long pole and their packs would swing from side to side as they trudged along. Men who had chickens or ducks had hastily put them into boxes and were carrying them. Some men had to pull the big trailers, so placed their kits aboard.

We couldn't guess what lay ahead of us. There were rumours of executions, and beatings, but despite it all, there was much cheery banter and leg pulling.

We arrived at the Selarang Barrack Square about 4 p.m. We were shown where to dump our things, and told not to move away from the spot. There was a continuous stream of men marching in and I began to wonder how room would be found for us all.

There were five blocks of buildings; each block, I was told, housed 170 men in peacetime.

The area was surrounded by a road with a malarial drain on each side, the drain on the inside being our boundary, and we were not allowed to cross the drain to the road. The Nips were using Sikhs as sentries and they constantly patrolled the roads. These men had been fighting on our side in the Indian Army, but had gone over to the Free Indian Army and were now with the Nips. In some cases they were worse to us than the Nips.

By 6 p.m. 15,000 men or more were enclosed in the small area, where normally about 1,000 were housed. We were in an awkward predicament – there were about four lavatories to each block, twenty lavatories for 15,000 men. Orders were given for working parties to be detailed immediately to dig latrine trenches in the Barrack Square. The Square was surfaced with hard macadam, making it a very difficult job and, as space was limited, cooking had to be done a few yards away from the latrines. The square was littered with temporary chicken runs, trailers, cooking gear, and piles of earth from the latrines on which men were working in shifts for twenty-four hours a day. Men had their bed spaces all over the place, and every available inch was taken up – parts of the square, on the roofs of the buildings – and anywhere that a man could stretch out, was occupied by someone.

The remainder of my platoon and I were given the corner of a passageway as our sleeping space. When we lay down for the night we were head to foot, and packed so tight together that one couldn't turn around without disturbing the others. The concrete was too hard for some, so they sat up most of the night. Many of the men had dysentery and many suffered from chronic diarrhoea.

It was a great relief when morning came. There was much suffering and anguish in that 'black hole' of ours. I had my little first aid bag with me and I was kept busy all day attending to one or another in the confined space.

The officers had taken the landing just above me for themselves, where they took up as much space for one as we had for four. Some had so much kit that it took up more room than one man's space!

Our cooks had rigged up the cooking gear and got the rice on. We had our water tank with us; it was full but it contained only

250 gallons of water which wouldn't go far. We had brought our rations with us, so had the officers, but theirs were more varied than ours. They couldn't possibly think of sharing with us, not even when we were in a hole like this. Part of our cooking gear had to be placed on one side for the officers' cooks. They had brought about a dozen ducks with them which they had reared at Changi, and these were prepared for the midday meal.

At midday we were served three-quarters of a pint of unflavoured boiled rice, a teaspoonful of sugar and, as water was short, we were given only half a pint of hot water. The officers came down to get their meal and passed us on their return with one mess tin of boiled duck, and one mess tin of rice. As they went by men started 'quack quacking'. Some of the officers seemed rather red-faced and looked ashamed – they with duck and we with plain rice.

During our first day in that hell, the Nips sent for some of our officers. They were taken down to the beach where a number of our men were lined up before a firing squad. These men had been escapees and, after being recaptured, had been sent to hospital. They were dragged from their hospital beds that morning and brought to that spot and shot as a warning to us all. One of the men was still alive after many shots had been fired at him and shouted 'You lousy bastards, why don't you shoot straight.' Needless to say, they were his last words.

On the third day we were still without a wash and shave, and there was very little or no water left. Rations were very low, sickness was on the increase, there was no firewood for cooking, and latrine diggers, though working night and day, weren't able to keep ahead of the work. Then we were told that the Nips had threatened that if we didn't sign the forms, they would bring all the hospital personnel, staff and patients into our crowded area. This would entail a heavy loss of life as there were so many very sick men there.

Then followed the order from our own Commanding Officer. He considered that, due to the latest threat, the increasing sickness and the danger of an epidemic, we must sign the form. He said that as we were signing under duress, our promise wouldn't mean anything, so he was now giving us an order to sign, and would take full responsibility for us doing so.

We all signed the form, vowing that should the occasion arise we would escape anyhow. A few hours later we were given orders to return to Changi. I never thought I would have ever been so delighted to return there.

Soon after our return, we learned of our General's death.

We held a memorial service on our recreation ground. All Padres took part and many Union Jacks covered the platform on which they stood. The service was indeed impressive and we were left feeling very downhearted. Most of us believed that perhaps the General had been tortured for some reason or other and had died as a result.

I managed to obtain a local paper at about this time called the *Nippon Times*, and one paragraph stated that prisoners of war were now being sent to Japan, where they would work for the great Japanese people for the rest of their natural lives. This was not very encouraging, following what the Japanese General had told our Commanding Officer at Selarang. His words were, 'It is useless for anyone to think of attempting to escape or hoping for release or help from your own people, because the Great Japanese Navy has utterly destroyed the American Navy and crippled the British Navy. We have defeated your Armies and now control all the Pacific.' It was remarkable the way our men laughed at this kind of news. They would always scoff and say, 'They hope, but wait until Churchill really gets going'.

The Forestry Party

I was given permission to go out with the forestry party as I was getting quite bored at being in camp day after day. Since I wasn't allowed to do heavy work, I knew I couldn't get a job with a working party. So I volunteered to go out one day a week as First Aid man with the woodcutters. This was accepted and we marched to where the rubber trees were being felled to make a clearing for a cemetery. I found the work interesting, and the day out made a grand break for me.

The trees were felled by men who first dug a clearance around the roots and, when sufficient earth had been removed and roots cut, a rope was attached to the tree about ten feet from the ground. About twenty or more men then grabbed the rope and pulled, as in a tug-o-war, until over came the tree, and the men scampered in all directions out of its way as it crashed down.

In the branches of the trees were many ants' nests, wonderfully made and each about the size of a football. Needless to say, when the trees came crashing down, the nests burst and out came thousands of red ants, a good half-inch long, mad as hell and ready to bite anything in sight with their tweezer-like jaws!

I became very interested in the vast range of insects and reptiles in that humid land. Almost all could bite, as we learned to our acute discomfort, and several were lethal!

While on that party I managed to purchase a camera and a film and, though it was rather a risk, I chanced a few snaps of the men at work, the little cemetery, our camp, our church and of other scenes of interest. When I had used up the film I sealed it, made it waterproof, and placed it in a tin I had prepared with a false bottom. This tin I half filled with palm oil and it survived many Nip searches, eventually getting it home safely to England only to find that the film had been destroyed by its own chemical composition.

As the rubber trees got used up and the plantations cleared, the forestry party had to move further afield and eventually made a camp on the site of their work. So, sadly, my little outings came to an end and I had to put up with the monotony and the routine of camp life again.

The Terror of India Lines

That routine, boring though it often was, had its lighter moments and one or two real highlights, such as the arrival of a Red Cross ship in the harbour and our first sacks of mail from home.

But it certainly had its black spots, one of which, the conduct of the Military Police, I have already described. A very similar black spot but one which lowered directly over our own lines was our Regimental Sergeant Major, the RSM or 'Tara' as we called him. The Army was that man's life and he saw himself as second only to God. Woe betide anyone who crossed him. He was dubbed 'The Terror of India Lines', and a terror he was, making an already miserable life more miserable for us all. Little wonder that several attempts were made to injure him, some of which, had they been successful, would have cost him his miserable life.

To be excessively 'regimental' in the circumstances in which we found ourselves would have been bad enough but Tara was just plain mean with no thought for anyone but himself.

Our latrines were a long way off from some of our huts and were the Asiatic 'squatter type'. As there were two damaged water closets near the huts, the REs repaired them so that the sick men, (many of whom were almost too weak to squat) could use them at night. As soon as the closets were useable, the RSM decided that they would be out of bounds to Other Ranks and were to be used by Sergeants and above only. Even the Sergeants saw the unfairness of this, but Tara had his way. Two days later, the closets were found to be smashed, the seats and pans were in little pieces and the cisterns damaged beyond repair.

I don't uphold such actions but our RSM was asking for trouble and it looked as though he was out to get it, by being such a persistent nuisance. He would snoop around the huts, listening to the men talking. As he often heard very uncomplimentary remarks about himself he would then punish the men in different ways until he became unbearable.

The first attempt to injure him, I remember, was when I heard a commotion during the night. Men were running and tripping over tins and so on, but as there were many practical jokes being played, I didn't take much notice. Next morning I saw that large lumps of concrete had been thrown through his window and had landed a few inches from his head with such force that the bed had collapsed. Tara did all he could to trace the culprits, but without success.

The last attempt on Tara's life was made during the last months of our first year at Changi. He and Staff Sergeant Gordon Davies were playing chess. Their heads were bent over the board studying the game when a large stone flashed between their heads and crashed into the room. The culprits were almost caught that time, but many men were shielding them and they got away.

Tara became very concerned about these attacks, but it didn't alter his ways a bit. In fact, I thought he became worse. My pal Gordon Davies went into the hospital with diphtheria at this time. I was very grieved and thought he was lost for sure, but he eventually came back to us, though very weak.

It is a long-standing tradition of the British Army that an officer's first concern is for the well-being of his men and that his own comfort and safety are invariably secondary to that. This fine tradition seemed to be quite unknown to the bulk of our officers in Changi. The RSM took on most of the officers' responsibilities and did a lot of their work for them. Small wonder then, that appeals to the officers about Tara's tyranny fell on stony ground.

Chapter Six

It Was Not All Gloom

Despite Tara and the Military Police, life in Changi had its brighter moments. One of these was the introduction of twice-weekly swimming parades. Under the watchful eye of Nip soldiers, parties, each under an officer, would march down to the coast and plunge into the sea, though forbidden to go more than fifty yards from the shore.

Not only were these outings a wonderful break from monotony but they had a great healing effect upon those with tropical skin diseases – the brine having a valuable therapeutic effect.

We took large water tanks with us, which were tied to trailers and parties of men pulled them to the water's edge, where they were filled with sea water. Back in camp these tanks of water were boiled for many hours, after which the water was baled out of the tanks and a thick layer of salt would be left at the bottom. The salt was used at our cookhouses and helped to improve the flavour of our meals, which would otherwise be saltless.

Those treasured outings were entirely dependent upon the whims of the Nips who would cancel one on the slightest pretext, causing us the most bitter disappointment.

Towards the end of September, we became very excited at the rumour that the Nips were going to allow Red Cross supplies to be sent in to us. That wonderful news would mean food, clothes, medical supplies and mail. The impact upon the whole camp was electric. Every man seemed to have taken a new lease of life, for we were going through a particularly bad time. Months of living on such poor food and on meagre rations even of that, had taken its toll and all sorts of measures had had to be taken to give the men the vitamins they needed to sustain life. We even ate fertilizer, awful though it tasted. Every man had to consume two tablespoons of rice polishings, which contained most of the vitamin B in rice, every day, before he was allowed to draw his meal, despite the fact that this bran-like substance was alive with maggots and weevils. We had also to consume half a pint of sour rice water daily. The administration of these awful medicines was carried out under the watchful eye of an officer. Many men forfeited their meals rather than take them, yet there can be no doubt that they did help to keep us going until that unforgettable day, 13 October 1942, when we were officially notified that a Red Cross ship had docked in the harbour.

Next day, all was hustle and bustle as we made spaces for the storage of this manna. Our own men unloaded the ship and brought back every trailer we possessed laden with precious supplies. What a day in the history of Changi!

That night we sat down to a meal of corned beef and rice rissoles, rice with a spoonful of jam, our issue of one pound of sweet biscuits, half a pound of vitamin sweets, to eat as we pleased, and a pint of sweet coffee to wash it all down. Then, to finish off, English cigarettes, sixty-five to each man. There were sighs of contentment everywhere. Our only disappointment was that there was no mail. There weren't any complaints that night, since we had been fed like lords and enjoyed a meal more than many could have enjoyed a banquet.

The supplies had come in bulk so cookhouses got the issue and distributed the food a little at a time, keeping some for Christmas. I don't remember seeing any clothes, but there were plenty of boots to go round.

There was quite a lot of hospital food and medical supplies. I think the chief vitamin food to come in was Marmite. This came in small jars packed in large cases and there was enough to last a long time. The whole lot went to the hospital and was issued to the malnutrition cases. However, many jars found their way to the billets of higher ranks. Another consignment of Red Cross supplies came in about a month later, but was so limited that it was hardly noticed.

Conditions became much better at about this time. We were

now receiving ten cents a day pay from the Nips and we were allowed canteens in the camp and organized parties of men were allowed to purchase goods from nearby villages to sell at the canteens. We got a limited supply of eggs, peanut toffee, sweet potatoes, rice flour, tapioca, fruit and Gula Malacca. These all helped to make the rice palatable and we began to look to the future with much more hope.

Our canteens flourished. Every man had a little to spend (one dollar every ten days), we had plenty of recreation and sport, and many concert parties which gave a good range of variety with plays, pantomimes, concerts and variety shows. To my mind, as things were, there wasn't much to complain of, considering that we were prisoners of war.

There were cases of bad beatings by the Nips and tales that working parties in other parts of Singapore were having a bad time. Occasionally a man returned to our hospital from these parties in an emaciated condition which would give us proof of this, but as far as we were concerned, most of us had got used to rice and were having a little food from the Red Cross issue each day. We had the canteen, where we could spend our dollar every ten days, we were free to study, to exercise, to entertain and be entertained, to take part in sport, look on, and were generally free inside the barbed wire. There wasn't much work, but each man had a job, and we had religious freedom, being able to attend the church of our choice. The extent of our religious freedom was shown by the fact that the Bishop of Singapore was allowed to visit our church at India Lines to conduct a confirmation service. Many of our men were confirmed that day and I was told that, on the same day, the Bishop ordained an officer, the only man I know of to be ordained in a prisoner of war camp.

As Christmas was getting near, preparations were being made to make it a Christmas to remember. There were to be pantomimes, afternoon sports, Christmas dinner from saved Red Cross food, and a religious service held at the little church (which was made from old pieces of wood, atap roofed with plane seats inside, a made-up wooden altar, and patched pulpit). Howell Griffiths and I went nightly to practise in the choir where Padre Haig, that distinguished singer, conducted and directed us in the singing of the Christmas carols.

Then, one day, we were given a card to send home. We could write twenty-four words on it but we were not allowed to say where we were or anything about it. There were so many things we couldn't write about that I almost despaired of writing the full twenty-four words. I spent more than an hour trying to fit in sentences and, after all the trouble I took over it, I was surprised when our censor sent my card back for me to delete one of the sentences. Eventually the cards went away, although I heard later that they remained in Singapore for quite a long time. Nevertheless, it made us a little easier in our minds about our relatives at home. We thought that the cards were on their way and at some time in the not too distant future, our people would know that we were still alive. We could only hope for their swift delivery.

I met Major Kennon about this time. He was in charge of a party of men who were felling trees to allow for an extension to our gardens. The Major was busy helping the men and I noticed that his legs were bandaged, so enquired about them. He told me that he had a few ulcers, so I examined them and found that they were very discoloured and seemed to be diphtheritic. I told the Major what I thought and said that he was in a serious condition and ought to see the MO straight away. He did, and was sent straight to the hospital where for many weeks he fought hard for his life.

Christmas

On Christmas Day he was moved to a ward and it was thought that he was strong enough to receive a few friends. Many went to see him and to wish him a Happy Christmas. They came back saying that he would soon be out of the hospital. We made Christmas Day as joyous as we could under the circumstances. For myself, my mind was at home. What I would have given to be there when the children awoke to see what Father Christmas had brought. That had always been a very happy moment for me, but I had to shake myself. Thinking of home would soon upset me, so I forced my thoughts to more material things.

On Christmas Eve, we held a midnight service in our church. It was packed out and we sang carols until about 1:30 a.m. It created a real Christmas feeling and spirit.

On Christmas morning, we had a pint of sweet porridge and sweetened coffee for breakfast. We went to church at 11:00 a.m. and, on our return, we had lunch – sweet potato chips, corned beef and a little pudding made to look like Christmas pudding, served in a small corned beef tin.

As we went in for dinner our officers stood at the entrance and handed a packet of cigarettes, five cheroots and a packet of dates to each man, then they waited at the table, which is the custom in the Army. I think that every man there enjoyed himself and for a little while forgot the misery of prison life as our Christmas feast progressed.

In the afternoon, we held a football match, then had tea. I don't remember what we had for tea, but I do remember that our cooks had worked miracles and had managed a riceless day for us. In the evening we held a mass concert on the field and the day ended having been an enormous success.

Boxing Day too was a holiday and, after a day of sports and games, we put on a show in the little theatre we had built ourselves.

The day was marred for many of us by the news of Major Kennon's death during the previous night. I was deeply saddened, as were all my friends who had served with him in 55 Company in France. No one who had seen him on the quay at Dunkirk would ever forget him. He was to us everything we wanted from our officers – a great leader, capable and deeply concerned for the welfare of his soldiers – always friendly and always ready to pitch in with a helping hand when the going was tough.

We at first decided to cancel the show as a mark of respect for him but our own Major insisted that Major Kennon would have wished it to go on as planned – so on we went. The show was a tremendous success, with an audience of about 400 officers and men.

This was the only time that I had attempted an effeminate part. Six of us rigged ourselves up as chorus girls and I had never seen such an unsightly lot of girls in my life. Red ink and chalk mixed with Vaseline made our rouge and lipstick, and soot our eyebrows. Kiss curls were well shaped with Vaseline and we wore a coloured cloth around our heads, with skirts and brassieres made from blue tent cloth. We were called the 'Beri Beri Girls'.

Our band consisted of a piano, an accordion and several

stringed instruments, made in the camp. They got the show going with a few snappy pieces. Then our compère started a near riot. Having failed to get a laugh with his jokes, he launched two well-aimed rotten eggs into the audience. The boys were rolling in the aisles and it was a good ten minutes before we could get the Beri Beri Girls on stage.

As soon as they saw us, the laughter broke out again. All went well and the lads loved it. The high spot was quite unintentional! I was the last off and, as I went, my brassiere slipped down to my waist and the stuffing fell out! The lads went crazy!

What an evening that was! There were nineteen of us in the party. Now, as I write, twelve are dead. Things that had brought us so close in friendship made the parting so hard to take when it came. If only I could recall their smiling faces as they were that night without the shadow of their deaths.

The New Year

The shenanigans went on and New Year's Day, 1 January 1943, was another riot of fun. Yet it was impossible not to wonder what the New Year would bring. What was in store for us? How would the war go? Would we be free at this time next year? Would we live to see our families again?

Two thirds of those laughing, rioting lads would be dead by the end of the year. Thank God we didn't know what was in store for us or we would surely have given up hope then and there.

The party that had gone to work in Singapore some months earlier returned during January and the rumours about the building of a railway in Siam reared their heads once more. But the delirium of receiving mail from home on 16 January blotted out all thoughts of anything else. Out of three or four mail bags I got seven letters.

I was one of the earliest to be in luck – a letter from an aunt and one from an uncle. Men came from all over the camp just to see and even feel the letters. I pinned them up so that everyone could see them. They were from dear old Blighty – that was all that mattered. I saw tears in many a hardened man's eyes that day.

Unfortunately, but inevitably, there was as much bad news as good. How can one forget those men with beaming faces rushing forward to receive a letter only to see their faces cloud over with misery a few moments later. Perhaps a loved one had died or a married man had received news of an unfaithful wife. Amongst the saddest were those who received no mail. They would suffer untold misery. No letter, no word of any sort and they could not write and ask why.

In the middle of February, another party was required for 'destination unknown' and, as we were short of fit men, most of the party that had returned from Singapore were detailed to go. I think they went as part of E Force. So I was parted again from friends who had only recently returned to camp. One was Gwyn Williams, who had been my pal for such a long time in England. We had been together as batmen, had shared the same room, then the same cabin during the voyage out to Singapore and now, for the second time, we were being parted again. We wondered if we would meet again and under what circumstances. We planned a meeting back home when the war was over, then said 'Farewell.' What more could we do?

The Memorial Service

In the following weeks I was kept busy doing the secretarial work for the Cymrodorians. Our memorial service was to take place on 1 March, St David's Day, and there was so much to prepare. When the day arrived, I was up early. My job was to help arrange the church, and be there to show everyone to their places. Over fifty invitations had been printed and sent out with a souvenir programme. Arrangements had been made for Welshmen to have the day off and for them to be marched in from the adjoining areas. After the memorial service there would be the unveiling of plaques, one with the names of the Welsh dead at Singapore, one with the names of the dead of the 77 Heavy AA Regiment, and one in memory of General Beckwith-Smith who had commanded the Welsh Guards.

While I was showing the men to their places, Howell Griffiths (who came from Llanelly) was arranging a roll of honour in the front of the Church. The Australian Welsh had just arrived and a young fellow asked me who it was that was putting up the roll of honour. I told him who it was, to which he replied, 'I thought I recognized him, I was twelve when I left Llanelly for Australia, and he and I went to school together.' I watched as he approached Howell, who seemed sceptical at first and then his eyes flew open wide with recognition. The two boys almost cried in the joy of meeting again after so many years.

Many men wore imitation leeks made from cloth and for about two hours we all existed in the 'Land of our Fathers', in mind and spirit. We were all back in Wales, we had Welsh prayers and Welsh singing of national songs and hymns. We finished with our national anthem, *Mae-hen-wlad-fy-Nhadue*.

That evening we attended the opening night of our musical concert with full orchestra, male voice choir and soloists. It was as any Welshman could have wished on the day of his patron saint, to pay homage to our dead heroes and to sing and listen to music and song. It made me feel good inside when I sang with the choir. When our Padre, John Foster Haig, sang, he was called back seven times and, as I heard a Welshman say, 'There was singing for you, Mum'.

Time to Go

Not many days after we had celebrated St David's day, we heard rumours that the whole camp was going to move. Later the rumours changed and I heard that 7,000 men were wanted for a working party. Then we got the official news: the Nips had sent in for 7,000 men to which our Command had replied that we didn't have 7,000 fit men. The Nips said that they wanted 7,000 men, be they fit or otherwise, as they were sending them up north to a camp where the climate was more suitable, food more plentiful, and the camp would be as at Changi, not a working camp. Sick men could go, as there would be no marching and transport would be provided for kits that couldn't be carried. This seemed too good to be true, but most of the senior ranks were going and men who held key jobs were volunteering. Practically all of my Company were detailed to go, so we all began to get ready for the big move. We were glad of the chance to get away to anywhere from the confined space we had been living in for the past thirteen months. So it was with a light feeling, as of adventure, that we all set to pack. All our books were collected to form a library at the other end and all the cookhouse gear was packed away tidily. My medical kit was packed in a special box, and I put all my personal kit in with it for safety. I painted a big red cross on the box and nailed down the lid, then painted my name and unit on it. I then packed a smaller box with small bottles of different concentrated liquids, and packed my little bag to carry with me.

Everything was now ready for us to leave Changi. I was feeling pleased to leave this prison camp, but always at the back of my mind were the words of the Captain of the *Sobieski* when he wished us farewell at Halifax. 'You are going on a very mysterious journey, where you will end up I cannot guess, but I wish you luck'. I hadn't come to the end of that journey yet, and I wondered where it would end and how. We were now about to go away with F Force.

Part Two

Life and Death on the Railway

In the fell clutch of circumstance
I have not winced nor cried aloud.
Under the bludgeonings of chance
My head is bloody but unbowed.

William Ernest Henley

Chapter Seven

By Rail to Thailand

I had been to the hospital and said my goodbyes and many of my friends and acquaintances there had expressed a wish to be coming with me on this journey to the wonderful new camp that we had been promised. I consoled them by saying that they would probably follow me with the next party and we would meet again under more pleasant circumstances.

My kit and small store of 'medics' were all packed away and I was lying on the floor of my little room trying to get some rest before leaving in the early hours. At about 9 p.m. Staff Sergeant Jock Campbell shook me and asked if I had anything I could give him for his stomach. He said that he had a bad bilious attack and that he was almost doubled up with pain. I explained to him that I had only my First Aid outfit handy and, as everything was packed away and nailed down, I couldn't possibly unpack just to get him a dose of powder, which was inferior stuff anyway and probably wouldn't be of any use to him. But he pleaded, stressing that he could never start on this long journey feeling as he did. Wouldn't I unpack as a special favour to him? He reminded me how he had once saved me while in Belgium. So I said 'OK, you win' and, in a joking manner, told him where he could go. Then I said 'Come back in about ten minutes and I'll have something for you'. So away he went and I lay there a little longer, thinking of the incident in which Jock had saved my mate and me from almost certain capture by the Germans in May 1940.

My heavily overladen lorry, which had covered a vast mileage over the past few weeks and developed an engine knock, had finally broken down with a main bearing gone. My mate, Charlie Sands, and I managed to get it off the road under some trees and hidden from marauding Jerry aircraft and sat down to wait for help to arrive from our Company, 55 (Ammunition) Company RASC, which was somewhere outside Dunkirk. Suddenly we heard tanks approaching and five Jerry *Panzers* pulled up on the crossroads nearby. Fortunately, they moved off up the road along which we had been driving, towards Poperinghe.

After a couple of hours, we decided that the only thing to do was to set fire to the lorry and make our way to the Company on foot. Just as we were going to do this, we heard a vehicle approaching. To our immense relief, it was our Company break-down wagon, with Jock Campbell in charge.

Jock was amazed to see us as he had narrowly missed the Jerry tanks as they went through Poperinghe. Thanks to him and his driver, Fred Jackson, we were soon back with the Company, just as the lads were beginning to destroy all our kit and vehicles to deny them to the enemy.

Forty-eight hours later, after going through the madness of Dunkirk, we were safely home in England. So I owed Jock a great deal.

I got up to get Jock his powder and found that my box had been taken away in preparation for the move. Jock had had it. However, I thought to myself, 'I'll mix him something, but he won't know that it isn't the right stuff. Thinking he had taken something for his indigestion might help him a bit.' I got a piece of clean chalk and ground it to a powder. Then I got a small amount of toothpaste which had a mint flavour and mixed the chalk and paste with water. When Jock came back, I handed him the mixture and told him what a confounded nuisance he was. He was very apologetic and took the dose in one gulp saying 'It tasted good'. He then shouted 'Thanks' and dashed off. That was that, I thought, 'Perhaps now I will get a bit more rest.' But it wasn't to be. In came the QM, who said that each man was to carry three cans of rations and presented me with mine. I had one can of Bully, one tin of butter and a tin of fish. It amazed me. I wondered where they could have come from. We hadn't seen anything like this for months and didn't know there were any tins in the camp. I could only assume that they had been stored away and were being used by someone in authority. Now, if we didn't carry them, they would be left behind.

Each man had to sign for the tins he was to carry and would be held responsible for their safe delivery to the QM on arrival at the new camp. Many men said what they would do with the tins rather than carry them for the use of higher ranks. One of our officers came and gave us an explanation, saying that the tinned rations were kept for emergency and if anyone failed to deliver the tins he would be for it.

Later on, boots were distributed. Many men's boots were in a bad state, but we had not been allowed to change them for new ones. Now orders were that we were to carry the Red Cross surplus boots and hand them in at our destination with the tinned food. To prevent us from wearing the boots, we were each given two right or two left. We were none too pleased about this, but had to obey orders.

Soon the order came for us to parade on the recreation ground. It was 1:45 a.m. We struggled with our packs and kits and found our way in the dark to the recreation ground where we formed up in parties of twenty-six. Each party was to be one truck load and from then on would be known by its truck and train number. I was in truck 13 of train No. 7, so our party was known as 13/7. The trains were leaving almost every other day. There were thirteen trains in all, each carrying about 500–600 men.

Our heavy baggage had been taken during the day to the RASC car park. So as soon as we had been checked we started to march off in numerical order of trucks to the car park. Jim Payne, my pal who had served with me in France and had worked with me in Changi, now gave me a help with my load. I had my big pack, small pack, medical bag and small box of medical supplies. This box was a treasure as it contained bottles of concentrated macluachrome, acriflavine, iodine and many other useful items for medical work. The men of my Company had offered to help carry it in turn if necessary. In addition to my kit, I had a half gallon water bottle. I had to carry extra as I might need water for sick men. Everyone also took with them pots, pans, bowls, buckets and anything that might hold water for washing or cooking.

So we started off. We looked a funny sight with all kinds of utensils hanging from our kit. The pots and buckets would be swinging and clanking. Some marched in pairs, their kits slung over a pole, the ends of the pole resting on their shoulders, their loads swinging from side to side as they went.

Old Bob had to have his little say 'Ho, ho!' he shouted, 'Any old rags or bones,' and, referring to his clanging tins, he said 'Can you hear my medals clinking? I won them in Fred Carno's Army. If Old Nip saw me now with this outfit and my bare knees he would pack it in from fright. Up my lucky lads, anyone would think you were all back at your civvy jobs.' He kept up a continuous flow of banter like this all the time and, although most men were finding it painful and difficult to trudge along, they couldn't help laughing at him.

We were all very glad when we eventually arrived at the car park and dumped our kit. We still kept in our groups of twenty-six, and found that quite a lot of extra articles had been placed in position for each party to take in their trucks with them. We had table tops and stands and a few large cases. I couldn't guess how we would find room for this stuff, but I hoped that the trucks would be fairly big.

Many men who were remaining in camp turned out to see us off, as well as quite a number of those who were to follow on in later trains. I was having a glance round when I saw Staff Sergeant Jock Campbell coming in my direction. I thought, 'Now I'm for it, he's still got a stomach ache.' But Jock was beaming, and said 'Have you got any of that stomach powder handy, because I'd like some to carry with me. I've never had such quick and complete relief. It was marvellous stuff.' He wanted to know what it was and I had to tell him that I had forgotten the name. Many months later, I told him about the trick I had played on him and he just rolled up with laughter.

The lorries were due to pick us up at 4:15 a.m. At 4:10 they started coming in and we began loading. Some lorries were used for the cookhouse gear and extra stores. There was even a piano to be loaded, which, I learned later, was the best we had at Changi and was being taken so that we could carry on with our musical shows at the new camp.

How we all managed to pack onto the small lorry, I can never explain. But all twenty-six of us piled on, on top of our kits and the extra stores, with a Nip guard sitting on the roof of the cab facing us, as we bumped and swayed on the first stage of our journey.

I remember looking at that Nip. He was staring back over our heads, and his face was one of the ugliest I have ever seen. He sat there motionless, like an Egyptian mummy, his slit eyes almost closed. I wondered what mercy we could expect from him. He looked so cruel, arrogant and proud, which didn't suit his small stature. All the way to the station at Singapore (a distance of about fifteen miles) I swear that man never moved except with the sway of the lorry and though our party was laughing and joking, his glum expression never changed. We had the RSM in charge of our truck and he at once became a nuisance. We discovered that he was nervous. He didn't like the Nip guard so he didn't like anything we did that might disturb him. He got restless when we laughed and joked and ordered us to be quiet, although the Nip's face remained like a mask.

I couldn't see much of the countryside as it was early morning and visibility was very poor. We arrived at Singapore Station at about 5:30 a.m. and went straight over to the train. The trucks were smaller than I had expected and I knew that we were in for an unpleasant time. We found No.13 truck and all scrambled in. Once all were inside, we discovered that we were crowded even standing up. Of course our kit and the QM kit took up a lot of room, so we set about trying to hang it up. Our buckets, tins, cans and so forth were all hung on hooks outside the truck, and such things as packs, on a long rope inside the truck, the remainder being left on the floor. We then just managed to find room to sit down. However, if we wanted to stretch our legs, someone would have to move. It seemed ridiculous to think that we would have a long journey to travel in such a cramped position. We were horrified to learn that we were to remain in the trucks for about a week. There was no alternative, so we had to make the best of it.

It became rather stuffy, so we looked around for ventilation, only to discover that the truck was made of steel and the only openings were two sliding doors, one on each side about 4 feet 6 inches square. We hoped it wouldn't be too bad once the train had started.

The train pulled out at about 7 a.m. and the cool morning

breeze that came through the doors was very welcome and refreshing. The RSM had thought of this and placed himself near one of the doors from where he was able to keep an eye on his brood. He snarled at us if we came near the door, dubbing us fools for taking the risk of falling out.

We progressed very slowly going north, leaving Singapore Island behind us as we crossed over the causeway that was supposed to have been blown up by our Sappers. Little or no damage had been done to the causeway and little sign of any repairs.

As we entered the station of Johore Bahru, with Singapore disappearing behind us, my thoughts went back over the months I had spent at Changi and of the men we had left behind in the cemetery. Thank God we were going to a better camp, even though travel conditions were rough. There is an old saying 'Live and learn', and this applied to me at that moment. I was going to live and learn a lot in the next few months.

On we travelled though very slowly, on the single track railway, sometimes waiting for hours at sidings for other trains to come through, all trains having priority over ours.

As the hours passed and the sun came out, our truck became stiflingly hot. We discovered that the steel had become so hot that we couldn't lean against it or even bear our hands on it. The truck became like an oven. By midday, two men had fainted.

We had to be very sparing with the water as we didn't know when we would get a chance of any more. All on the train were suffering alike and I thought that there must be serious results, as all our men were suffering from some form of malnutrition. Many had not been long out of the hospital and weren't strong. Most had diarrhoea or dysentery and were weak, so the terrific heat just bowled them over.

It was during some of the waits at sidings that men were allowed to leave the trucks for a few minutes and I saw many with fouled clothes having to throw them away as there was no means of washing them.

There were many signs of the other trains having stopped at these places as there was excreta and litter all along the line, with clouds of flies. Although the men were suffering from the terrific heat, pain and discomfort, our plight seemed to give them reason for joking each time we stopped and were able to get together. One poor fellow had a bad bout of dysentery and I heard two men making bets on whether he would mess himself before we got to the next stop. Old Bob remarked about such an incident and said that he laughed so much that he had messed his own trousers. The cause of his merriment was over one of the fellows who was being held out of one of the doorways to relieve himself, as the train moved along. Old Bob said, 'I've learned my lesson. I'll look the other way in future.'

It seemed as though the Nips weren't going to give us any food or drink because night came on without any sign of either. We were glad of the night though if only because we would be free from the sun. But it brought its own misery. The men at the end of the truck, away from the engine, got what little draught there was from the open doors, but there never seemed to be any circulation to the forward end with the result that we just had to sit there cramped and sore, aching in every joint and sweating in the stinking and stifling heat, trying to get a little sleep.

During the night, someone with the urge of nature would try to make his way in the dark to the door, stepping on everyone in his path, then the poor fellow with dysentery couldn't wait to pick his footsteps, and just made a dash for the door, leaving us to put up with the ensuing unpleasantness. The natives working on the rail tracks, as the trains went by, got many sudden dousings.

At 2 a.m. we pulled into Kuala Lumpur station and were told to roll out and bring our mess gear, as there was a meal for us. Everyone searched and scrambled in the dark for their mess gear and, when found, dashed out of the truck in a state of undress. It was very funny to see them dashing up the platform, some of them almost naked, their hair ruffled, eyes bleary and staggering along.

We filled our water bottles and were issued with our meal, which consisted of about a pint of curried rice and half a pint of hot water. I was famished but I couldn't eat the rice for, at the first mouthful, I nearly choked. The stuff was on fire, or I thought so. There must have been as much curry as rice and most of us put the meal in the swill bins. Then we had to collect a pint of white rice and a small piece of dried salt fish which had to last us for the next twelve hours.

I passed most of that halt sitting against the cool brown

polished stones and dozing off. After about two hours, we were ordered to board the train again. The RSM would shout and bellow when we didn't get in quickly enough to suit him. He wanted us to be an example to the others by being first aboard and last out of the trucks when we stopped. Whenever a stop was made, the men from other trucks would jump out to find a convenient spot to ease themselves or for fresh air, or to get up to the engine to get water. But Tara would not let us out until he received orders to that effect from the OC of the train, Colonel Hinkson. Even though we pointed out to him that the Colonel's men were out of their truck, he would remain regimental to the end. The fact that men were on the point of fainting and gasping for fresh air and water didn't move him one iota.

When we stopped at night and the men with enteric troubles dashed out, the RSM would make us all number from 1 to 26 several times to make sure we had all returned. I often said that Tara should never have been given charge of men. He worried too much and, though nervous complaints are not contagious, we were all soon suffering from nerves through him.

When we arrived at Ipoh at about midday and stopped there for about two hours, permission was given by the Nip Sergeant for us to take a shower bath under the engine water feed pipe. Out we all dashed and, regardless of the many people standing around on the platforms, we all stood under the big leather pipe in turn and let the water pour down on us; it was a wonderfully exhilarating feeling after being so cramped up in the truck for so long without a wash or shave. We had no soap, so the water ran off our bodies, leaving grease-like trails where there were little blobs of perspiration. We all queued up and marched under the big pipe, just paused there and walked around again. The natives, men, women and children, all looked on at what must have appeared to them to be emaciated, hairy, naked, wild men having a shower, quite unashamed. When the order came for us to return to the trucks, we all dashed back. On our way we had to pass a big coal dump, where engines were coaling. They sent up clouds of black dust and we, wet and naked, all had to rush through them. Consequently, when we arrived at the trucks we were as black and grimy as the natives.

We put our few clothes back on and were waiting for the train to move off. I was peering over Tara's shoulder at the people on the crowded platform. There was a real mixture; Chinese, Malayans, and several types of Indian, all dressed in beautiful colours. There were a pair of Indian girls standing to one side. I caught their eyes, and they smiled, showing lovely white teeth. I winked back and smiled. They acted like two very shy children and I almost expected them to put their fingers in their mouths, but they just kept on rolling their large eyes and smiling. Tara, not knowing I was behind him, spotted the girls and must have thought that he had made a conquest as he said 'Look at these, aren't they lovely?' and leaned out and waved to them. This drew the attention of a Nip official who came up to us in a threatening attitude. Then with much shouting and jabbering he 'shoo'd' the girls off the platform.

We had been waiting for over half an hour and were longing for the train to move, so that we could have a little draught of air, when we were told that the train would be held up a while longer and we could sit about the platform. One of our men, Tommy Buckthorpe, made straight for the lavatory, which was in a terrible state, but, as he said, a man in his condition, which demanded quick action, couldn't be particular, so off he went and after a while came back and motioned for us to follow him into the truck. We followed him in. He was very excited and told us that a Chinese had followed him into the lavatory and slipped a piece of paper and a ten dollar bill into his hand. Tommy produced the paper which read something like this, 'Keep up your spirits. I know where you come from and I know where you are going. I belong to the guerrillas who are operating in the mountains near here. The news is good. Tripoli has fallen to our forces, we have invaded Burma and are now advancing down towards Malaya. Good luck to you all. Burn this paper.'

We all buzzed with excitement at this – we were going towards our advancing forces. This was great and, although the news proved later to be untrue, it certainly cheered us up for many days. It became second on our list of important subjects, or most discussed subjects of the day, food being the Number 1 subject. It is remarkable how the gnawing of a hungry stomach keeps one's mind on food. The most peculiar thing was that the prevailing subject, day in and day out in the barrack room (women), was now very rarely heard. Instead, everyone talked of food and the news or rumours.

We set off from Ipoh and our next short stop was at Prai. From there I could see Penang Island, only a short distance away. Prai station was very close up to the sea and the ferry boat could be seen on its short journey to Penang. Here our engine was un-coupled, turned and came to the rear end of our train. As we started off again I noticed a wonderful difference. We were now getting the draught at our end of the truck!

In a short while we were nearing the Thai border and a stop was made at Alor-Star. Here there was plenty of evidence that the other six trains had passed this way – smell and flies and, when walking about, one had to step with care. Of course, it couldn't be helped. Men weren't allowed to move far from the trains and these were the consequences.

The Nip in charge ordered that all men should have ten minutes physical training, and it struck me as very amusing. In truth, it was tragic to see the way we lined up in that clearing. The stench was enough to knock down a mule, and we all had to keep our eyes down to make sure we were treading on unfouled ground. The heat was terrific – 108° in the shade. Chickens that had been brought along by some of the more ambitious were dying, although they had been placed in the shade, and three of our men collapsed with sunstroke at this place.

The Nip now told us that soon we would be crossing into Siam – Thailand – where, he said, the police were very strict. So he would have to curtail the freedom that had been allowed us up until now. There was to be no singing or shouting. Men weren't to hang their legs over the sides. All pots, pans and buckets that were hanging outside the trucks were to be taken in. No one was to leave the trucks without his permission and, in general, everyone was to be on his best behaviour. If anyone misbehaved then all in the truck would suffer because, as punishment, he would shut the truck doors. This was a terrible threat, as it would mean death to many by suffocation, so after that we were very wary about what we did.

We had entered the land of plenty, or so it seemed, as wherever we stopped, the natives seemed to appear from every corner, laden with luscious mangos, papayas, bananas, and pineapples. They also had little cookies, fruit turnovers and small pies which had been fried in either peanut or coconut oil and contained a mysterious concoction with the flesh of almost any living thing, as always, hot with curry or chilli. Our men bought all they could. I am sure many overdid it, with the result that many had dysentery relapses next day.

As we travelled along, I was surprised by the natives' dress; European fashion, in very light material and narrow-rimmed slouch or straw hats. At the stations were many people who could easily have been mistaken for Europeans. They appeared very well fed and prosperous. They sauntered about looking very wise and important, but rarely gave us a glance. When they did, it would be with an air of condescension. They would smile as though it hurt them and pass on as if they had performed some very heavy and painful duty. No doubt they were 'big-wigs' in their little domain but we would have been very pleased to give them a healthy British punch on the nose or in those over-corpulant corporations of theirs.

As we travelled up the east coast, having crossed the peninsula in a north-easterly direction, our nights became more of a nightmare to us and our days an even greater torture. At night, the swaying and noisy trucks, the stuffy stinking heat and the cramp and broken sleep, with all those visits to the door. It was a nightmare, and that is putting it mildly. The days, living in an oven, suffocating and roasting, hungry and parched for a drink, were sheer hell. I know that if that journey had lasted much longer, there wouldn't have been half of us getting to this 'camp of promise' alive. It would have to be good to make this journey worthwhile.

There were many things that I would have enjoyed seeing under happier circumstances. The scenery, the teeming life of insects, animals and humans, the jungles, the paddy fields, the native boys on the elephants, the water buffaloes pulling ploughs that were under water, and the natives working up to their knees in mud and water. Queerly formed rocks rose like large ant hills all over the place. In some of the largest, I saw caves and what appeared to be dwellers in them. In one large block of rock, I saw a native shrine with steps cut out of the solid rock leading up to it. At another place, I saw what appeared like the giant's castle out of a fairy tale. It was built on the top of a rock with high towers and queer shaped doors and windows and hundreds of steps. The Buddhist priests lived there. There were many of them about, with shaven heads and all dressed in yellow robes.

I think I could write for a week on what I saw of interest on that journey, but although it was so interesting, it brings back the most painful memories of the appalling suffering endured by so many.

Chapter Eight

Bampong

For five days and nights we were tormented in those hellish trucks. Finally, on 29 April, we arrived at Bampong. Orders came for us to drop any kit we couldn't carry. It would be picked up and delivered to our camp later. Many men put everything out except their small pack and water bottle saying that they didn't even feel able to carry them and would take a chance on the kit being sent after them. I left my medical box but kept every other article of kit. We were then taken to the roadway outside the station where we formed up into five ranks and were kept standing there for over an hour in the blazing sun.

Opposite to where I stood was a native's open fruit stand displaying luscious tropical fruits. Just inside the door was a Siamese boy, about fourteen years of age, sitting in an armchair. He was horribly fat and looked like a mental case. He was grinning at us and, with a regular forward movement of his head, he spat into a spittoon placed there for his convenience – he was hideous. A woman, who seemed to be his mother came to the door and one of our men asked for water. I have often wondered what we must have looked like to those people. We were rough, unshaven, saturated with sweat and still reeking with the odour of the truck. We must have presented a frightful sight. The woman took the proffered bottle and filled it with water and then brought out several jugs of iced water. The squad of men next to us had the first lot, then came our turn. But the RSM took the jugs away saying we weren't to have the stuff as it might be contaminated. Our men simply raved, and the woman then offered to let the men fill their bottles and leave to get water was asked of the Nip guard. He consented to let two go at a time. While this was going on, a Nip Sergeant chased our men back into line and struck the guard a brutal blow in the face for allowing us to fill our bottles.

We were ordered to leave the remainder of our kit in the roadway and every man had to give a hand to unload the baggage trucks. We sweltered, sweated and swore as we toiled in the terrific heat. The men were in no condition to work but work they did. When our officer complained that the men were sick, the Nip in charge struck him with a golf club which he apparently carried for this purpose. Some of our men sustained very bad injuries from blows received from that club. It was maddening to see our weak men struggling and straining under heavy loads, with some dropping from heat and exhaustion, only to be struck and prodded by the demon with the club. How we all silently vowed vengeance. I promised myself to get him at some time, if I could.

When the unloading was completed, we stacked the boxes, and other things in an open space at the side of the main street. Lorries were dashing about and clouds of dust were rising from the sunbaked streets. In that dust we started what was supposed to be a short march to the camp. The short march proved to be about two miles, but it seemed like six. As I struggled along with my heavy kit weighing me down and sweat running down my forehead into my eyes, I noticed two men fall out and collapse. Then, as I neared a little shack of a shop, a native woman in spotless white clothes of very European cut, her hair greying and with tears running down her face, offered us bananas which she handed out and rushed back for more. But she soon realized that she couldn't get them quick enough to let all the men have a share, so she directed us to walk through the shop and pick up fruit as we passed through. All the time we were going through, the woman was wringing her hands and mumbling something in her language. To me she was a dear old lady who felt as any mother would to a son. And that day, whatever her religion may have been, she did a great Christian kindness in showing pity and sympathy to us at a time when we felt that both kindness and sympathy were dead. I had felt that every heart was hardened against us. We had suffered hell these last few days during which time people had just grinned at us, and now this dear old soul had given me new hope and new courage. Men went into the shop with long sullen hopeless faces and came out of the other door with a little gleam in their eyes, and I know that they felt just as I did. The Grace of God being administered through the medium of a lowly native woman. I feel very small and humble when I say 'May God bless her'.

We trudged on and eventually came to the camp where we all dropped down and rested. We had to await the pleasure of the Camp Commandant as he wouldn't deal with us until all our men had arrived, so we had to remain in the sun. A few of us got together and went back along the road to pick up those who had fallen exhausted by the way. I didn't go far because I picked up one of our Changi musicians, the brilliant pianist of our concert party. He was all in. I picked up his kit and took his arm over my shoulder and, with others, helped him into camp, where he slowly recovered. There were dozens of similar cases and, as they were brought in, the Nips merely grinned.

It was whispered that the Nips were going to search us, so I dipped into my pack and fished out my compass and hid it. I saw many things come out of the most unlikely places and pushed into the grass or into the ditch. However, a Nip turned up for another reason. We had to form up in single file and pass before him to receive a small piece of cloth on which was stamped our identity number by which we would be known in the future. So I became 298/7 – the 298th man of Train Seven. This cloth had to be worn so that it was visible at all times.

After that, we moved into the long huts and were each given a space 2 feet 6 inches by 6 feet long. I was settling down to my first stretch out for over a week when the Nips came in and chased us out while they searched our kits. The search over, we were allowed to return and after a while, a meal was served consisting of rice and stew. The stew was of marrows and a kind of parsnip boiled with eggs. I thought it tasted excellent. Later on, some small native boys came round with baskets full of hard boiled ducks' eggs at about 5 cents each. It was a wonderful treat and that night Jim Payne and I had a feed of hard boiled eggs and tea which we made, sweetened by Gula Malacca. We felt on top of the world again.

We were told by our officers that we were to move on from this camp very soon. We settled down for the night and I slept like a rock, having, at last, been able to stretch out and lie down. There was a lovely breeze coming through the openings in the sides of the hut. When I was awakened next morning, I could hear the howling in the hills just behind us of what seemed like coyotes, but I learned later that they were some kind of pariah dog.

That morning we got an order from the Nips that shook even the stoutest hearts among us. Our officer, Major Barber, called us on parade and told us that he had very grave news for us. He said 'We are ordered to prepare to march out of camp at 10 o'clock tonight on the first stage of a march of 150 miles into the jungle, where we are to assist in the building of a railway. We are to proceed in easy stages and refreshment will be provided at a halfway camp each night, tea being prepared for us by the people at these camps.' Major Barber said that Colonel Dillon, OC of 'F' Force, had objected, pointing out that two thirds of the men were unfit to march and that we had been promised a non-working camp as convalescence for our sick. The reply was to the point: 'We are in Thailand to build a railway and all the talk in the world will not help. If the men were sick it was too bad, if they died it was too bad, the honourable Japanese were velly solly.' Major Barber said that every man must stand up to this as a Britisher. It was going to be tough going but we had to go through with it. Everyone then returned to the huts and began sorting our kit. There were many sighs as men parted with precious kit which they could ill afford to be without but couldn't carry on a long march. The kit at the station was now given up as lost as most of the heavy stores had been looted overnight by the natives. I made enquiries about my medical box but got no satisfaction. One of the men was going to the station to do picket on the stores, so I asked him if he would look out for the box and he said, 'Your box is the most important so, if it's to be found, I'll find it.' He found it all right and delivered it to me at about 7 p.m.

When I opened it up, I considered it ridiculous even to think of trying to carry the box on the march, so I thought it would be a good idea to ask each man to carry one of the precious bottles. Men offered to dump some of their kit to make room for any bottles I might have left over. This was appreciation indeed for the little I had done for them. It meant much to me to find every man I asked so willing to spare some of his precious carrying space for my bottles. I hadn't worked hard tending to these men when they were sick for nothing, and they knew that in helping me get the bottles to our destination, they also helped themselves. I also distributed bottles among the Sergeants and then got the RSM to take my only bottle of iodine, which was concentrated and very strong. I told him not to use it as it would burn him and he vowed that he would get it safely to me at the other end.

Major Barber was very complimentary about this idea and offered to carry a bottle himself. There was so much willingness to help that I let men carry some of the dressings as well, warning them that they must see them safely delivered to me at the other end. I marked each of my bottles so that only I would know what they contained. I did this as a precaution against the men turning amateur doctors and using the contents of the bottles for themselves or for others. The most important thing was to get the stuff through to the new camp because, from what I could see, it was going to be a long time before supplies of any kind would be sent after us.

Someone shouted out 'Does anybody want boots?' and there was a general move to where all the surplus kit had been thrown. Now that each man was left to please himself what he carried, the boots had been thrown into a heap and men started trying to sort out the lefts and rights in their sizes. I don't think that any man found a suitable pair of boots; anyway this was no time to start 'breaking in' a pair of new boots. The pile was left for the natives, the result of negligence and sheer bad management by those in charge of us.

Many natives came to buy our surplus kit and it became like an oriental marketplace, despite the efforts of the Nips and Thai Police to keep the natives away. Men trying to sell would hold the articles up, and natives, half hidden in the bushes, would then bid by a show of fingers for the number of dollars meant. There was much head wagging and nodding with the number of fingers increasing or decreasing. Then, when both parties had reached an agreement, the native would dash forward, grab the articles and drop the money, and run as if all hell was after him, often with Nips and Thai police shouting in full pursuit. I would sit and watch business being done. When both parties nodded agreement,

I shouted for the boys to see the sprint and chase. It was a really good laugh.

All over our camp were piles of things that men had thrown away. I checked and re-checked my kit, sorting it out and reluctantly placing things on one side that I thought might make my load too heavy for the march. Jim and I tried and re-tried our packs on, adjusting and re-adjusting the straps to make the bag light and comfortable for the long journey. Many treasures were sacrificed. Books we could do without; out they all went and, as many others thought the same, our plans for a library were doomed. The three tins of food were next. We decided that one was as much as we would carry so I kept the tin of butter and the other tins were opened for supper that night.

All that evening we sat and juggled with our kit. When even the most unimportant article normally became most important to us in our circumstances, the difficulty of making up one's mind about what to part with was really painful. Even a small tin was of great value as a container for boiling water and many other uses.

Jim and I had finally finished our packing and decided that we could carry our packs the distance we had been told we were to march that night, so we took a stroll around our hut and, to my great delight, I found Gwyn Williams about to enter the hut in search of me. We were both delighted at meeting again, though we could only have a few minutes. He had come with an earlier party who were all in camps in and around Bampong. Three of his party had died a few days previously from food poisoning. They had bought and eaten some yak meat and had died as a result in terrible pain about twenty-four to forty-eight hours later. Gwyn was a lorry driver and said that the Nip that travelled around with him was treating him very well and had allowed him to come in search of me. As Gwyn was lorry driving, there was a chance that he might come up later to the camp for which I was bound, so we parted expressing the hope that this would be soon.

Chapter Nine

The March I
Bampong to Tarsoa

Hills don't seem so steep to climb when climbing with a friend.
Roads won't seem so rough, and long, although they twist and
*   bend,*
If you have for your companion someone dear to you,
One in tune with every mood: a friend sincere and true.
Burdens will not be so crushing, nor so hard to bear
If there's someone at your side the heavy weight to share.

Patience Strong

At 9 p.m. we were ordered to move out, into the roadway. So we
paraded with our kit, ready for the march. I was feeling very
uneasy about the outcome of it and could see from the appearance of some of the lads that they too were filled with foreboding.

We formed up in groups of twenty-six, as we had for the train.
At 10 p.m. we got the order to 'Get dressed'. We put on our packs
and started off into the dark night and the unknown. For a while
we passed huts and shacks until we left the town and then we came
to rather wild looking country, or so it appeared to me from what
I could see of it by straining my eyes in the dark. The road was in
pretty good condition and not too bad for marching, but I
couldn't help thinking and wondering how the men were going to

99

stand up to this long march. We had all been confined in a small area with little or no heavy work for fourteen months, during which time we had suffered from ailments caused through semi-starvation. Many men were weak and some were still ill. All had been aggravated by the train journey and now we were faced with a march that would make the strongest of men quail.

When we started marching, I congratulated myself that I had filled my pack to the right weight and made the straps comfortable. However, before we got our first ten minutes rest, I was in agony and kept wriggling and twisting in my straps to ease the strain, as they seemed to be cutting into my shoulders. There were hard bumps in my pack that kept sticking into my back. I was beginning to feel generally uncomfortable and wondering if we would be given a rest at all when I heard the Nip guard on ahead shout '*Yasumi*'. Down I flopped with Jim and Gordon Davies beside me. We didn't waste any time with talk but frantically set about adjusting our straps. I pulled out a pair of old socks and doubled them over and padded my shoulder straps, then laid back to enjoy the rest but, as I sighed at the pleasure of stretching myself out and resting, so the order was shouted down the column 'Get dressed', and up we had to get, helping each other on with our packs and off again for another fifty minutes. We were marching for about fifty minutes and resting ten.

On we went through the night with Thais sometimes keeping pace with us and wanting to carry our kit. Some lads rashly handed over their packs to them. They walked beside the column for a little while and then quickly disappeared into the jungle, knowing that our men dared not follow. We were learning! Later when a native joined us and tried to get a bag to carry, we crowded him in and for a while all one could hear was the jabbering of a very excited Thai who was getting kicked and knee'd and punched. He couldn't get out of the ring of men who kept marching and were dealing out some hefty kicks and punches. When the Thai did liberate himself, being helped with a good push as he fell into the undergrowth and a few hearty laughs and jibes from the men, he got to his feet and moved off faster than I've seen a native move before or since. He meant to get away from us as fast as he could.

At 3 a.m. I was very glad to hear '*Yasumi*' being shouted again, after we had been led into the grounds of a big oriental house. Down we all flopped on the grass. We were all bunched together, steaming and sweating, sore and tired, but this was where we were to get tea and tea was more valuable than gold. But first, off with my boots, as many others were doing. Things weren't as they should be down in those boots. My toes were getting chafed. I had a small blister on each heel and my right heel was becoming very sore. I straightened out the creases in my socks and put my boots back on, an operation that proved extremely painful. Then, as the men began to line up for tea, I took Jim's mug with mine and joined the queue. Jim remained to look after the kit.

At the head of the queue were two large torches which threw a flickering eerie light over the boiler where a native laboured stoking the fire in an effort to boil the water. He must have given it up as a bad job because he picked up his ladle (which was half a coconut shell) and started issuing half a pint of lukewarm water per man. My vision of a nice cup of tea disappeared into thin air! I received our issue and returned to Jim. Although it tasted vile, we drank it with a gulp and Jim returned to get another two mugs, after which we laid down to make the most of our short rest. We had half an hour here before the dreaded 'Get dressed'.

As we started off again, I thought that my aches and pains had increased a hundredfold but they gradually wore off as we progressed. But I began to feel rather queer inside. There was something wrong with me and I couldn't make it out. I felt very lightheaded and had a very sickly feeling, with an emptiness in the upper part of my stomach, which persisted and became worse. I thought that the warm water had upset me and I wanted to lie down until this awful feeling of weakness passed over, but I dared not. I said to myself over and over again 'I'm not going to give in, I have never really fainted in my life and I am not going to now'. Just then 'Yasumi' was shouted down the line, so I rested and felt a little better when we started off again. Two men failed to start off, being too exhausted to pick up their kit. Their kit was thrown away and the men with their arms placed around the necks of two stronger men, walked and stumbled along like that.

Day was breaking when I felt I couldn't do another step. We had marched about twenty-two miles. I was feeling all in and really wild with myself. I had thought I could manage the march.

There were so many others who were ill and weak but were still forging ahead, although looking as though they were biting their tongues in an effort to hold themselves together and keep going. I tried to steady myself but stumbled and almost fell. I knew that if I fell I wouldn't be able to get up again. It was awful and I didn't know what to do with myself.

Just then Jim spotted me and wanted to know if I was all right. I assured him that I was, then took a couple of steps and rolled over. The maddening thing about it was that I was conscious but my brain seemed lazy, it just would not work and though I tried to struggle to get up, my limbs wouldn't work: in my weakness I remember uttering a jumble of words – I couldn't even get words out properly. I noticed two men stop and bend over me, a little water was splashed on my head and I saw Dave Ellis and Dyke, two of my old patients, pick up my kit and add it to theirs, telling Gordon Davies that they would see my kit all right. Then I was heaved up, Gordon had my arm over his shoulder and was half carrying, half dragging me along. The rear Jap guard caught up with us and with a grin gave me a dig with the butt of his rifle and said '*Biochi huh, no good iguh*', meaning 'Sick huh, no good'. He passed on and left us to follow as best we could.

I recovered sufficiently to walk by myself the last few hundred yards and arrived at a little wayside clearing where there was a large building, its roof supported by four large pillars. Under this roof were collected some of the sick men who had failed to go any further and who belonged to one of the first six trains.

Tariwa – First Rest Camp

An Australian MO had been left in charge of the sick and when Gordon helped me in I lay down in the pathway under the roof. The MO was busy attending to his patients so I stopped where I was and, after taking a drink of water, I went off to sleep. I awoke at about 2 p.m. with the pitiless sun shining down on me. I was in a bath of perspiration but felt stronger. I moved into the shade but after a little while I had to make a dash to the latrine and from then on I had no rest. I had another dose of dysentery and there followed the regular dashes to the latrine and over-powering weakness.

102

To make matters worse, my right heel had become one large blister, my toes were raw and my left foot skinned in several places. Most of the men were suffering with their feet in similar ways. I realized that my blister would have to be removed, as experience had taught me that in this hellish climate, if I didn't, the water beneath the skin would soon turn to yellow pus and I would find myself with a septic blister. Gordon and Jim also had bad feet so I attended to them and a few others who were near and then I got Gordon to remove the skin from my heel. I instructed him during the operation, which was very painful, but felt much easier when the water and skin were removed: it left me with a raw patch about the size of a five shilling piece. I placed a pad on it but it was too painful for me to bear my weight and I limped about all that afternoon. This made my journeys to and from the latrine something I will never forget.

I have tried to describe my condition and feelings on the first stage of our march in the hope that I can make it clear how, not only I suffered, for I was just one in thousands, but how we all suffered on that nightmare. I was in good condition compared with many, at least I had started off feeling pretty strong, but many were weak and ill at the start and so suffered even more pain, weakness and exhaustion than I. This had the effect of turning our column into a shambles.

The nightly marches that followed became even worse, with desperate men shouting for help, men collapsing, men cursing and steaming with sweat, and then, above all this, one could see the men who were trying to cheer the sick. Although they themselves were overburdened, they would perhaps be carrying part of another man's kit or carrying between them the sick who had fallen along the way.

All through that day the sun poured down on us pitilessly, and we were glad when the Nips gave us permission to bathe in the river which ran beside our camp. I hobbled over and lay in the water as long as I could and felt very refreshed. When I got back, Gordon had visited a native canteen and had purchased a four-egg omelette for me with a mug of hot coffee. I thought I had never tasted anything like it and felt so much stronger afterwards.

I then went to see the MO and he advised me to carry on to the next camp if I could as there were no facilities at this place.

So, though not feeling up to it, I had to march that night.

A small motor truck had been hired by Major Barber to take our kit on to the next stop. Every man had to pay twenty cents and when the kit had been loaded there was enough room for about six sick men, and six who considered themselves the worst were asked to step forward. Tara, our RSM was one of the first. He said that his heel was so bad that he could hardly walk. He offered to take charge of the truck. Five other men who had stepped forward and who were genuinely ill went with him: they left in the early evening for the next camp which was called Kamburi, about twenty miles away.

At 9 p.m. we started out ourselves feeling a lot lighter without our kit. However, I soon found that it was a painful job walking on the toes of my right foot and, after a few miles, my legs ached from toes to thigh with my heel throbbing and my toes increasingly painful with the extra pressure of my walking on them. I managed to keep marching the full fifty minutes but had to dash into the jungle when the yell '*Yasumi*' went up. This meant that I wasn't getting a rest as the others were. The dysentery was making me so awfully weak that by the time we had been marching for four hours and had stopped for our third ten-minute break, I had almost fainted off in the ditch and was being helped back on to the road when the order to move off came. Two other men had collapsed and were being supported or carried when a lorry came along driven by a POW. Seeing the plight we were in, he asked his Nip guard if he could pick up the sick men. The Nip consented and so he stopped and informed the officer in charge. There was a mad rush and everyone tried to get on the lorry. When order was restored, the Nip ordered them all off again. I was lifted bodily by someone onto the lorry and I remember the rocking and bumping and the lorry packed with men: two men messed themselves.

Kamburi – Second Rest Camp

We arrived at the camp at Kamburi and were shown where our kits were. We had to be there until the main party arrived later in the morning. I approached the pile of kit in the hope of seeing my pack and getting my blanket and ground sheet to lie on. I felt weak, sick and dizzy and found it hard to keep on my feet. I saw my pack, recognizing it by the red paint mark I had put on it. It was in a place easy to see. I went forward to pull it out of the pile when I heard Tara's voice rasp out 'Keep away from there. You cannot touch that kit until morning.' I explained that I could see my kit and that I had nothing to sleep on. Tara walked forward (and, I noticed, without the limp) and told me in his best barrack square bullying manner that he didn't care if I hadn't a rag to my back, he wasn't going to let me touch any of that kit until morning. So I said 'Will you lend me one of your blankets then?' He nearly had a blue fit and cursed me for a fool.

After this there was no alternative but for us to lie down on the hard sun-baked ground and shiver the night away. The strange thing about our Tara was that he called the Nips all kinds of evil names for their arrogance and acts of cruelty yet he acted in this way himself.

At daybreak, when the marching party arrived, we were all sent into the bush to sleep. There the men rigged up all kinds of shelters to protect themselves from the sun. They used blankets and groundsheets to make a roof for shade, the roof being more important than having something to lie on. The sun became so terrifically hot that it was impossible to sleep. The temperature that day I was told was 144° in the sun and 112° in the shade.

The wells at this camp were some distance away and had become dry so there was a great shortage of water and we had to manage on what was sold to us by natives. An old building was being used to house the sick, but it was just a roof supported by pillars, and the hard earthy floor was the only place for the sick to lie. I didn't pay much attention to the sick bay that day, as I found plenty to do in attending to the feet of our men. I felt that I would drop at any moment. I felt ridiculously weak and light-headed, but I had had a few hours rest and these fellows had been marching all night, so I sat under a bush and did what I could.

The men's feet almost made me vomit. There being no water for them to wash with, they came with dirty, smelly, sweaty and bloody feet. For some I had to cut away socks which had stuck to raw places and these men would have to keep marching. I thought to myself, 'This being our condition on the second stage of the march and we have only covered about forty-five miles, what were we going to be like at the end of 150?' It didn't bear thinking about. It was an enormous relief to us all when we were told that we were to rest there for one night.

That day we lay in whatever shade we could make or find and baked and sweated. We couldn't rest as we were being tortured by the heat and thousands of flies. The sanitary conditions of the camp were too disgusting to describe fully. The latrines were in the centre of our camp space and being over-full, had contaminated the ground for many yards around, with the result that we couldn't get within yards of them, even if we had wanted to, as had the parties that had been here before us. We had to use the privacy offered by the bushes and there was hardly a square yard of uncontaminated ground upon which we could make our bed spaces. Between the awful smell, the flies, the heat, the lack of water and food, we couldn't make up our minds whether we would rather be on the march again in preference to remaining in this awful place. But that night I slept well despite the many urges from my enteric complaint.

Next morning we were all paraded at 10 a.m. by the Nips and marched three miles to a big house, which was being used as a Nip hospital. I shall never forget that march – my foot and heel gave me hell. That, coupled with my other complaint, my weakness and the sun, brought me to my knees before arriving at the hospital. I was helped into the hospital yard where Jim got me some water and then, like many others, I lay in the sun for over an hour. It seemed as though the sun was sucking away what little energy I had left. Then we had to fall into single file and pass the Nip MOs. The first one took a blood test. The second tested us for enteric diseases. The third injected dysentery serum and so it went on until we had passed six doctors. I thought that perhaps we were being used for experiments and, from what followed later on, I do believe we were used as guinea pigs. As I passed each MO, he grinned evilly. I was their guinea pig and they probed and pricked with a kind of evil delight. When they had finished, we started the agonizing march back to camp.

When I reached camp, I was too weak to stand for long so I very reluctantly reported to the MO. By doing this I knew that I would be kept behind in the sick bay and perhaps be separated from all my friends. But if I attempted to carry on and march out

106

that night, I would be a burden to my pals, for I knew they would stand by me. When I reported to Major Rogers, an Australian MO, he told me that had I gone on in my present state, I would have died. When the party moved out that night, I was to move in under the roof of his sick bay.

While I was at the sick bay that morning, the men of No. 8 train arrived. They looked a very sorry sight and soon dispersed into the bushes to sleep.

During the afternoon, the Nips told us that, as water was so scarce, they would take us to the river if we wished to go for a wash. I thought I might feel better if I had a dip and, in any case, I had to get water as I had run out. Jim and Gordon Davies, who were also ill, decided that they too would try to make the distance, which we were told was only half a mile.

We fell in with the others and made our way to the river, which proved to be over two miles away. The march nearly killed us but, once there, we lay in the cool, swift running stream.

At the riverside were many natives who lived in funny little huts, built on rafts. They had apparently been expecting us because they had bamboo stalls rigged up with a display of fruit for sale. They also made a drink from half a lime, a teaspoon of sugar, and hot water – it was delicious. I noticed that they got their water from the sand at the riverside. They dug a hole in the sand until it was below water level, then the water from the river seeped through as clear as crystal. We filled our bottles from this hole, but to be sure about it, I added a tablet of chlorine.

It would have been a grand outing if it hadn't been for the march, which meant agony to most of us. Like the old saying 'It never rains but it pours', to increase our misery on the return journey, a big black cloud, which had been hovering overhead for over an hour, now opened up and down came the rain in torrents. We weren't wearing much clothing to worry about getting wet, but it was remarkable how quickly we changed from being over-heated and sweating to cold and shivering. I was glad when the camp came in sight, and wondered if anyone had picked up my kit and put it in the shelter of the sick bay. When I limped into the camp, I nearly cried with dismay for the campsite was under about two feet of water. Most of the men had crowded under cover in the sick bay, but as the rain was being blown in all directions the roof afforded very little cover. Jim and I squeezed in as far as we could and then enquired about our kit. No one knew anything about it, so we gave it up as lost in the flood. Articles of kit could be seen floating on the water which was also carrying the residue of the latrines. The place was in an indescribably filthy mess. We stood shivering as we clung tightly to one another, with the rain driving in on us.

Night came on and our train party had to move on. I don't think I've ever seen such hopeless misery. No. 7 train party, with most of my friends, were leaving in the pouring rain. Their kits, or what they had managed to salvage from the water, were now wet through and triple their normal weight. The men, shivering and wet, started off into the night to do another twenty miles march or more. They left with their heads down, looking dejected and miserable. The only sounds to be heard were the sucking and squelching of their boots and feet in the mud and the howl of the wind and the rain. That night was one of the most miserable I have ever spent, feeling so ill and having to stand in about a foot of mud, shivering and wet, until morning.

During the early hours the rain ceased. In the morning, with the sun out, the ground that a short while ago had been mud and slush now became a hard cake again. With latrine residue spread all over the place, the camp was smelling foul.

To my great relief I found that Jim had remained behind, having developed a fever. He came over to me and suggested that we make a search for our kit. We made for the spot where we had left it and I found my pack caught in the bushes, hanging about a foot from the ground. My blanket was in a bush about five yards away and other articles were all scattered around but my ground-sheet had disappeared.

I picked up my kit and hobbled back to the sick bay, where some kind of order was being restored and the place was being tidied up. I put my things out in the sun to dry. My treasured photographs seemed to be ruined, but I managed to save some of them, though they were very discoloured. I returned to the sick bay and found a small space where Jim and I could lie down. There I lay all day in a semi-coma. Jim brought some rice and thin soup, but I couldn't persuade my stomach to hold it, so I gave up the job. Jim told me that there were quite a number of our men left behind. After a little while, a few of them came to see me. It gave me courage to find that a few of my friends were left here with me, though they were all ill. There was Gordon Davies, Staff Sergeant Bill Langley, Sergeant Colmer, Dick Sabin, Jim Payne, H. Powell, Allington, Captain Wadesley, Padre Cordingly, Corporal Bedford and a few others whose names I do not remember. Seeing them meant that I wasn't alone and I felt a lot easier. We all agreed that we would try to stay together. Major Rogers, the MO promised to do what he could about that.

I missed Old Bob and his continuous banter, but I saw him before he left with the party and shook hands with him. He assured me, as always he did, that we'd be out in six months. 'There is nothing to worry about,' he said. He was soaked through and standing in six inches of mud with a twenty mile all-night march in front of him. 'Nothing to worry about!' What a man! What a spirit! As he left, he said 'I'll be seeing you and if I run into our troops I'll tell them you are down here,' then he was gone. I missed him terribly and hoped that I would catch up with him soon.

The men of No. 8 train party had come and gone and now the men of No. 9 train were in camp and were going on the next night. On the night of 5 May, Gordon, Jim, Colmer, Allington and Sabin had been signed off as fit to march that night. I was still too sick but I didn't intend to stay behind if I could help it. So I asked Major Rogers if I could go. He said 'All right, it's your funeral laddie.' So it was all settled and at 10 p.m. that night we started off, with Jim and Gordon either side of me making sure I was all right, although they were still pretty weak themselves. We marched our first period of fifty minutes then, while we rested, the Nips sent round the message that we would soon be in wild country and must beware of snakes, tigers and wild natives. From then on, the Nips carried big flaming torches. It was a weird spectacle, this long column of miserable, dirty, sweaty men all struggling along, straining under their loads, swearing and shouting as they stumbled over rock or root – 'Rock here, Look out for this root,' and everyone hurrying to try and get to the front. Tins and cans were clanging, as they swung about and the very dark jungle closing in on both sides, with the shadows cast by the flare of the torches in front and behind, and the Nips as they shouted to each other sounding like this 'Whata-whata-wooe.' Then the longed for 'Yasumi' would be shouted by the Nip in front and repeated by our men all along the column, and down we would drop wherever we were. Many times during that march, after rain had fallen, we would flop down in deep mud or, after a hot day, the track would be inches thick with dust. As we marched along, clouds of this dust flew into the air, into our nostrils, eyes, ears and throat, making us choke and gasp, adding to our terrible thirst. When we got 'Yasumi', down we would flop into the dust, our bodies soaked with sweat so that when we got up again, we were covered with a scale like cement.

During the night, we would get separated from one another as we marched. When we stopped, one could hear the names of different men being shouted all down the line. Then, on recognizing the voice or call, we would make for the place it came from until we got the 'Get dressed' order. 'Yasumi' was always the signal to start dozens of men yelling out their own names or the names of those with whom they had lost contact.

Temple Camp

Friendship is the best of all gifts that God bestows
Lonely cold and empty is the heart that never knows
What it means to have a friend: a good friend all the way.
Keeping step beside you whether it be night or day.

Patience Strong

The march was becoming hell to most of us but I was pleased with myself up to the fourth stage of that first night out of Kamburi, as my heel was much better after the few days' rest. However, the exertion of the march started my stomach pains again and I went from bad to worse. By 6 a.m. I was all in, and being supported by Gordon and Jim, with Dick Sabin carrying my small pack.

We arrived at Temple Camp at about 9 a.m. My legs had completely refused to function and when we stopped outside the camp, I lay on the ground while the Nips made a check. One Nip came up and rolled me over with his foot. I faintly remember him doing it, then Gordon and Jim picked me up and helped me

110

down some steps onto the grounds of an old temple and into the bushes as a protection from the sun. They then went to buy coffee and little sweetmeats from some natives who had come into the camp to sell to us. I was given a mug of coffee and then slept until the heat of the sun made it impossible. I got up and hopped down to the river where I lay in the cool water for a long time.

My feet were in a bad state again and my socks, like those of many others, were soaked in blood. When Gordon, Jim and Dick joined me, I noticed that their feet were also in a very bad state.

As we sat in the water, we saw a number of natives go out into the stream with nets and then witnessed a wonderful display of fish catching. Two natives, one on each end of a thirty foot net, held it like a low fence in the water. Then another two, one on each end of a net about forty foot long, went up stream about 500 yards and, with the net stretched out full length, started running back towards the other two, their net slowly shaping into a half-circle. As they pulled the net completely round the two stationary men, the fish were trapped and all they had to do was to work the net under the fish and pull it up. I was amazed at their dexterity. There was a native boy ready with a large earthenware jar. As the fish were picked out of the net, so they were placed in the jar. This was done quickly and expertly. The natives repeated the trapping many times until the jar was full. Then they came ashore and cleaned the fish, fried them in oil and sold them to us at a ridiculously low price.

It was fortunate for us that the natives charged so very little for their wares as we didn't have much money and what we had was rapidly dwindling away. Many men had sold their kit or other articles of value, such as pens or watches, which were always in great demand. The Nips would approach us saying 'Watchee, watchee, Parker pen' and, if a man was foolish enough to produce either pen or watch, it would be taken away and perhaps a few cigarettes or cheroots given in exchange. The Nip would walk away grinning, leaving a very riled man who was helpless to do anything about it. There were cases where Nip guards gave the price asked for but the natives were the best to deal with. They would always pay up after bargaining, and we had much amusement doing trade with them, overcoming the language difficulty by using signs and showing fingers to represent the number of dollars.

When a man had used up all his money, he would look for something to sell, and after the sale he would be able to buy something to eat at native bazaars or stalls which were set up in the first few camps on our way. The more extravagant men, who believed in selling all their kit and spending their money carelessly, became rather a menace. A man with no kit to sell and without money would be on the lookout for something he could pick up to exchange for food or money and theft became rampant and a source of much annoyance.

We were now marching with No. 9 train party, commanded by Major Hyde, and during the first few hours I learned that much thieving had taken place during the march. This became very apparent as the march progressed, and it became unsafe to leave an article of kit out of sight. If we wanted to go for a wash or anything that would take us away from our kit, we had to be sure that someone was left on guard. Nips had been a source of trouble in this respect, as they strolled around while we slept and took anything they saw of any value lying about. Then there were the natives who grabbed the kit off men while on the march, and now our own men had become the worst menace of all.

The OC of the train threatened all kinds of punishment to anyone caught thieving, but this had no effect. I have seen men in tears who have had their wallets or packs stolen which contained many personal belongings of sentimental value such as family photographs. Many offers of forgiveness were advertised for the return of these things but rarely, if ever, was anything returned. It was a cruel blow to men to have things like this stolen after having kept them through such trying and difficult times. I am sure that had a man been proven guilty of theft, he would have had very rough treatment at the hands of his mates, for to steal a man's belongings (under these extreme circumstances) might well mean the loser's life. Any article of kit now became very valuable and once lost there was no means of replacement.

That night we had an offer to have our kit carried to the next camp by a team of native yak drivers, but many men hesitated. It meant that we could march without the encumbrance of our packs but we stood a good chance of losing our kit. I set the ball rolling by saying that as my kit was usually carried by others at the end of the march, I would chance mine, and seeing mine go on, others

112

added theirs. When we started out on our march we had nine yak carts following us loaded high with our kit.

At 9 p.m. we set out. My feet were giving me hell and it seemed that many others were suffering in a similar way. Some had decided to carry their boots, and had bandaged their feet with puttees and rags. Many of us had bamboo sticks for support and through the suffocating blinding dust we marched on and on, with the usual yells and cries, and always the cries of the yak drivers in our rear.

At about 1 a.m. it started to rain and soon it was teeming down. At first I welcomed it as it was so cooling and it damped the dust, but it wasn't long before I thought I'd prefer the dust as what had been six inches or more of dust now became mud, making each step an agony. As we trudged through the mud, each step became deeper and more sloshy. The rain put our guards' torches out so all we could do was to follow the noises of clanging tins and the sucking noises caused by the suction of the men's boots in the mud. We lost the sound of the yak carts and, through the pitch darkness, we almost lost each other. My little gang kept shouting to each other, other gangs did the same, and the night became one hell of a noise of shouting, straining, suffering men. I thought 'God, will this ever end?' It was beyond human endurance. Yet we held on and, through mud sometimes knee deep, we followed the many noises. Many times we had to stop and pull out men who had got too deep in the mud to extricate themselves.

On one occasion, while crossing a narrow ravine where tree trunks had been felled to make a kind of bridge (it was very difficult and we had to perform a balancing act in the dark), a Nip who had remained there to see us safely across, suddenly grunted as I passed by him and disappeared into the ravine. He might have slipped and on the other hand it was a simple matter to bump him so that he would lose his balance. However, he disappeared. Soon after this, I saw lights in the distance and hoped it was the halfway halt. My hope was realized, for soon we came to a clearing and I could see black shiny faces and googily eyes peering out at us from behind spluttering smelly torches. The natives were squatting, and around them they had an assortment of food for sale, slices of toasted coconut, fried bananas, warm coffee and a big container with water for our bottles lay before us.

After we had rested, we were allowed to buy and, having

completed our business, we lay down in the mud to rest again. The yak carts had not caught up with us and we were told that we could rest for two hours. Being soaking wet, I began to lose my body heat and to shiver. Everyone was the same and so, as if by some understanding, we bunched up together and lay in the mud, huddled together for warmth, just as animals do. I felt very disturbed about this. It seemed that the further we went into the jungle the more like animals we became in almost every way. We were living on food that dogs would spurn. Men, when they received it, would gulp it down and many would snarl and almost fight over extra food. Self-preservation seemed to have become everyone's greatest concern. I am sure many men were losing their reason. As much as I detested it, I found myself in the middle of a bunch of men whose bodies were wet and sticky with cold sweat and mud. The stench gave me a terrible sickly feeling, but we were getting some warmth this way and I got in a bit of sleep.

We were awakened by the noisy arrival of the yak carts. I shall never forget the torture of that hurried move from the roadway. I was stiff and sore, aching in every joint and my feet were caked with dry blood. There were agonizing groans and moans on all sides.

I have often thought of how I pitied a corporal of the RAMC who, while we rested, was told to return along the track to look for a man who had fallen by the way and was now missing. He struggled to his feet and, with another RAMC lad, departed to look for the lost man. Though tired and weary, they sacrificed their short rest period. When I got to know the corporal better, he told me about that journey. He and his companion had struggled back through mud and slush on their hopeless task. When they had gone a considerable distance, they felt too exhausted to go any further. So they slowly made their way back, only to find on their arrival that the party was ready to move off again. Without any rest, they had to fall in and continue marching with the group. Next morning, they learned that the man had been with the party all the time. He had been completely exhausted, was sleeping and hadn't heard his name called.

Inevitably, the march was bringing out the good and bad in the marchers. The 'bad' men were those who shirked their share of those essential duties which were essential to the welfare of us all.

For example, we had with us a number of 6-gallon containers. With these, we got water from wells or streams for general distribution. While the main party was resting, small parties would have to go forward with the containers to get water and then issue it. In addition, as the Nips had no containers, ours were also used for collecting the rice or other food when we were in one of the camps. So those containers were extremely valuable to us. The problem was that they had to be carried on the march. To ensure that this task was fairly shared, everyone was given a number. As we marched, the numbers of those next for duty in carrying the containers would be shouted out by an NCO. Men worked in pairs, each pair carrying four containers slung on a long bamboo pole which they balanced on their shoulders. Pairs changed every fifteen minutes on a shout of 'Change over' from the NCO.

The task grew increasingly burdensome. The further we marched, the weaker we all grew, for we were all exhausted and overloaded and virtually every man was sick. Many men shirked their term of duty when their number was called, leaving the men who were due for relief shouting frantically for them. Inevitably, tempers got very frayed and all too often, the exhausted carriers would simply dump their containers on the track, where those following stumbled and fell over them. Many containers were lost in that way. In consequence, we soon did not have enough to cope with the water issues and men went short.

Sick men had to be helped and the fittest and strongest were asked to assist and support the sick men in turns. There again, men shirked their turn and the sick became a great burden to the willing helpers.

The camp duties also became extremely arduous. Exhausted, weary, and ill though the men were, when we arrived at a camp, someone would have to collect the rations; someone had to do the menial jobs, and although men were fairly detailed for these jobs, many were missing when their turn came. The result was that some would have double the work to do and soon many of the fittest became ill. Many normally willing men became very reluctant to do for the dodgers.

The good in men was also shown in many ways. Many made themselves ill by helping others. To help another on this agonizing march demanded a great effort of self-sacrifice because if a man succumbed to weakness and fell by the way, he would be likely to lose his kit, as helpers couldn't carry the kit as well as the man. To assist another, they were giving away precious strength which was already overtaxed. But, even so, no sick man was left wanting. If a man fell exhausted by the wayside, many hands would reach out to help him up and words of encouragement would be offered. There were many acts of bravery, of sacrifice and mercy, by heroes who will never be known. Many acts of unselfish thoughtfulness and kindness that were overlooked and barely mentioned. Little acts of kindness such as when a man fell exhausted, another picked him up and shared his last drops of water with him or dampened a piece of rag with those last few drops and wiped the man's forehead. Then he lifted him on to his feet, supported him and helped him along, after becoming so weakened by the effort that he had to be assisted himself later on. I was helped in this way, picked up when I fell exhausted, my kit taken and carried, and I was given a friendly shoulder to lean on. My pals Gordon Davies and Jim Payne rarely left my side and they saw to it that I wasn't left behind. I owe them gratitude that will never die. Gordon, not very strong himself, had to be assisted towards the end of this leg of the march.

Bridge Camp

The yak carts now kept up with us and the drivers could be heard crying out to the beasts. The rain had stopped but the mud seemed to get worse, becoming even stickier as it dried and calling for agonizing effort when marching through it. Several of the men who had completely collapsed were now riding with the load of kit on the yak carts. I too began to feel the distance was too great for me and, like the night before, I collapsed near the end of the march. Half carried and half dragged, I arrived at the Bridge camp with Jim Payne and Gordon Davies, my saviours once again. I remember staggering down a long steep incline into a narrow valley and wondering which was worse – ascending or descending hills. When ascending, one struggled and strove to climb. In descending, it took all one's effort to hold back, causing one's full weight to be thrown on sore and painful legs and feet. As I descended that hill, my knees, all wobbly, and my head feeling too heavy to carry, I noticed the high bridge that was in the course of construction. It was of wood and I pitied the men who might be working on the construction as it seemed so dangerous. We passed quite close to it and crossed over a stream by a small wooden bridge then up the bank on the other side of the valley to an open space where we were halted. I just sprawled out where I was and lay there for quite some time. I noticed many others doing the same – men with hollow cheeks and sunken darkened eyes, who looked filthy, weary and miserable.

After Gordon and Jim had found a place in the bushes nearby, they helped me to the spot and then left in search of the kit. They found ours in a big heap and, on returning with it, told me that we were lucky. One yak cart was missing with its load, and consequently there were many who were now minus their kit and sorry that they had trusted the yak drivers.

At about 10 a.m. we were given a meal of rice and vegetable water. The sun had come out and the heat prevented sleep, but we all lay down and tried to rest, though we rolled and turned and perspired. At midday we were called on parade by the Nips. We hobbled into ranks and when the Nip arrived on the scene, we had to salute. The Nip told us that he was very angry with us as someone had stolen articles from the cookhouse. If the articles weren't returned, we wouldn't be given any more food. He said that a meal had been prepared for us. As soon as the articles were returned, the food would be issued. Major Hyde then gave us a good lecture about thieving, and suggested that the thief should leave the articles with him. He would chance taking any punishment the Nips might mete out.

We returned to our shelter and cursed the bunch of thieves that were making themselves a real nuisance. The meal was not served until 7:30 p.m. We paraded and were issued with half a pint of rice as a haversack ration. Then we picked up our kit and started off on another stage of our journey. As we picked our way painfully down the side of the valley, Nip guards stood every few yards with bamboo sticks and, for seemingly no reason at all, poked or struck us as we passed by. It was just like running the gauntlet, punishing us for the theft.

Some of our men had brought dogs with them. Two dogs I knew were with us. One was a puppy about three months old, and its owner must have truly loved it. During the day the pup could be seen curled up close to its master. If anyone approached, he would prick up his ear and growl in a puppy way. He became quite a favourite with the men. His owner could be seen sharing his food and drink with it and many times carried the little body when it seemed that his little legs couldn't take anymore. The little thing seemed almost human and copied us in many ways. On the march he would flop down as soon as he heard the shout 'Yasumi' come from the Nips and always seemed like a spoiled child when we moved off again. He would grunt and yawn and had to be coaxed to start off once more. We all became very attached to him. He was in the lead with his master when we started down the slope. When I reached the bottom of the incline, I could hear the puppy yelping and crying out. I came to an ugly looking Nip who stood grinning at us as we passed and at the yelping struggling little pup which he held prisoner. He had apparently taken it away from its master, pushed his stick through its collar and stuck the stick into the ground and was holding it there, causing the collar to be twisted and the pup much pain with his little head forced to the ground. I have never felt more like committing murder than I did at that moment. That ugly grinning face would have provoked a saint. As we passed by I heard many mutter about what they would some day do to that Nip, and for quite a time we could hear the pitiful yelps of the pup whose fate was certain, as the Nips were fond of dog meat. Later while resting, I heard the owner of the pup sobbing and I am sure that many shed a silent tear in sympathy. That poor little pup, another innocent and undeserving victim of our horrible circumstance.

As we marched, the demand for help became more and more urgent. As we left each camp, men joined us who had been left behind by previous train parties because they were too ill to go on and we left our very sick in their place. The sick that joined us were given a place at the head of the column so that if they collapsed, men would not have to walk back to give them assistance.

Tarsoa

I felt pleased with myself next morning when we arrived at Tarsoa camp and I hadn't collapsed. I had been very near it but had

118

managed to make it. Tarsoa was as far as the railway had been built and a big junction was being made there. I swore to myself when I realized that the Nips could have brought us this far by train. The devils should pay for this if I had any say in the matter.

As we approached the place where we were to rest for the day, we passed a bamboo enclosure and inside, leaning over the bamboo fence were men of my Company who had left Changi in the early days. We were elated to meet again and managed to shake hands through the fence and exchange a few words of greeting and news. My courage was badly shaken when they told me that we were going to a place called Nieke which was about 150 miles further in the jungle. They tried to console us by saying that they had heard the grub was all right up there. The Nips then came and chased them from the fence with bamboo canes and I heard many whacks as the sticks landed on bare bodies.

Then we passed the Nip officers' quarters. They too had turned out to see us go by and all wore that hateful Japanese grin which exposed their gold teeth. I thought of the pleasure I would get one day in knocking those smiles off. I never lost that feeling and I never lost faith that one day I would be free to do it. I could have killed those officers without the least compunction. That they should stand there and laugh at men struggling along as we were in the last stages of exhaustion, limping and hobbling, dirty and sweaty, and bent under our loads, trying to keep on our feet until we got to the spot where we were to rest, was intolerable. And those maniacs were grinning at us. I don't know which was more provoking – they, or the Nip with the pup.

When we reached the spot in the jungle where we were to rest, I saw Colonel Harris and Colonel Dillon watching our arrival and thought that they would now be told the facts of our march and something might be done about it. Later we received word from them to say that they had begged the Nips to do something about it, only to be threatened with violence and told that we would have to carry on.

I met Doc Sillman with whom I had worked at Changi. He had been kept back from No. 7 train to administer to the sick as they arrived at Tarsoa. He was unable to treat the men of my party as he had run out of medical supplies and was leaving to go elsewhere very soon. I told him that I still had my bag and he asked

119

me to do what I could for the sick. So I found myself with a long queue of men suffering chiefly from foot troubles. Some were in an awful mess and, with Gordon and Jim's help, I did what I could. I then realized that I could never cope with them all and get a bit of sleep in (we were marching off again that night), so I issued a little of my stuff to each one and let them attend themselves. Then I flopped out again and woke up just in time to parade for the march out again that night.

As I left the camp, I looked back along the railway which had been laid this far. It seemed like a switchback, and I wondered how they expected trains to run on so uneven a track. But apparently they were relying on the weight of the trains to help set the foundations.

Off we started on our next stage, with men who were almost unable to start, being too ill and weak. Our officers had asked for them to be left behind, but the Nips would not allow it. They didn't like having sick men near this big junction.

Chapter Ten

The March II
Tarsoa to Neiki

It is almost impossible to describe the suffering endured by the men on the remaining stages of the march. The march that was to be of 150 miles became almost 250. The fit men became sick, the sick became worse and many died, their various complaints aggravated by the rigours of the march. If I attempted to describe all the incidents or sufferings of the men, I would no doubt be accused of gross exaggeration and possibly bore my readers by the sameness of the prolonged sufferings and incidents. So I have explained roughly how I and my companions came through the first stages and they will have given some idea how things developed as it progressed. I will leave the actual march to their imagination and describe a few scenes and incidents that occurred between Tarsoa and Sonkurai No. 2 Camp between 7 and 17 May 1943.

Branchali

After leaving Tarsoa, I lost count of time. It seemed as if I had been marching for ever. Though marching in a half delirious state, there were many things that occurred that I shall always remember. The 'Hitler's Camp' for instance. That I shall never forget. We had marched through Kenwyn on to Kinsayo where we stopped one night, then on to Wopin and then to Branchali (or

Regimental camp, and as we called it 'Hitler's Camp'), named 'Regimental', because everything was run strictly to time and was very regimental, by the Nip NCO in charge. I was told that he had belonged to the Guards of the Emperor's Palace in Japan, had been disgraced and was sent to Branchali as punishment. So, being a bitter man, he meant to make everybody else's life a misery. From what I saw of him he was succeeding.

We had arrived in the early hours and were sitting outside the camp waiting to be checked, when one of the Nips from the camp came out and started taking down the numbers of the men by merely looking at the number on the piece of cloth which we had been given at Bampong. Unfortunately, I had lost mine during one of my momentary collapses. When the Nip discovered this, I was cracked over the head with his stick and fell over. Luckily, I did not lose consciousness but was left with a nasty scrape on my skull.

After the check, we were allowed to pick our places in the bushes to rest for the day. We remained there until 10 a.m. when we were all called out into the clearing to parade in front of the Nip NCO. He was standing on top of a large anthill and looked amazingly like Adolf Hitler. He was leaning on a long bamboo cane and kept grinning evilly at us. When we had all assembled, he spoke to us in Japanese, which was translated by our interpreter. We were told that food would be given to us in return for work and the rules of the camp were read out. We were to be treated as coolies and all orders were for coolies and prisoners of war.

Our first jobs were to start immediately and parties were detailed off for latrine digging, water carrying, tidying up the camp, woodcutting and cookhouse fatigues. Jim, Gordon and I were on the latrine digging party. How we found sufficient energy to do the digging remains a mystery to me. We worked in gangs of eight with four in the trench at a time working fifteen minutes and resting fifteen minutes with a Nip looking on and grinning all the time. The sun was scorching and the flies tormented us. During our fifteen minute rest period, the Nip guard tried to make conversation. We understood him through a few understandable words and signs. He was pleased to inform us that the great Japanese Air Force had reduced New York to ruins and that soon the world would be asking Japan for mercy. He also told us that our Air Force was no good, explaining, by moving his hand slowly across the front of his face and making a droning noise with his mouth, that our planes flew at great height and took a straight course, dropping their bombs 'boom, boom' from too great a height to be effective. Our RAF was afraid to come down he said, but the Japanese Air Force (his hand moving from above his head swiftly down to his feet and a zooming noise from his mouth), would dive and bomb 'boom, boom like that'. The IJAF was the best in the world, he said. He kept up this line of conversation all the morning and seemed delighted when we nodded as if in agreement.

When the men who had been detailed to get the midday meal shouted to 'come and get it', our Nip told us to pack up and took us to get our meal. He filled our mess tins brim full of ripe and weak vegetable stew saying 'Plenty food for hard workers'. Our other men were lined up by 'Little Hitler' in eights, four baskets of rice were placed at convenient spots and Little Hitler stood there holding out a long cane in front of the men and gloating at them. He raised his cane and the first rank of eight would step forward, two to either of the baskets, then the stick would fall back into place to hold back the men. When men moved a little too far forward they would be rewarded with a 'smack' from the stick. He seemed to find great pleasure in viciously jabbing or striking our men with that long bamboo cane. One of the men who was serving the rice found that he was running short, so he pointed out the fact to the Nip, who promptly set about him, beating him unmercifully for not being more careful. Many men had red welts on their bodies after that meal.

I thought the Nips would have let us rest that afternoon, but it wasn't to be. They shouted for us to turn out on parade again, but many men were sleeping and sprawled all over the place and didn't hear the command, although even if they had heard it, they couldn't have understood it. The Nip in charge seemed to go mad and stamped and raved, ending up by picking up a long bamboo pole about fifteen feet long and charging the places where our men lay sleeping. I am sure he would have run them through had he caught any, but the end of the pole caught in a root and it split giving the men time to get on parade before he could find another weapon. There were many who had to be brought in in a fainting condition that afternoon. To expect men to work all day in the terrific heat after a long night's march was too much. At about 4 p.m. we were allowed to get some rest and were told that we would stay the night at the camp.

During the evening, a very peculiar and persistent buzzing noise came from the surrounding jungle. It started like the buzzing of telephone wires when struck by a slight breeze. It grew in volume and echoed and re-echoed through the jungle. We couldn't understand it, but some of the men said the noise was caused by millions of insects. I was rather keen to see the creature that made that noise and in later months had a grand opportunity of studying that peculiar bee-like insect. But on that evening, they were a real nuisance and their ceaseless noise became very irritating.

Late that evening, Little Hitler stood on his anthill keeping his eye on the camp and though our men kept out of his way, he found many with whom to have fault and used his cane frequently. I had a very unpleasant experience during the evening meal. We had been served with a pint of dry boiled rice with no salt or sugar to flavour it. It was very unappetizing and tasted musty, but I was hungry and had to eat something. I found it very difficult to swallow and had only a very little water with which to wash it down. I nearly choked when some of it stuck in my throat, which must have been too dry to allow the sticky rice to pass. I had almost suffocated before I had drawn attention to my predicament and water had been brought to me. Even then it was a long time before I could clear the blockage and the struggle and pain left me weak and ill. It was fortunate that we were staying that night or I am afraid that I would have remained behind.

The night's rest did us all a lot of good and the next morning I felt much better. I had just finished my rice breakfast when I noticed that No. 10 train party men were arriving. They were just as we had been; men being carried or supported, and many collapsed on arrival. After they had been checked, it was discovered that one man was missing and, until the man was found, they had to remain seated in the sun. About an hour later, one of their officers with a Nip guard and the missing man came into camp (he had fallen asleep during one of the rest periods and not awakened when the others moved off). Little Hitler walked over to them and after a few questions he beat the man brutally until he collapsed and then he kicked him, after which some of our men carried him into the shelter of the trees. The men of No. 10 train were then allowed to go into the bushes for shelter from the sun and a little later they were called to get their meal with Little Hitler supervising the issue. Most of the men, being exhausted, had fallen asleep, and didn't answer the call quick enough for Little Hitler, so he dashed amongst them striking about him in a mad frenzy. Those who were a little late were given a hiding and sent back without food.

We were glad when the time drew near for us to march away from that camp of beatings and we all hoped that one day that beast of a man would be brought to justice. Before we left, I saw him inspect a small company of Nips, who were on their way to Burma and had stopped for food and rest at this camp. He lectured and bullied them and ended by making them repeat allegiance to their Emperor; they half turned and faced the east and though I heard it repeated many times, I did not hear it ever sound any different to this, 'ijee, ijor, ijoh, ovis'. They repeated this about a dozen times and then bowed solemnly. It sounded very queer with the whole crowd of them producing those queer guttural sounds in their funny little voices. After the ceremony, they made the half turn to the rear, saluted and bowed to the Little Hitler three times, then saluted and bowed to their NCO twice, and broke off by saluting and bowing to each other. They then took their places around a little cart which was loaded with their kit and arms. About twenty of them grasped the rope at the front, a long rope that had lengths of rope spliced to it so that each man had a length to himself. This rope was placed over his shoulder and grasped firmly in both hands at the front. When they started off, they would bend low and then rise, levering themselves forward, sometimes breaking into a trot. When they came to a hill, they would start chanting a weird song that grew faster as they moved faster to clear the hill, then slowed as they slowed up. Many times during the march I felt a cold shiver in the region of my spine when I heard the chanting of the Nips in the dead of night coming from somewhere in the dense jungle ahead or behind us. There was something so mournful about it, and I knew when I heard it that they were struggling and

125

straining at the ropes of their carts. The NCO in charge of them usually rode a horse.

When we lined up to leave Little Hitler's camp, we looked a sorry sight. Some men had managed to wash, others were dirty, but there was a certain amount of spirit left as it seemed the men wanted to show defiance for, as we moved off, the men at the front of the column started singing 'Colonel Bogey'. If Little Hitler thought he had broken our spirits this was indeed a rebuff to him and I was expecting him to order our return, but we kept going unmolested.

Rain started again, and I was informed by a man, who said he knew all about it, that the monsoons were starting and soon it would rain all day and every day. This was indeed a bad outlook for us, and it did much to increase our misery. During one of the stops we made, I picked up a few small wild mangos. They were about the size of bantams' eggs, had very little flesh and seemed all skin and stone. The stone was rather large, but I found that by keeping it in my mouth (like the old soldier's tale about sucking a pebble), I didn't become so thirsty. It had rather a sharp, bitter taste making it quite pleasant to suck.

As we marched along, drums could be heard in the jungle. We could hear them off and on all night and, on one occasion, we came pretty near a camp where the drums were being beaten and our men started humming in time with the drums. The natives must have heard us for they stopped beating the drums and a few seconds later started up again with 'tom-tiddley-om-pom, pom-pom'. They must have known who we were. As we advanced further and further into the jungle, the sound and sight of natives became less and less until we were about halfway, when it became very noticeable that there weren't any natives living in this region. It seemed as though we were going further away from human habitation with every step that we took.

The mosquitos were becoming more and more troublesome and the insects buzzed and buzzed, the crickets rattled their peculiar noises, the bullfrogs croaked hollowly and there were many un-familiar noises in the jungle mingling with the noises of our column. It was a strain for the strongest of nerves. As we marched, tigers were heard loping along and crashing through the bushes, but always keeping out of sight and away from the torches we carried. The Nip guards marched in the middle of the column, being careful that they weren't at any vantage spot for attack by tigers.

Each time we stopped for a rest, fires had to be started for protection, and the Nips became very agitated and jumpy. During one rest period, we were told that we could rest for an hour as we had made good time. After shouting pretty hard, I directed Gordon and Jim to where I was and we then prepared to make ourselves comfortable. I had stopped near a pile of fallen bamboo branches, so I slung my pack on the pile and lay down on the track with my head on my pack. The others did likewise and after a short while Gordon wanted to know who was moving the bamboo branches. We all denied being the culprits so he got up to look into the matter, and shouted, 'Look out, snake'. I jumped up and saw what I thought was one of the bamboo branches moving away. It was a large snake, like a python, and was very slowly moving from under my pack. We had all rested our heads on it and it hadn't attacked us!

We rested at that spot for over an hour and then came the dreaded order 'Get dressed' and we were off again. During the following days and nights we grew more weary and ill. We were leaving more and more men behind at different stops and, as the country grew wilder, so the stops became less suitable for the sick. Now, when men became too ill to carry on, they would stay on at the spot where they rested, and relied on other sick men for help. Heavy showers had become more frequent so those sick men, left with only the cover of the trees, had to endure the tortures of the sun and of the heavy downpours. Many, dismayed by being parted from their friends, exhausted and ill, lost all hope and gave up, dying where they lay and being buried by the men of the following trains. Now men remained behind only when they couldn't possibly go forward and many kept going when they should have remained at the last stop. The number of sick increased to such an extent that they could hardly be supported and we longed and prayed for the march to end.

During one of the last stages of the march, when we entered a clearing and made our stop for the day, I found that it was my turn to go with a group of men to fetch food from the Nip cook-house about a mile away. Picking up the large dixies, we moved off and eventually found the place where rice, and a kind of stew, was being cooked for us. To my great surprise and delight, I found Old Bob there. He saw me and came over, his face beaming, and wanted to know how everyone on the party was faring. He said 'Welcome to our wayside cafe, I suppose you are hiking to Burma, sly old fox, but didn't let me know that you were coming so that I could have the place all comfy for you, and a nice cup of tea ready.' He kept on in this strain and had us all roaring with laughter in a very short time. He moved away as a Nip showed up but came back again in a few minutes and reaching down, picked up one of my containers, winking as he left with it. I looked down and in the container that he had left was a lump of cooked meat and a handful of rice. The Nip had been looking our way but hadn't seen the sleight of hand. I hadn't seen it myself, but there was the meat and the rice to be got rid of before the Nip saw it, so I hurriedly disappeared into the bushes. Then, after a few minutes I returned feeling much better for having had the most tasty portion of food in months. As we left with the containers of food, Old Bob said 'Keep going and keep your pecker up, remember the further you go in the direction you're going the nearer you are to our troops.' He pointed across the river and said 'Just think of it, fifty miles away is Moulmein, in that direction, and our troops are not far from there.' He shouted after me as I departed that he hoped my 'plates of meat' (feet) weren't as tender and sore as his.

I shall always remember Old Bob as one of the best. Jolly under all circumstances, he always appeared to me to be a typical Tommy, typified in the 1914–18 war, by the men who joked under heavy bombardment. I didn't realize when I left him in that little corner of the jungle that I would never hear his cracks, jokes and witticisms again, never hear that chuckling laugh of his, or even see him again. But perhaps it was a good thing that none of us could visualize the future. God bless good Old Bob!

Konkoita

On we went, from camp to camp, wending our tortuous way up hill and down dale, through thick jungle and clearing, through bogs and marshes, encountering seemingly insurmountable

128

obstacles, but winning through in the end. We thought when we arrived at Konkoita that we were at the end of our tether. It seemed that we couldn't go any further. They said the distance would be 150 miles. Why, it seemed as though we had already covered about 300 miles, though in truth we had come about 200. This seemed like the end. We had started off the night before at 7 p.m., had marched all night and were still marching at 10 a.m. in the blazing sun. One man, Harry Barlow, fell against me as we marched along. I almost fell with him. His lips were swollen and his tongue dry between his lips, and he was murmuring 'Water, water'. I had a little in my bottle, wet his lips and poured a little into his mouth. He gurgled, but it revived him enough to carry on for another mile. Poor fellow, he was overexhausted. He had strained his heart. He never seemed to get over it and lingered between life and death for about the next six months before he died.

We arrived at a clearing and were told that we would rest there for the day. We were too exhausted to make ourselves a shelter from the sun, and so we just lay where we could. After about an hour I felt rested and roused Jim, Gordon and Dick Sabin. While they made a shelter I took all our water bottles to try and find water. I had noticed a river about a mile back on our left, so I thought that if I walked into the jungle to the left, I would be bound to find the river. I kept going deeper and deeper into the jungle but there was no sign of the river. I had been walking for about ten minutes when I thought that I had better not go any further or I wouldn't find my way back. I turned to retrace my steps and discovered that something had been following me. I could see the thick undergrowth moving about ten yards away, as if a large body was moving there. I became transfixed. I couldn't move. What was I to do? If I shouted there was no one to hear me. I tried to think of everything I had read about adventures in the jungle, but couldn't remember reading anything that would be of use now. The movements were getting nearer. I had to do something. I didn't have anything that could be used as a weapon and very unsettling thoughts passed quickly through my mind of being mauled or bitten to death. I was in a bath of sweat and terrified. I did what any child would have done. I looked for a tree to climb. There were plenty of these but they were so covered with thorny creepers that it looked hopeless. I moved to back away from the unseen terror and trod on a rotten branch. I stooped quickly and picked it up, but it was covered with all kinds of crawly things and a large centipede was making its way along it towards my hand, so I threw the stick as hard as I could in the direction of the disturbed underbush. The movements stopped. I stood there waiting and holding my breath, but nothing happened, so after a while I moved quietly away. I realized then what a fool I had been to risk coming so far into the jungle alone. As I made my way back I kept looking round in fear, expecting to hear a crash of bushes and to be pounced on any minute.

I realized that if I kept on like this, my nerves would give out for I was letting my fear and imagination work me into a state of hysteria. I was in the worst funk I had ever been in, so I stopped and tried to pull myself together. I reasoned with myself and felt better for it. I decided that I wouldn't look back any more and found it helped immensely. However, a new fear was forming. I wasn't getting back to the clearing in the time I had taken to enter. I kept going but everywhere looked alike. Above, tall trees with large hanging creepers kept out the sun, and below, wild banana trees and thick bushes with creepers. How had I got into this place? The real problem was how was I to get out? I had read about walking in circles; was I doing this? I must have been travelling back now for over half an hour and I had only walked about ten minutes into the jungle. There was something wrong somewhere and I had nothing to help me for direction. If the Nips found me they would think I was escaping and probably shoot me, so I dared not shout in case I drew their attention. On the other hand, I might disturb some sleeping animal. I sat down and tried hard to think of some way out. I had never felt so lonely or so scared. Was this to be my end to the mysterious journey? I thought, 'Not if I can help it'. I listened hard to see if I could hear any sound of our men, but the noises in the jungle drowned out all else. I couldn't go forward as the undergrowth was too thick. I would have to go back the way I had come and try to find the little track I had followed when I entered the jungle. But what about the hidden danger in the undergrowth? I considered this a little longer and decided that I would have to chance it, so I cautiously turned to go back the way I had come, when my blood seemed to freeze in my veins. There, only a few feet away, was a large snake. I could only see its head at first and as it came out from behind the log I had been sitting on its body seemed to get thicker. I couldn't move and perhaps I did the right thing by standing perfectly still as the snake approached to within a foot or so of me. Then it turned over a rotten piece of wood and disappeared into the undergrowth. It was at least ten feet long. As soon as I thought it safe, I moved. I would have run if I could, but it was as much as I could do to walk through the thick bushes.

Two narrow escapes in such a short time and I was still lost! I began to go cautiously again, as in my mind was ever the thought of the hidden terror in the bushes. Just then I noticed it was getting much lighter and on looking up I could see patches of blue sky through the tall trees. Soon I arrived at a clearing, and at the other end I saw our men and their quaint shelters. Never had I experienced such a feeling of relief. I hurriedly found my shelter where the boys were sleeping soundly. They hadn't even missed me! I had been away two hours and they had been about the worst two hours in my life. What puzzled me was that when I had thought I was going deeper into the jungle, I had actually been on my way back!

I told the boys of my adventures when they woke up. They were quite concerned at first, but ragged me about it afterwards. No one will ever know what a feeling of helpless terror I had experienced during those two hours while I was lost only a short distance from my pals. I will never know what it was that moved in the undergrowth, or why it stopped when I threw the stick.

After a few hours, we were awakened and instructed to fall in for our meal. We would march back along the track two miles to get it. We collected our mess gear and, as the cookhouse was near the river, I grabbed the water bottle and my towel and off we went. I felt dopey after such an unsettled sleep, although by now we were getting used to marching while feeling in some kind of stupor. We arrived at the place where rice was being prepared for us and were told that we would have to wait an hour or more as the rice wasn't quite ready. This was very annoying as every minute spent away from the temporary stop meant sleep lost and every minute of sleep and rest was extremely valuable.

Gordon, Jim and I walked to the river and soaked ourselves in the cool water while we waited for the rice. After our refreshing bath, we filled our water bottles from the cleanest of the muddy water in the river. I added chlorine to our water and then one of our MOs, who was standing near, shouted to all around that we were to be extremely careful with the water as he had received information that cholera had broken out in this camp among the natives who were working here. The MO shouted to a man who was swimming that he should not swim or allow the river water near his mouth. The man replied that it was no concern of the MOs. If he died it was his own business, and what was life worth anyhow? The MO answered that at least the man might think of his people at home and of the danger to his mates if he should fall a victim to cholera. This seemed to make the man think a bit because he came out of the water. He belonged to the Manchester Regiment and died within weeks. I believe he was the first of No. 9 train to succumb to cholera – that dreaded disease.

We collected our meal and devoured it. Then we received our pint of rice as haversack rations and made our way back to camp. When I arrived back, I visited some of the sick and found that they had been placed in the bushes where they had to fend for themselves. Some had been there since the early parties had passed through and were in an awful state. They were too weak and ill to walk into the bushes so had messed themselves and were lying in filth with no one to care for them. They were simply left to die. I thought 'Good God, what an end'. The next party to come through would probably find these fellows dead and would bury them. The poor devils were at the end of their tether. They had stopped behind to rest to try to regain sufficient strength to march on with a later party. As they saw each party come and go, they lost all hope and grew weaker and weaker as each day passed. They were too weak to walk the distance to the cookhouse. Unless people from the parties passing thereafter visited them and collected their food for them, they went without. As it was, there was rice, days old and sour, in the mess tins. I spoke to one. He raised his sunken eyes, and gasped out my name. I was surprised and looked closer then recognized him as one of my old patients. I was shocked by the change in him. He had been a hefty fellow, and now he was a mere shadow. His cheeks were hollow, his eyes sunken and his voice husky and weak as he asked me for water. I found that his bottle was dry, so I raised him to give him a drink and found that he was caked in his own excreta. Flies were about in their thousands to torture that poor sick man.

What could I do for these men? What could anybody do? They were dying without a doubt but what torture to spend one's last moments like this. I left him my water, after wiping his face with a damp rag and went to find the MO who was with our party. The MO was sleeping, so I woke him up and got told off for my pains. He said he knew about the sick, but what could he do? I realized that he was quite right. Our MOs had had a hell of a time on the march, attending to the sick as we marched along and sometimes having to come back from the head of the column to the rear to see a man who had collapsed, and doing this extra walking must have been a great ordeal. Then, immediately after we arrived at a stop, an MO would be seen attending to the sick while others were resting. They did all they could. How they kept going I can never guess. It must have been disheartening to see so many helpless and dying and be unable to do anything for them.

I heard later that our MOs and officers had asked the Nips to let the men remain here to rest for a while, explaining that owing to the cholera outbreak in the camp, it would mean that our men might take the disease with them to the camps further up. The Nips wouldn't hear of it, so we had to keep going on with no knowledge of how much further we had to go. So, that night, sick, weak and weary, and sick at heart about the plight of the men we were leaving behind, we started off again.

After a short time, I think my mind must have been wandering because I faintly remember seeing a river running down between two mountains. We were walking down the side of one of the mountains and must have been going west as the sun was setting and we were walking towards it. The sunset was reflected on the river and the small tufts of cloud around the sun were coloured in the most beautiful array of colours I have ever seen. The colours were also reflected on the water and with the mountains dark and overshadowing the river, and jungle on each side, which seemed to take on the reflecting colours, I have never seen such a wonderful sight. So wonderful did it appear that I still think it was the turmoil of my mind playing tricks of fancy on me, but there was no fancy about the aches and pains and the torment I was enduring at the time. I asked many men afterwards if they had noticed the wonderful sunset. Some said 'I had too much on my mind to think of sunsets'. Others said that they thought they remembered something about it, but I found no one that could describe it as I saw it. Perhaps it was an hallucination after all.

As the night progressed, a new torture emerged. The rains had made the jungle stink of rot, and steam or mist seemed to hang about low over the ground and between the trees and under-growth. With this dampness had come clouds of midges or sandflies, so small that they could hardly be seen. They got in our eyes, ears, nose, hair and between tightly closed lips into the mouth. Although we wrapped our heads with what available pieces of cloth we had, these tormentors got under it somehow and the situation then became worse as we couldn't get our fingers under the wrappings to scratch them away. When first we en-countered them, they buzzed about our ears and it seemed as though we had suddenly developed a very irritating skin rash; thousands of them biting simultaneously. It was after an hour or so of this torture that one of our party went rather queer and, I think, lost his reason. No doubt this awful experience had upset his mental balance. He threw his kit from him and tore at his hair. His eyes seemed bright and wild. He kept shouting 'Take me home. Let me go home', ending up by bursting into a fit of sobbing.

This addition to our troubles seemed the last straw and, to have their arms free to battle with these midget flies, men threw away kit that hampered them. Arms and legs also became easy prey and everyone seemed to be smacking and scratching all night long. As dawn broke, the midges eased off, leaving the men very silent. There was no longer the shouting and noise that there had been in the earlier stages, and all that could be heard now were the weary steps we took, the jangle of the tins, the laboured breathing and, occasionally, a half-suppressed groan. Men were now suffering in silence, each with his own particular aches and pains, his own thoughts and so terribly exhausted. I only knew that my whole body seemed to be on fire. My head, like a drum, seemed to be rolling about uncontrollably, my eyes seemed raw and were kept open with the utmost difficulty. My shoulders were skinned and raw from the chafing shoulder straps of my pack, which was worsened by the loss of flesh. Each day brought an increase in the protrusion of my bones, the gnawing pain in my stomach, my knees ready to give way at every step and my feet like lumps of raw beef. This is no exaggeration, and I was in good condition compared with some. Any survivor of this march will no doubt say that I haven't told the half of it. This will be understood when I say that most of the men had skin diseases which gave hellish irritation as soon as they perspired, or perhaps they had rashes or eruptions in the arm pits or crotch which had become raw through continuous chafing. In many cases these had turned septic, with running sores, making every step more agonizing. Others had malaria, dengue, or some other form of mysterious jungle fever. All were emaciated and starving, no one could ever describe their real suffering. Ask the survivors what kept them going, and many will say they don't know. Their steps became automatic and they moved forward blindly. Others will say that they had willed themselves to get back home to their loved ones and so kept going with that one aim in view.

I have compared notes with my pals who marched with me and it seems most peculiar that our notes are strangely alike. Our minds seemed to work and react similarly to the changing conditions. As we advanced, stage by stage, into the jungle during the last marches, when we were in the last stages of exhaustion, we each had a feeling as though we were home among our families and near the ones we loved. I have heard that a drowning man lives his past again in a few seconds before oblivion. That is what made me pull myself together many times. My mind was wandering and it seemed that I was half asleep, yet I was dimly conscious of my aching body as something that was pulling me down, or holding me back. In front was home and, strangely enough, I was in the home of my childhood days with my dear mother and father, or I was home with my wife and children. I saw them quite clearly and then dimly. It was during the time that they were dim that the aches and pains seemed to be holding back the most. Then I would make an effort and everything would be clear again.

This must sound very phoney to any sensible person. I would probably think so myself if someone else told me that it had happened to them. However, when I had rested and thought about it at the camp at Neiki, I decided that it was too clear to be fancy, so I thought my mental faculties were being affected by the

135

strain. When, with great concern, I told one of my pals and explained my fears, he looked enormously relieved, and said that he too was worried because he had also had a similar experience. This gave me the idea of checking with the others later on and I was surprised by the number who had felt as I had.

Neiki

When we arrived at Neiki, I saw that a large camp was being built. Many long huts were near completion, some with only the upright bamboo poles in position. Our party moved into one of these half completed huts and my pals and I immediately got down and slept. We woke up at about midday with rain pouring down on us. All we could do was to rig our groundsheets so that the rain would not beat directly on us. After doing that we foraged round for something to eat and managed to get a meal of rice and watery stew. I then discovered that the parties from Nos. 7 and 8 trains were in the camp. They had been waiting for us to catch up in order to go forward as one party to the camp which was our destination. At last we were coming to the end of our march, though I found it hard to believe any statement made by the Nips. We were given orders that afternoon to form up in order of train parties to move off that night and march to No. 1 and No. 2 camps. The Australians were to take over No. 1 camp and the British No. 2. No. 1 camp was about five miles away and No. 2 a further five miles after that.

Colonel Dillon made a speech and told us that the hell we were enduring would not be forgotten, and that he was doing his best for us. Colonel Harris said that the Nips had a lot to answer for but we were lucky in that here there was a reasonably decent Nip, Colonel Bano – who would be in charge of Nos. 1, 2, 3, 4 and 5 camps, to which 'F' Force had been allocated. Colonel Harris had been promised that all that was possible would be done for us, and that when we had settled in the various camps, canteens would be arranged, blankets and warm clothes and mosquito nets would be issued. He said that Colonel Bano, the Nip, had given up some of his own tinned milk to our sick at this camp, which proved that his intentions were good.

Colonel Harris then said that we had a little further to march but that we would go from here in short easy stages, as the distance from Neiki to No. 2 Camp was nothing compared with the distances we had been marching. 'So cheer up, just one more short march and you will be at the end of your journey.' I am fully convinced that the Colonel thought that he was telling us the truth about the distance, and again we believed that 'Tonight wouldn't be so bad', so we were easy in our minds for the remainder of that day. Except for the scare about cholera, I think we were rather cheerful.

During the day an Australian near me had collapsed and I had rushed over and picked him up. He said his head was throbbing and he wanted to vomit. He was frothing at the mouth and complained of cramps in the upper part of his legs. I guessed he had cholera, for those are the dreaded symptoms. This was the first case of cholera I had seen. I recognized the symptoms since I had read quite a lot about it. I got one of the fellows to help me and we carried him to the sick bay.

The Australians had come to this camp first and had got busy with a pretty well organized sick bay. It was a hut with an atap roof, and the sick were lying on bays that were built off the ground. The stench was dreadful. It was a smell that stayed with me for a long time; the smell of death. Men were dead and dying there. Cholera was taking its toll.

We were told by an MO to lie the man on the floor. Then we were to rub our hands in lime, wash them, and get the hell out of there. We got out quickly but were badly shaken and though we tried, got very little rest.

I was surprised that night when they ordered us out to start the march at about 9 p.m. 'Why so early, if the distance is so short?' was the question in our minds. Off we went and it wasn't long before the men started pulling out and the usual marching troubles began. We had covered about eight miles when the Australians turned off to go to their camp, and there were shouts of 'Good luck' and good wishes exchanged. The Australians shouted 'Get the railway finished soon, you Pommy bastards so that we can get out of here'. We shouted back that if they worked like they could shout, the job would soon be done. It was all good raillery, such as always occurred when we and the Australians met or parted.

The rumour had got around that the road and railway had to be built by us and that we would return to Singapore as soon as we had completed the job. On we marched, soon realizing that the ten miles was another catch. A most remarkable sight that night were the glow-worms and fireflies. One tree was covered with fireflies. There must have been thousands of them, flickering in and out giving the tree a fairyland appearance. The glow worms were everywhere. This, with the high toned chirrup of the crickets and croaks of the frogs and numerous other sounds, made the scene seem creepy. In the distance the deep, full throated bark of what sounded like gorillas drew us closer together, though we were getting to care less and less about anything.

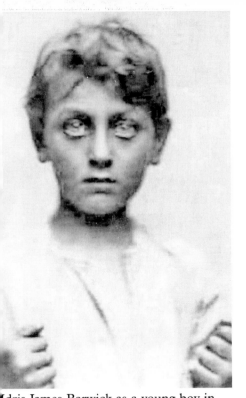

Idris James Barwick as a young boy in Wales, circa 1915. *(Author's collection)*

2. Idris Barwick as a young man, circa 1930. *(Author's collection)*

4. Enduring the Blitz at home were Idris's three children, Isobel, Anne and Bob. He had three more children after the war. *(Author's collection)*

dris and his first wife, Ruby Jones. *(Author's collection)*

5. Bobby Barwick in Dad's gear. This is the photo that was taken from Idris and thrown into the road by a Japanese soldier. *(Author's collection)*

6. Idris Barwick in uniform. *(Author's collecti*

7. At the Officers' Mess, Winslow, before leaving England for the Far East. *(Author's collecti*

8. Idris at Holland Road camp, Singapore, just before the surrender to the Japanese. *(Author's collection)*

9. Changi jail. *(Author's collection)*

10. Japanese ID tag assigned to Idris Barwick. *(Author's collection)*

11. Idris Barwick's 'kit'. *(Author's collection)*

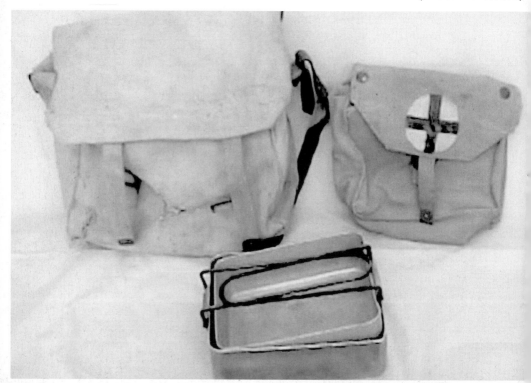

2. POWs building the Tamarkan Bridge on the Burma – Thailand railway.

(Author's collection)

3. A section of the 'Death Railway'.　　　　　　*(Author's collection)*

14. Above: POWs working on the railway. *(Author's collection)*

15. Left: Prisoners laying track on the railway. *(Author's collection)*

16. Below: Graves in the jungle. *(Author's collection)*

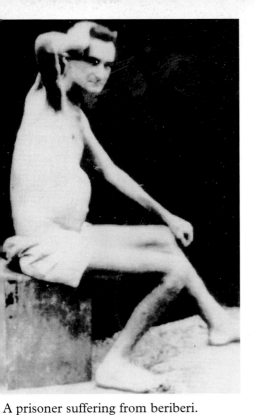

A prisoner suffering from beriberi.
(Author's collection)

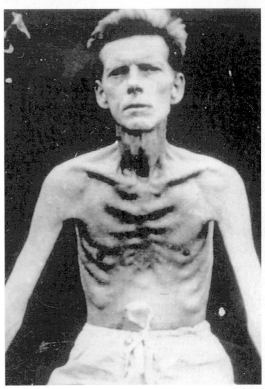

18. The effects of starvation on an unknown POW. *(Author's collection)*

A camp hospital. *(Author's collection)*

20. Left: Making grave
markers in Chan...
(Author's collectio...

21. Below: Mass bur...
in Singapore.
(Author's collectio...

22. Changi jail on liberation day, August 1945.   *(Author's collection)*

23. Survivors.   *(Author's collection)*

24. A medical officer examining a prisoner who has had his leg amputated.

(Author's collection)

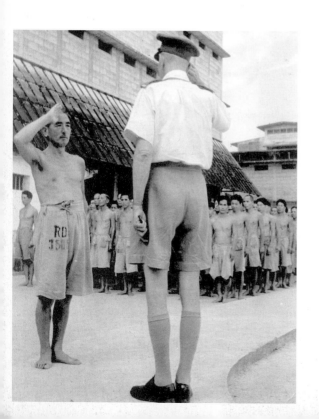

25. Japanese prisoners
parade at Changi jail
while awaiting trial.
(Author's collection)

. A Japanese POW. (Author's collection)

27. Japanese Sergeant Seiichi Okada, also known as Doctor Death, was responsible for the deaths of many POWs.

(Author's collection)

Prisoners awaiting execution at Changi jail.

(Author's collection)

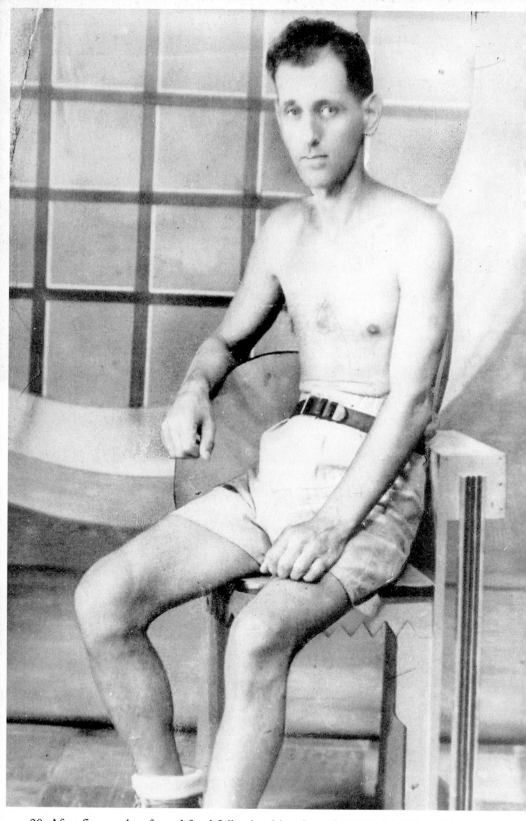

29. After five weeks of good food following his release in 1945, Idris Barwick had brought his weight up to ninety-five pounds when this photo was taken.

(Author's collection)

30. HRH The Duke of Edinburgh chats with former POWs at the Empire Theatre, Leicester Square on 15 October, 1953. Idris Barwick is second from the right.
(Author's collection)

31. A group of ex-POWs gather to see *A Town Like Alice* in 1956. Idris Barwick is in the front row, second from the right. *(Author's collection)*

32. Idris Barwick *(right)* at a Returned POW exhibition. *(Author's collect*

33. After losing his first wife and moving to the United States, Idris Barwick married Barbara Oberdorfer in 1961.
(Author's collection)

34. Idris and Barbara's adopted son David with their daughter, Elizabeth, who wa born in 1962. They also had another Bill, born in 1969. *(Author's collect*

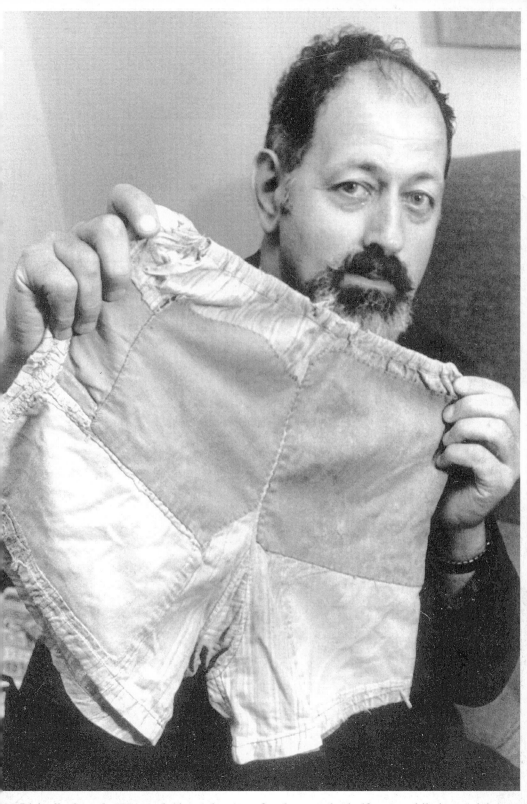

35. Idris displays the 20-patch shorts he wore for three and a half years while in captivity.
(Printed with the permission of the Akron Beacon Journal, Akron, Ohio, USA. Photographer: Bill Samaras.)

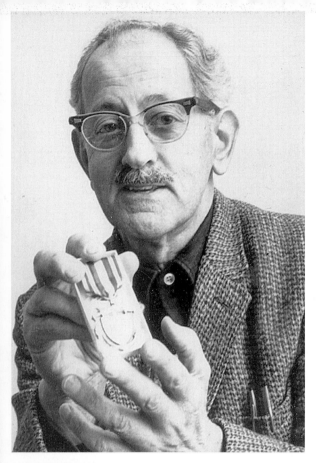

36. Idris holds the medal he received from the people of Dunkirk, France for helping to evacuate wounded soldiers from the beaches on 31 May 1940. This photo was taken in 1973 two years before his death.
(Printed with the permission of the Akron Beacon Journal, Akron, Ohio, USA)

37. Five of Idris Barwick's six children celebrating daughter Elizabeth's wedding in 2001. *Left to right:* Anne, Isobel, Elizabeth, Bob and Bill.   *(Author's collection)*

Chapter Eleven

No. 2 Camp: Sonkurai

The last stage of the march was made worse by the fact that the Nip guide twice lost his way so that we had to retrace our steps to the point at which we had gone wrong. For this to happen to us in our condition was more than our weary bodies could stand. I heard more than one man sobbing in despair, but we plodded on. It was on this march that I contacted Padre John Foster Haig again. He was with No. 8 train and it was indeed a comfort to be near him. He did his best to help cheer the men, though I am afraid that most were past hearing or noticing him. Occasionally I heard him speaking sharply, telling men to pull themselves together and brace themselves for a last effort. He consoled us saying that he thought we must be near the camp and it couldn't be far now. But on and on we went through the night, suffering the endless and increasing tortures until about 10 a.m. on the morning of 17 May, when we were told to halt after crossing a rough log bridge over a fast running stream. Nearby I noticed one roughly built hut and a few under construction. This was Sonkurai or No. 2 Camp.

We were herded together in groups of about fifty and told to sit and wait. After a short while, three Nips came from the rough hut, and true to form, looked at us and grinned evilly. Seeing one of our men to whom he apparently took an instant dislike, one Nip moved over and hit the man several slashes with a long bamboo cane. The blows were struck viciously and were meant to do damage. Each blow, aimed indiscriminately at the head and shoulders, could be heard as they landed with a resounding 'thwak'. The man raised his arms to protect himself and was beaten the more for his action. Eventually he collapsed under the savage attack. The Nip then left him and lashed out at anyone near him. I thought 'God help us if we have to live under this tyrant'. Unfortunately it turned out to be so, for we were to live under him for many months in Sonkurai, the 'Horror Camp of the Thai Jungle', as it was known later, where many of our men died under the most dreadful conditions imaginable. I know I could never describe adequately those horrors or paint a picture to enable anyone to see clearly the terror of the life we lived over the next few months at that camp.

Right at the start we had witnessed and suffered those beatings. They were our introduction to months of similar beatings, starvation, slavery and sickness which ended in the deaths of over two-thirds of our number.

We were shown our bed spaces in what were going to be huts. There was the framework of huts and bays about 12 feet long by 12 feet wide made of bamboo looking very much like a raised platform. Into each of these bays twenty men had to find room to keep their kit and make a sleeping space. We could stretch out and lie down but if anyone turned over, it meant touching the man on either side, as there was barely 18 inches to each man. When, in trying to sort ourselves out, we stopped to complain of the ridiculousness of crowding us in so tight, the Nip came with his stick and shouted and raved at us until we were glad to get down anywhere.

We had to lie on strips of very uneven bamboo and, as there were no roofs to the huts, we were now tortured with sun and rain alike. We made protection from those elements our first consideration. We joined our groundsheets together and cut poles to support them, like a large marquee, and then lay down to get some rest. In trying to rest we found that we had to cover ourselves as protection against giant horseflies, which were about the size of bumblebees. We hadn't known of their presence until we felt their bite, which was like a prick from a very blunt needle.

After a few hours of terrific sun, the rain came pouring down. Just as we were congratulating ourselves on the worthiness of our groundsheet roof, there appeared a big swelling in one of our groundsheets. I realized it was filling with water and then, without any warning, the whole structure collapsed, bringing down many

140

gallons of water, which gave us all a very untimely bath. The lads in the other bays roared with laughter at our struggles to extricate ourselves from the sodden sheets. We must have presented a very funny spectacle, but it was amazing how quickly these march weary men came to life and jumped to it when the deluge landed on them. I saw the men laugh for the first time in many days as other temporary roofs collapsed, splashing water over the men below. But laughter soon changed to misery again, as we were soaking wet and chilled and there seemed no way of getting any comfort for the night.

Our cooks were concerned with building a shelter to cover the boilers which they had fixed up. Then they had to carry water from the river, and men were detailed to gather wood. This had to be done as soon as we entered the camp, so those men hadn't been allowed to rest after the long march and had to keep going until a meal of rice had been served.

We got our meal in the dark that night and had to stand in mud at least a foot deep while queuing to be served. During the serving of the meal our officers told us that the Nips were giving us the morrow off to rest but would start us working the following day. Although our CO, Colonel Hinkson, had pleaded with them and told them that the men were not fit to do the heavy work, the Nips stated that we had been brought here to work, and work we would – even if it killed us all. So things didn't look too good.

That night we built a big fire. Although it kept raining, we managed to keep the fire going and got a little warmth from it. We also were able to dry some of our clothes by it when the rain ceased. After a restless and miserable night, we were glad when day broke and the sun came out again.

The day of 18 May was spent in trying to put the camp in order. Latrines had to be dug, paths made in the jungle, as it had only been cleared to make room for the huts, and wood had to be collected for the cookhouse. The Nips would not allow us tools so we had to collect rotting wood so that we could break it into pieces to burn under the boilers. All that could be done by worn out and tired men to make his camp habitable was done, but the job was hopeless without tools and with only one day allowed us to do it in. Consequently, we utterly failed to make the camp into anything like a fit place in which to live. We had three huts constructed on the side of a hill between two deep gullies down which flowed fast flowing streams. The hill was matted with jungle growth which was now steaming from the heat and rain. Two of the huts were for the use of the men. They were parallel across the hillside and with thick undergrowth between. The length of the huts was between 250 and 300 feet, and about 25 feet wide, with raised platforms each side of a passage, which ran up the middle of the hut and was about 7 feet wide.

Our officers were given the only hut with a completed roof. The Nip guards occupied the extreme end of it. A clearance had been made for a road and this ran along the side of the camp. On the other side of the road was a roofed hut which housed the natives who had been preparing the camp. Near their hut they kept their yaks and carts. These yak carts were the only means of transport for the hauling of stones or timber, and they were required for the building of the railway and road.

The Nips wanted all available men for work and said that only a certain number would be allowed in camp. Work would start at 5:30 next morning and every man must turn out on parade. If he was ill, he would be sent back off parade if the Nips considered him unfit for work. So we looked to the morrow with great foreboding.

During the day, the men of No. 12 train stopped at our camp on their way to No. 3 camp, which was about eight miles further on. Some of them were left at our camp to increase our numbers to about 1,800.

After another miserable night, we turned out at 5 a.m. in the rain and drew our pint of rice to eat, and another pint to take with us on the working party. At 6 a.m. we fell in and were formed into parties of about fifty. Each of these parties moved off with a Nip in charge and drew tools for the particular job for which they were detailed. The jobs were: clearing the jungle; felling suitable trees for bridge building; shaping timber with axes and saws; road shaping; quarry work and cutting and blasting stone for road foundations. Only a few men were left in camp, and these were either sick or doing the cooking, except of course the surplus officers and warrant officers. Tara had taken charge and kept a little set of warrant officers for administration. They saw to it that each day the men were up at reveille and made sure that the correct number went out on the different parties. Otherwise the Nips might have taken them to fill the quota.

I kept with my pals as much as I was allowed. On the first day I went with the party that was detailed for tree felling. We started off at 6:30 a.m. with our tools; rain was dropping in a steady drizzle. The tools were carefully checked before leaving and we were warned that we would be held responsible for their safe return and cleanliness.

As there were virtually no means of keeping our clothes dry, most men went out wearing as little as possible. I wore hat, shorts, socks and boots, and my groundsheet. I considered that though cold to start off with, we would soon be working hard enough to keep ourselves warm. I also carried my small pack in which I had my mess tin with midday meal of cold rice, and my water bottle. Most of us were dressed this way. We splashed along in the mud to the guard room where we were checked out and then slithered and stumbled to the site of our work for the day.

Everyone complained of an awful feeling of lassitude. Our legs seemed to be too heavy, but we reasoned that we were still weary from the march and thought we would brighten up after a while. But the feeling persisted, and everything was too much trouble, every job too heavy, every movement so great an effort.

We had marched about two miles, then halted, and the Nip in charge gave us our jobs. We were to work in parties of five and our job was to cut down trees as near as possible to 12 inches thick, and 15 feet long to be used for bridge structure, and a number of thinner trees to be used as scaffolding for bridge building. To get suitable trees we had to cover a wide area, but I always kept the other parties in sight. One experience of being lost in the jungle had been enough for me! With me were Dick Sabin, Dick Richards and two other men. Although we felt so languid, we were glad to work as we were feeling so cold. One of my party was very pale and kept having bouts of shivering. As we walked through the underbrush we trod on rotting wood and soft marshy, spongy ground, which sent up a nauseating stench and thousands of midges and mosquitoes buzzed around us as we disturbed them.

As we felled our first tree, many insects, including numerous unknown species, dropped on us and into the underbush at each

143

blow of the axe. We were badly bitten so decided it would be better to saw down the trees as the saw would not shake the tree like the axe. The rain came down in a heavy drizzle all day. Everything we handled was wet, and heavy, and the logs, being slippery to handle, became very dangerous.

The further we travelled to search for suitable trees, the further we had to carry them back to the Nip. The logs were taken by yak carts from our dump to the camp where they were shaped and cut to size for the bridge we were soon to build. Apparently our job at this camp was to build a railroad halfway to the camps ahead and behind us. Owing to the uneven country, it would mean many bridges and cuttings, and as we had a deep ravine running down beside our camp, it meant that we would have rather a high bridge to build for the railway and a strong bridge for the road. We had an enormous task ahead of us and my heart almost sank at the thought of the months and months it would take us to complete the job.

At midday we stopped a short while to eat our now sour rice, and tried to light a fire to warm ourselves. Everything was too wet and we shivered more and more as the pouring rain chilled us. The fellow who was having the shivering bouts, Wright, collapsed. All we could do for him was to cover him with our groundsheets. He seemed to have a bad dose of malaria. At 5 p.m. the Nip in charge ordered us to collect our tools as we would start back to camp early owing to the rain. We started out on our way and when we had covered about half the distance we met another party working on the road. Their head Nip spoke to our Nip and between them they decided that it was too early to return to camp so we had to restart work in that area. We eventually returned to camp at about 7.30 p.m. It was now dark and still raining. All we had to look forward to was a roofless hut and, probably, wet or damp blankets to lie on. Our meal, which was served in the rain, consisted of one pint of boiled rice and half a pint of thin soup. We were glad to lie down in the dark, even though our roof was only made of leaking groundsheets.

That night I developed a fever. When I paraded for work at 5 a.m., the MO ordered me back to my bed space. The fever turned out to be a form of dengue and my condition was worsened by a further relapse of dysentery. So I had a day in camp and, with a few other men, managed to erect a tent. Although the Nips had only a few, they had offered them to the sick if we could carry them from their stores and rig them up ourselves. There were no poles issued, so we had to tie the tents to trees. There being no tools with which to cut poles for this purpose, tying was the only way by which we could put them up. Our tent kept us dry and that was a comfort. I went out and got some grass which I scattered over the floor. It was sodden wet but soft to lie on, so I spread my groundsheet out in one corner and lay down. Everything was damp or wet and miserable but I thought myself very lucky that at least I had shelter from the rain. When my mates returned to camp after a day with the working party, they managed to squeeze in under the tent roof. In all, seven of us used this as our sleeping place. During the day, other sick men who had been left in camp struggled to the Nip stores to collect tentage and placed it over the roof framework of the lower hut at the extreme end, nearest to No. 3 stream. There were about fifty sick men lying in the bays at that end.

The tentage kept the rain out for a little while but it soon began to sag and great bulges appeared in the gaps between the framework. The water gathered in these bulges and eventually became so heavy that the hut collapsed completely. Really it was tragic, yet almost everyone roared with laughter as the hut on its high bamboo supports slowly heeled over gracefully and, amid shouts and laughter, crashed down, jerking the tentage loose and tipping a few hundred gallons of water on to the men below. They merely wrung out their wet clothes and lay back in the wreckage. The lassitude of which we all now complained gave us the desire to lie down and remain in that position. This awful feeling, coupled with the many illnesses that were prevalent, rendered the sufferers almost helpless. They wouldn't get up to collect their food and, as in the case of the collapsed hut, they just lay back where they were, soaking wet and cold with no will for anything but to lie down. A Medical Officer told me that he thought the cause of this awful languid feeling was the fact that we were very high above sea level and we lacked oxygen. I think he must have been right because that lassitude lasted for the whole time that we were at the camp.

Tara had got himself fixed up in the officers' hut and immediately started looking after himself. He sent for me and I found that

145

it was as much as I could do to climb the hill to his hut. When I arrived, he informed me that he knew I was ill but, as I could get about a bit, he proposed giving me the job of looking after him. I was to get up each morning in time to light a fire and boil him water. He wasn't going to risk washing in unboiled water for fear of cholera infection. I had to take the water to him so that he could have a wash before seeing the working parties off each morning, and then, if I wasn't sent out with a working party, I was to boil more water for him.

When we arrived at Sonkurai we were short of containers for carrying the food to and from the cookhouse to the serving point, and the few we did have were also used for carrying water from the river to the cookhouse. Men had brought small pots, buckets, tins, and so on, but these were either commandeered or confiscated by our administrative staff, leaving the men with very meagre means for boiling water for themselves. This situation left very few suitable tins or bowls in which to collect water for ablutions. Mess tins became general purpose receptacles and were used for containing food or fetching and boiling water. Later they were put to many other uses. What particularly annoyed me was that Tara had a bucket to himself, as did many of the officers. There they were, in the dry and, for the most part lying about all day. I know they felt ill. I know they suffered from the awful lassitude, but so did their men, and those men were working from 6 a.m. until, sometimes, 2 a.m. the next day. They would arrive back off some parties at any time from 8 p.m. up to 2 a.m. or even 3 a.m. Then they would have to turn out at 5 a.m. for work again. They had no dry place in which to sleep, no dry clothes to wear, and were feeling weak and ill, hopeless, discouraged and miserable. These men had no hot water provided for them, but our Tara and most of the officers had hot water in the early hours and after their meagre breakfast, went back for another sleep. Meanwhile their men were working their lives away in that hellish jungle.

The monsoon season had started with a vengeance. It rained all day and every day. Our CO pleaded with the Nips to provide dry quarters for the men. They said they would do what they could. After a few weeks, the natives, or Bongs as we called them, who were living in the hut across the road and in comparative luxury

146

to us, came over to put atap on the roofs of our huts. Although much of the rain still found its way through, this helped a great deal and gave the men a chance to keep their kit in the dry. Large fires were now kept going day and night in the central gangway of the huts. So, if they weren't too exhausted, men managed to dry their clothes at night. Those fires were also the only means of illumination during the hours of darkness.

Then came the dreaded day when a few of our men collapsed with cholera and died within forty-eight hours. The number of sick men increased each day and, by now, half the lower hut was occupied with sick and dying men. Cholera began taking its toll, at first with one and then three or more each day. The first casualty from my Company was Redman (who had been one of the Beri Beri girls in our show at Changi). He reported sick on the evening of 26 May and died the next morning.

I had to go out with the work parties again and, on returning to camp one evening, I felt sick. My stomach felt tight and queer pains were developing in the lower abdomen. The dysentery seemed to get worse. I got scared and thought, 'This is it this time. If I've got cholera I'm done for. In twenty-four hours I shall probably be dead.' I went to see the MO and when I explained the symptoms, he sent me to the sick bay as a cholera patient. When I got there I enquired about the treatment and was told there wasn't any. If I had cholera it was just too bad. I thought over everything I had read about the disease; the word 'cholera' in the English dictionary is explained as bilious vomiting and purging, which is a mild explanation of the actual thing. The men in the sick bay were in an awful mess and sickening to look at. Their eyes seemed to sink deep into their sockets and became dark all around. Their faces became drawn with pain and weakness and most of them were still covered with the dirt from the work parties, as they hadn't washed for days. Their hair was dishevelled and matted and their bodies covered in the bile and mess that they had vomited over themselves, or by the men who lay beside them. They suffered from uncontrollable and unrestrained attacks of the most violent vomiting, which was always accompanied by 'hair raising' screaming and groaning, due to the awful pain and strain of retching. To make matters worse, they would probably be lying in their own excreta. Being so weak and helpless, with severe

147

cramps in the upper leg muscles, they had been unable to move when the awful purging took place.

Those poor men were unrecognizable. As I entered the sick bay, one called to me in a weak croaky voice, 'Taff, have you got some water?' I emptied some into his mug and looked hard at him, suddenly realizing that it was Dyke, one of the men who had helped to carry my kit when I had collapsed on the first stage of the march. But what a change in the man in so short a time. He was dying and knew it, poor fellow. In my feeling for him I realized that perhaps I would be in a similar condition very soon. I was horrified at the thought of it and I decided then and there that I wouldn't lie down while I could do something to prevent an end like that. I had read about saline transfusion and doses of saline as treatment for cholera. Fortunately I had a few calomel tablets in my bag. I knew it was dangerous to take an overdose of calomel, but my condition was so dangerous, that it called for risks to be taken. I took three tablets at once, hoping to clear myself of the awful pains in my stomach. Then I got out my bottle of salt which I had carried all the way from Changi, and mixed a good proportion with a pint of water and swallowed the lot. I became violently sick, but immediately took another pint which stayed down. I kept this up every hour and though I spent most of the night in great distress and at the latrine, I kept on my feet as much as I could. I thought to myself, 'If I lie down, I'll never get up again'. It was probably enough to kill a man, but I was desperate. Then more salt water. I kept on taking the saline until my supply gave out, and then I had a blackout. I came to hours later and was in an awful mess. But I felt strangely relieved. The pain had eased and I closed my eyes and thanked God. I felt I had won through, and sure enough the pain didn't return. The purging eased off and in two days I was sipping rice water, liking it and wanting more. In fourteen days I was out of that Chamber of Horrors.

I wondered many things – what had brought me through? Was it my own very feeble efforts? If so, it was a miracle. My thoughts turned to home where I knew that my dear old mother never ceased praying for my safety. Here were her prayers answered indeed. I had often accompanied mother to morning service at the little village church that she loved so well and did so during the few hours I had spent with her while I was on embarkation leave, on the occasion of her seventieth birthday. I will never forget how we walked there, with mother holding my arm. In the porch we stopped and, with a catch in her voice, she pointed saying, 'Look, my boy, you see we always remember you in our prayers'. There hanging up in the porch was a roll of honour with the names of the men of the village who were serving with the Forces, and who were mentioned in the prayers at that little church every time the people gathered together in prayer – and my name was amongst them.

In my case I think a miracle had happened. Here I was alive and walking about when men who had been with me in the sick bay a week before were now dead and buried. Of the six men who had used the tent with me, just two of us, Dick Sabin and I, now remained alive, and the death roll within the camp was getting higher each day. I got a dose of malaria before I was discharged from the sick bay, and so had to remain there. But I was separated from the cholera patients. I was given nine quinine tablets a day, and for seven days I was like a drunken man. One of my old friends, Darky Ross, was brought in with dysentery while I was ill and was put by my side. He told me that men were falling sick by the dozen and now dying at the rate of ten a night. While I lay there, Captain Sillman, the MO of Changi days, came around and recognizing me, stopped to enquire how I was. He gave me an examination and said that I would soon get over the malaria, but would take a long time to pick up on the present diet. He added that he didn't want me to do any hard work for a long time owing to my condition, and also because any injury to the hernia would be bad, as there was no hope for operations at Sonkurai, with no equipment, no anaesthetic and, I believe, no surgeons. Anyone who received an injury or anything that required surgical treatment was unlucky. Many died when an operation might have saved them. However, the MO said that as staff were so short in the sick bay, perhaps, when I felt strong enough, I would give them a hand.

I mentioned that I had quite a lot of medical stuff in my little bag, and that if he could only speak to the men on parade some of the bottles I had given them might be recovered. He was delighted at the prospect of getting anything in the way of antiseptics and

149

drugs, and almost jumped for joy when I produced tubes of morphia with needle complete. A check was made and I was amazed to find that some of my bottles had arrived safely, although many men had lost their kits completely, with my bottles going the way of the kit. Some men who had thrown away kit, when feeling too ill to carry it any further, had kept my bottles. When I realized the great sacrifice made by such men to get my bottles safely through, it gave me a feeling of warmth and pride. I then asked Tara if he still had the bottle of concentrated iodine. He laughed and said 'No, I used it all on my feet on the march'. I said that what he had used would have done for about 200 men. He answered 'But it cured my feet'.

A few days later I was taken on by RSM Childs RAMC to work in the sick bay. Most of the RAMC personnel, though non-combatants, were being used on road and rail construction, so the sick bay, with its ever increasing number of sick men, became ridiculously understaffed. I was a welcome addition to the few who were trying to administer to the many, and the only way I could be kept there to help was by keeping me in as a very sick man. It was just as well that I was kept in, because I had relapse upon relapse of malaria, and was under treatment all the time I was there.

When I started my duties in the sick bay I found that Jim Payne was there as a patient. He was suffering from continued weakness and blackouts caused by a severe attack of rheumatic fever at one time. Now it was aggravated by the march and the existing conditions. He too was kept in to assist and his job was to keep a record of the men and their ailments. At this time it seemed that organization and enforced discipline were mastering the disorder and chaotic condition that had prevailed during the first weeks in this horror camp. Where the men with all sorts of complaints (most of them contagious) were lying side by side and mixed up before, they were now sorted out and the sections that they occupied became known as 'Fever Ward,' 'Dysentery Ward,' 'Cholera Ward,' and, later, the 'Ulcer Ward'. While the contagious cases weren't isolated, at least they weren't mixed up with the non-contagious cases and efforts were being made to persuade the Nips to allow a place for isolation. The difficulties that we had to contend with were:

150

OVERCROWDING. Men lay side by side, head to foot in double rows along the bays and so close together that they frequently covered each other with their excretions.

WATER, so necessary for patients with terrific thirst when in a high fever, and also for the purpose of washing, boiling and sterilization, was difficult to get. This came about through an order from the Nips that, due to the cholera outbreak, no one except cooks would be allowed to draw water from the river. In the wards we had to manage for a long time on what we could gather from the rain. However, as we had but one bucket allocated to the ward, it became almost impossible to sterilize by boiling, as there was not sufficient water for the needs of the sick.

FOOD. The rice allowed each worker was one pint for breakfast, one pint for lunch and a pint of rice and half a pint of stew for the evening meal. The morning rice was usually cooked, then burned brown or black on a big hot plate for taste. Lunch was plain rice, and as already mentioned, stew and rice at night. This diet was useless for men working as ours were, and resulted in the men being unable to work and coming into the hospital where they could never improve on the food. The only advantage of being in the hospital was for rest – if one could ever get it in our crowded wards. Rice allowed for each sick man was half a pint for breakfast: for lunch, half a pint of water (taken from boiled greens): evening meal, half a pint of stew. A little of the workers' rice was used to supplement the sick men's issue.

BEDDING AND CLOTHES. The Nips had promised us clothes and blankets but, even though the climate was cold and wet, we had less clothes than at Singapore, where it was almost always hot and dry. Very few men had shirts and many who had boots had by now worn them out on the long march. Many boots had fallen to pieces after being worn in water and mud for days on end with the result that many men were barefooted when they went out on working parties.

LIGHTING AND HEAT. The only sources of light and heat were the large fires we kept going day and night in the central gangway of the huts and, due to lack of staff and tools, it became very difficult to obtain sufficient wood. There was more wood in the jungle outside than we could ever hope to burn, but it was big stuff. We had burned up the loose, small, moveable wood, in hut and cookhouse fires, and the Nips would not allow us choppers and saws for getting the bigger stuff in. We had to ask sick men to spend an hour a day collecting firewood. As the sick increased, it became more and more necessary to have a large fire at night so that the orderlies could have some illumination to enable them to work.

MEDICAL EQUIPMENT. The small amount of medical equipment and supplies that had been brought by the men was inadequate even for first aid treatment. The few thermometers were soon broken and instruments were very scarce, there being only the few that had been brought by men of the RAMC. I had a few, but all were in constant use, which resulted in loss and breakage. There weren't any bedpans, although we had a few made out of bamboo. They were made by slitting down the middle of a rather thick branch, then cutting the sections, leaving a hollow trough about 4 inches wide by 3 inches deep and 14 inches long. They served the purpose, though they were not very hygienic. Bowls were almost non-existent, and men had often to use their mess tins to bathe septic sores and for similar tasks. Many very primitive utensils were invented for use in the wards.

MEDICINES. These became in very short supply and of poor variety. Antiseptics, disinfectants, ointments, bandages, drugs, anaesthetics, all extremely important in a hospital, were scarce and when the little we had was used up, no further supplies were available.

These were the conditions that I found when I started work in the Fever Ward. Long will I remember the suffering endured by the patients, often through lack of proper equipment and medical supplies. I started as Day Orderly. My duties began at daylight and, if I could get around to all my patients, I could leave off work at dark. But I lived in the ward, so was on call at all times. When I say that I was on duty all the time, it would be no exaggeration. I lived in the atmosphere of sickness and death for many months, and I, who had been a 'softy' and had never seen a lifeless body until this war, soon became hardened to it all. It sickened me at first, but it was probably worse for me because I was ill almost all the time I was there, dysentery and malaria taking it in turn, and sometimes both together. But I always found it better to fight off the awful feeling of languor and keep on my feet doing something. Many men came into the ward ill and lay down, never to get off their bed space until they were carried off, having died.

Our camp didn't get that name 'Horror Camp of the Thai Jungle' for nothing. The name is right, for the figures prove that at the end of it all, there were only 250 survivors, of the 1,800 who had entered the camp. Only God knows what the dead had suffered, the torment of mind and body, the daily slavery, beatings and tortures by the Nips, and the fevers and diseases. The jungle was also a factor. It led men to give up all hope, to lie down and die or to walk into the jungle, if only to die in freedom. Some escaped, never to be heard of again. Others escaped only to be recaptured and punished horribly. Still others escaped and died horrible deaths. Those who survived are lucky if they retained health in body or mind, because the experience alone was enough to shatter one's health or reason.

Chapter Twelve

Life in the Jungle Hospital
17 May – 5 September 1943

It had quickly become obvious that a further ward was needed to cope with the massive problem of tropical ulcers. As I had made a special study and had some experience of coping with ulcers, I was put to work in the Ulcer Ward.

My duty in the ward was to care for the patients with skin complaints – rashes, sores and ulcers. After a week or more, I was given the care of about sixty patients who were considered to be the worst ulcer cases. Anybody having seen or experienced tropical ulcers will appreciate the difficult task I had, considering the lack of supplies and equipment. The fact that the food was so poor and the patients so weak, meant that they had very little resistance to any infection. In such circumstances, the treatment of ulcers was very difficult. Once an ulcer formed, it was almost impossible to check or heal and, through having little or no disinfectant or antiseptics, infections were inevitably spread from one patient to another. Although I boiled water continuously and kept my forceps, tweezers and scissors sterilized and as clean as I possibly could, I knew that it was impossible to avoid spreading the infection.

One patient, named Canns, who was in an emaciated condition and had a bad dose of malaria, was put in my ward and assigned to me as a special patient. When I examined him, I almost vomited. I had an unavoidable feeling of nausea at what I saw – he had thirty-two large ulcers in different places from his chest to his feet, the smallest was as large as a half-crown, and they hadn't been attended to for days. He also had a touch of dysentery, all of which had made the poor fellow wish for death. It was as much as I could do to persuade him that I might be able to help him. He had attempted to cover the largest ulcers, situated on the calf of each leg, with his puttees, which were now saturated with discharge. The smell nearly bowled me over. However, I kept my nausea hidden, tried to comfort the man and set about cleaning him up. I spent the whole morning with him using his own mess tin to boil water and an old salmon tin with WSP as an antiseptic. That completed, I had to find something to cover the ulcers. As there were no dressings available, I took off the sleeves of my shirt and used them. The only healer I could use was WS powder mixed in water, making a mixture like Eusol. Once the dressings had been soaked in the mixture, I applied them to the ulcers and as there was very little adhesive tape, the dressings were left to adhere to the ulcers themselves. I washed his dirty puttees so that I could use them again later.

That poor fellow must have suffered agonies during the regular morning clean-up and although I handled him as gently as I could, I know he suffered. But he rarely made a sound, and told me that he knew I was doing my best for him and wouldn't make a fuss so as not to hurt my feelings. He, like most of my patients, was tremendously grateful for what was done for him, and, in his case, I was promised a partnership in his confectionery business, somewhere near Olympia, when we got out of this. It always pleased these patients when their offers were accepted. We would pass the time by dreaming of the day when we were free and made a great many plans for the future. I have no doubt that, at the time, they were feeling so low that they would have given almost anything they possessed in return for a little sympathy and kindness.

The one thing these men suffered from most was a lack of care and understanding. They had been taken from their homes and families to a hostile land and forced to endure hatred, cruelty and death, day in and day out, and to top all that, they became ill with little chance of survival. It is no wonder they craved attention. Some felt reunion with their loving Creator was the only way out of this horror. To take notice of a patient was always rewarded by him being attentive and helpful. I got to know about their families, all about their home life, their hopes and fears and, in most cases, it always ended up by them making me ridiculous promises of reward. While I had no wish to take anything for what I did for those fellows, it was very gratifying to know that they were so grateful at the time. It helped me many times to work on hour after hour always with the feeling, 'I can't let these fellows down'.

Canns was one of my worst cases, but I had many almost as bad. The difficulty was to get round to them all in the hours of daylight. After attending to one I had about twenty others to see to and found it very difficult. They were all over the place and I had to keep boiling water and washing dressings for re-use. I told the MO of my difficulties and he later arranged for all my ulcer patients to be put together and got one of the men, who was not so sick but almost blind (a malnutrition case), to follow me around with hot water. This man entered the hut as a suspected diphtheria case and I had been told to keep my eye on him.

The first time I saw him was when I went to take 'pulse and temperature'. I saw a huddled-up form of what appeared to be a little wise old man. When I spoke to him, he answered in a low weak voice, and expressed his concern about the trouble he was causing. When he had the strength to walk about he insisted on helping in the wards. We called him 'the little old man', and I can vouch for him that he never lay down while he was able to help. We became firm friends, especially when I found that his home was only a few miles from my own, in Kent, and we planned many joyous times when we returned to dear old England. His name was John Hawkins of Sidcup. The very sad thing was that he was losing his sight, caused by the malnutrition, but he was always smiling and was a great lad in the ward. He is one of the men I'll swear came through by sheer will power and dogged spirit.

I asked the patients to help by partly cleaning themselves before I got to them. Those that could walk, I helped down to the stream that ran at the end of the ward (No. 3 stream). Although they suffered because of the great effort they had to make, it was worth it when they got there. They lay in the stream and it helped to wash their ulcers. They could also wash themselves and their dressings at the same time.

I seemed to be making headway with some of my cases but most of them were getting worse and many were dying. Death was chiefly due not to one ailment but to the many from which they suffered. The camp had become the 'Camp of Death'. Men were now dying at the rate of thirty-two a night. We went round each morning at daybreak and anyone who seemed strangely quiet or still we examined to see if he was dead. Often, when I felt for the pulse of a strangely inert form, he would rouse and say 'Not this morning, Taff. Perhaps some other time.' I always dreaded waking a man like that because he knew what I was doing. If the test proved a man dead, the body would be taken by shoulders and feet and carried outside and, if there were others, they would be laid in a row side by side. We couldn't spare a blanket so they lay there looking a dreadful sight, emaciated, with bones protruding, eyes open and staring glassily. They lay with the rain beating down on them. God, what an end.

As morning progressed, medical staff would line up with stretchers made of two poles pushed through a sack. A dead man would be put on the stretcher and, as the sack wasn't long enough to support the whole body, the head and legs would hang loosely and swing to the movement of the carriers as they carried the body over the road to the cemetery, or crematorium. There weren't enough men or tools for grave digging. In any case, as the men had died of contagious diseases, it was best to have them cremated. Pyres were built of wet wood and here was another difficulty; there were only a few men to keep those pyres going, and much wood was required with very few tools, if any, for cutting it. Furthermore, the rain continued unceasingly, which put out the fires. The result was that the bodies lay in rows of sometimes as many as thirty or forty, for days, waiting to be cremated. The men doing this gruesome job worked night and day and were always in danger of infection from the bodies they handled. Constantly to be found at this terrible work were our two padres, Padre Duckworth and Padre Foster Haigh.

It seemed that most of us were no longer our normal selves for we went about performing these gruesome tasks as though we had been used to it all our lives. The feeling of repugnance wore off as we settled down to each day's work of horror, with a numbed and empty sensation in the tummy, and the thought ever persistent in our minds that 'It might be my turn next'.

Work was going ahead on both road and railway and, after many weeks, lorries managed to get through on the rough track that had been cleared for them. Finally, we got supplies of food through. The lorries had great difficulty in getting to this camp because of the waterlogged condition of the track. As the monsoon rains increased, they failed to get through to us at all. Rivers were flooded, roads blocked and deep in mud, and we were virtually cut off from the outside world to starve and die in that hellhole.

Small parties often went off into the jungle in the hope that they would escape, but were never heard of again. One morning, there was a great stir in the camp when it was learned that a party of officers had left overnight. They had taken a supply of rice and beans, and made for the coast, bordering the Indian Ocean. There they hoped to get a boat somehow to take them out to sea in the hope that they would be picked up by one of our ships.

Three of the officers I knew very well, having worked with them when I was attached to their Company. One of them left a note, of which I found a copy. This is how it ran:

I am writing an explanation of the action I am about to undertake from this 'hell hole' in the midst of the Burmese jungle. Food is short, health is failing, sickness such as Beri-Beri, Cholera, Malaria, Small Pox, Dysentery, and Diphtheria, is prevalent. Some 220 officers and men have died since our arrival here about five weeks ago. Work from eleven hours a day under the worst possible conditions and under the most extreme task masters continues, therefore, I consider, with some of my fellow companions, that the risk we were about to take, be it life or death, is to some purpose if only to get away from here. Our main desire is, of course, to get back to our loved ones. I trust that my strength is sufficient and that God is with me in this escape.

That party consisted of one Colonel, seven other officers, and one OR. Their experiences in the jungle would read like a thriller, but were actually tragic. This is the story, as given to me by one of the survivors. They struggled through the dense jungle for days on end, ran short of food, and some went down with fever and died. The

158

party then came to a river where they made themselves a raft which ran into a rapid, struck a jagged jutting rock and broke to pieces, throwing them and their kit into the rushing waters. They managed to scramble ashore where the dense jungle allowed them very little movement, and they remained there without food for many days until they saw 'head hunters' in their little boats sailing by on the river. They attracted their attention and were taken off. Later, the natives took them to a nearby village, where, after a rest, they travelled on to another village. There a native policeman took them into custody and handed the three surviving escapers over to the Nips. These three survivors were then taken to Moulmein and on to Singapore. They were about to be shot several times, and were eventually sentenced in Singapore to five years or more in prison. The officer who wrote the farewell letter died in the jungle. This is but one tale of the tragic happenings of our men.

Work started on the foundations of the bridge and the already swollen river was drained on one side. A wall of sandbags made an effective breakwater, deflecting the stream and leaving a small area dry. Using an antiquated method, boring was then started in the rock bottom. Sledge and drill were used, one man holding and turning the drill while another did the striking with the sledge. When enough holes had been bored, charges of explosives were placed in the holes and set off to make piles of blasted and smashed rock which had to be moved by hand.

When holes had been made in the rock, tree trunks cut and shaped to size were placed in position in preparation for their final emplacement in the hole. A strong rope was then attached to the top end of each log, the other end of the rope being thrown over a primitively made sheerlegs or derrick which reached high above the hole. Then, by a steady pulling and manoeuvring, our men guided the bottom end of the log into the hole. The fit was always very tight and the log always had to be forced into the hole. To do this the Nips built a very primitive hammer: a framework of poles was placed round the upright log and the sheerlegs placed around and above the framework. A large stone was then attached to the end of the rope and placed inside the framework. Our men, who were wading up to their waist in the cold river, were then given a whistle signal by a Nip who was perched high on top of the scaffolding. At this signal, they grabbed the rope and pulled, stumbled and splashed as they moved back in the water, heaving the stone to the top of the framework. The Nip would then give another signal for them to release the rope and the stone dropped with a resounding whack on the log.

That was how all the supports were sunk for the wooden structure of the bridge, the large primitive hammer being kept going for weeks while our men toiled, shivered and groaned as the Nip gave his shrill whistles, one to pull and two to let go. They worked like the slaves of old, no stop for rest, often no stop for food. Frequently men who were dying, worked and slaved in that awful river until they died.

Then there was the work in the quarries, boring, blasting and carrying all the broken stone by two handled baskets. A chain of men moved to and from the quarry, two men to a basket, working from early morning until late at night, carrying and cutting stone for the road foundation, every piece handled and carried by our dying men.

When men didn't move quickly enough they were kicked and beaten, often being kicked or struck on ulcers. One man, sick and weak with dysentery, was unable to get to the privacy of the trees and messed in the road. The Nip beat him until he fell, face down and unconscious, in the mud. Then the Nip promptly placed his foot on the unfortunate man's head and pressed it further into the mud. Two of our men, at the risk of being beaten off, then picked up the man before he suffocated.

Men with bare feet walked to and fro in that endless chain stepping on the sharp-edged stones of the quarry. Despite this, they were forced to keep moving with cut and bleeding feet and, at the end of the day's work, had to walk miles back to camp.

The forestry workers were made to carry the trunks they had cut and always with too few men. In their weakness, and due to the overload, they often collapsed and fell, only to be beaten and made to pick up the tree trunks again. Many got crushed under the weight they had failed to carry and some were killed. One man fell awkwardly and the log he was carrying broke his neck. He was carried back to camp where his brother, on seeing the shapeless tortured body, seemed to lose his reason and babbled incoherently for days afterwards.

There were many such tragic incidents during the building of that bridge. When it was up to its third tier and about thirty-five feet high, one of our men was hanging over the side working when a Nip leaned over to beat him. The man grabbed him and they both fell to their deaths in the torrent below. Another man, fixing iron retainers, or 'dogs', over the side, was being beaten by a Nip with a large stick. There was a danger that he might lose his hold and drop into the water to his death, so our officer in charge of the party came up and told the Nip that if he wanted to beat the man to get him up where he wouldn't be in danger of falling in the river. The Nip then turned and struck the officer on the head. My pal, who was standing nearby, saw the officer, with his hands over his eyes, stumbling around and about to step over the side of the bridge, so he grabbed him. He found that the officer had been temporarily blinded by the blow.

This was the type of horror experienced on the working parties. I could write a book on working party tortures alone and the misery these men experienced during their short time in camp, but time and space won't allow. It is sufficient to say that when ill, and they had to be very ill to be sent into our hospital, they were crowded in between the other patients with hardly enough room to turn. I have seen men come into the wards at night after returning from a working party, sobbing – yes, sobbing – in their weakness and exhaustion, and from the pain of their many afflictions. How these men felt and suffered, as they fought for life, and lay dying, can only be imagined.

Our cooks worked shorthanded and endlessly. With rice to prepare for three meals a day, water to carry from the river and wood to gather for fuel, they had their hands full. One afternoon I visited the cookhouse looking for the water drained from the drying rice, which was given to the patients and seemed to do them some good. As I approached, I glanced down into the boilers and thought the insides of the boilers were moving until I got closer and saw that white maggots were moving in a mass up the sides of the boiler. They were all coming away from the little pieces of meat lying in the water at the bottom. Apparently this meat had been given to us by the Nips, who had stored it away until it could have walked out by itself. The meat was unfit to eat as it was but if the maggots could be removed, the meat would be edible and the men would have some extra nutrition they otherwise wouldn't have had. In an effort to encourage the maggots to leave the meat, the cooks warmed up the pot and it was succeeding. The maggots were moving as fast as they could, up and over the sides of the boiler. The meat, when issued in a stew that evening, was delicious.

While visiting the cookhouse, I was given a whole dried salted fish by the cook. The fish was also full of life but, on my return, I visited the small stream and scraped the maggots out. The fish then proved a marvellous feed for about eight of my patients and myself.

The staff of the hospital ward lived in one of the bays at the extreme end of the lower hut nearest No. 3 stream, and the rest of the hut housed the very sick. A special hut had been built near the cemetery for isolation cases, chiefly cholera, and the idea behind it was gruesome. It meant that, as the men died, there was little distance to carry their bodies to be cremated or buried. Men, many of them acquaintances and friends of mine, who showed symptoms of cholera were carried away to isolation where many died. The horror of it was that the patient knew that when he was carried over there he would never come back. My heart ached for them. Dyke, who had helped me on the road, and a boy who had been through the Belgian-Dunkirk campaign with me, were both carried away together to the isolation hut on 29 May. I saw them off and tried to comfort them, giving them both a drink of boiled water, and I'll never forget the look in their eyes as they each said, 'Goodbye, Taff' in voices so weak that they were almost inaudible. We each knew that they were going to their deaths, cut down in the prime of their lives. Many a hardened man turned in this hour of need to his Maker and prayed for help, safety and guidance, but strangest of all, when our Padre held his little services in the ward, the men, in their final hours, prayed so sincerely, not for themselves, but rather for the safety of their loved ones at home, whom they would not see again until they met in Heaven.

I lived with the ward staff in their bay. Jim was with me, also Les Brand (the Sergeant who had to make the return march for lost men), and we worked together in the same ward. My job was getting to be more than I could manage, due to the increase in ulcer cases, so a man was brought in to help me. His name was Aubrey King (the tenor who sang at Padre J. Foster Haig's concerts) but he always seemed ill and easily gave way to the languid feeling. He had great difficulty to keep working and seemed to get worse, always worrying about himself. But, despite this, he tried sincerely to help me.

I think it is as well now to describe some of the cases I handled so that you will have a little idea of the suffering, of the effects of starvation and of the difficulties we confronted. We were often overwhelmed by the helplessness we felt and the hopelessness of our task. I prayed each night for guidance and help in administering to these suffering men, for patience, as God knows I needed it, and for the health and strength to carry on doing this work. I despaired, trying to heal the wounded lives that had been so severely injured that many of my patients had lost all desire to live.

Chapter Thirteen

My Patients

We fought against hopeless odds to check or cure those dreaded tropical diseases, only to find when we thought there was improvement, the patients would pass away without warning. If ever a hell on earth existed, this was it.

Our MOs worked night and day, as did the staff. Many were criticized severely, but they had a job beyond all human ability, yet they kept on trying even when they were very ill themselves. As a little example, I myself can account for eight attacks of malaria, with relapses, two relapses of dysentery, cholera and other minor ailments, during the four months at Sonkurai, which meant that I was ill practically all the time. But so was almost everyone, and as someone had to keep things going, the work went on somehow.

My own first case was a man who had come in with a sore throat. I was still a patient myself so was told by the Staff Sergeant to keep an eye on the chap as he had been sleeping (or unconscious) for two days. About half an hour later, I thought he seemed strange, so I moved over to take a look at him. He had started giving the last movements of his life. His head slightly jerking back, as his mouth opened and then closed, repeating the movements without seeming to breathe. I rushed for the Staff Sergeant and told him. He replied 'Don't get excited, the man is dying. Go back to the patient and when he dies report back to me.' This order shocked me. I thought, 'What utter callousness,' but when I had more time to think about it, and had more experience, I realized that the Staff Sergeant couldn't do a thing for the chap anyhow, so it would have been useless to have tried. I sat by the man until the gasping movements had stopped then felt for pulse and respiratory movements, but there weren't any of either. The man had been a victim of diphtheria.

The next patient to die was a beriberi case and, in all my experience, I never saw such a shocking death. The man was bloated in face, body and legs, like a grotesque balloon. He was so filled with fluid that his skin was shining tight with pressure from within. His was the worst beriberi case I'd seen. His eyes were almost closed with the puffiness all around them, and large bags had formed below them. When handling this patient, my hands sank sickeningly into the part where I applied pressure and when I took my hand away, a deep indentation was left. He had complained of pains in his chest and head during the afternoon. I was on duty until 10 p.m. at the time. When the MO came on his round at 4 p.m., I told him about this patient. He gave him a look over and, after hearing about the location of the pains, took me aside and told me that the man would die before morning. I was instructed to prop him up in a sitting position and, if necessary, tie him so that he would remain upright. The job became very difficult owing to the crowded condition of the bay for, as we lifted him, we were stepping over other patients who lay too ill and too weak to move out of our way. The job done, I returned to attend to other patients. All my ulcer patients had to have the affected parts soaked with Eusol. This was done by making an opening in the top of the bandage and pouring down the cool Eusol. Patients suffering agonies from highly inflamed infections would sigh with relief at the cooling effect and the ease it gave. They waited patiently for this nightly treatment and, though in agonies of pain, would rarely bother the orderly unduly to hurry. I had just completed this treatment when the beriberi case started gurgling. I rushed over to him but it was only a mild attack. It was explained to me by Sergeant Brand that water had now reached the man's lungs, and that it would have the same effect on the patient as if he were drowning.

I was relieved at 10 p.m. and the night orderlies took over the ward. A little later I lay down in my bay, which was next to the bay where the beriberi patient was. Being so near, I had very little rest when the patient started struggling. I had to get up three times to assist the other orderlies in holding him down. During the few remaining hours of his life, he fought like a drowning man, and with amazing strength. While he slowly smothered, he screamed and raved, struggled and kicked, and vomited and messed the whole place. For three hours the fight went on. For mercy's sake I wished the poor suffering man dead many times. It was the most ghastly form of death I have ever witnessed and he must have suffered tortures in hours of agony while suffocating. It took four men to carry the body away.

During June and July the Nips started employing drastic methods to force our sick men out to work. The men had been getting weaker and weaker under the harsh, brutal treatment they were receiving and the number in the hospital had increased with alarming rapidity. The result was that the numbers of men on working parties were not only reduced to a minimum, but certain working parties had to be cancelled because there were no men to make up the parties for those particular jobs. The Nips started putting the screw on, first by cutting down the hospital rations by half, saying, 'No work, no food'. They contended that many men in the hospital were pretending and weren't sick at all. If they wanted food, whether or not they were sick they would have to earn it by working. This cut in the rations was tragic as the men weren't having enough to keep up their strength as it was. Now they would have only half a pint of rice at each meal.

From then on I noticed the deterioration of my ulcer patients. They became too weak to stand the strain of being cleaned each day. Previously patient and uncomplaining, they now became irritable and hopeless, with the result that the ulcers failed to respond to treatment and grew much worse. Many who used to prepare themselves for treatment now became victims of languor. They lost all hope and lay without the strength or will even to eat the small portion of rice now allotted to them. So I had the bitter experience of seeing men, who I had thought were pulling through and with whom I had become so friendly, now slipping away, weary of everything and desiring above everything only to be left alone. All the work and time spent on them was to no avail. I often returned to my bay at night tired out and ill, and cried at the hopelessness of it all. It might have been childish to cry but I couldn't help myself. I tried very hard to remain strong to fight these emotional moments, but when I had lost several patients who had become part of my life, who had been a responsibility and with whom I had shared the struggle and fight for recovery, had shared their thoughts, hopes, fears and ambitions, had heard of their home life so often that I felt I had known them for years, perhaps I can be excused for giving way to tears, at a time when emotions were all too often aroused and easily gained sway.

Starving the patients in order to drive them to work did not have the desired results, so the Nips tried another stunt. They issued a warning to the MOs that if the required number of men weren't on parade for work next morning, they would take the men out of the hospital. So that night there were hurried consultations among the MOs with the result that the sick were graded. Those able to walk about and do a little for themselves were Grade 1, those able to move about were Grade 2 and the bed-down patients Grade 3. Each grade was then graded again, according to the particular ailments, Grade 1A, 1B, and so on, so that if the Nips did enforce the threat, the MOs were ready with a list of men that could at least walk out with the party. However, the Nips were appeased somehow, or perhaps they hesitated when they saw a row of bodies lying in the rain awaiting cremation next morning – about thirty to add to those already at the crematorium.

A few days after the warning, the Nips held a medical inspection of their own. Two Nip MOs had somehow got through to our camp, and would examine our men. Two Nip guards came into the hospital and gave the order for everyone to turn out to be examined. Most of our men were too ill to move off the bays. This didn't satisfy the Nips, so they started beating the dying men with bamboo sticks. Many made a great effort to get up. Others lay still and took the beatings with hardly a murmur, and these had to be carried out for the inspection. The only patients left were the diphtheritic cases in a bay of their own. The Nips were afraid to go anywhere near them and always kept at a respectful distance from them.

The examination having taken place, the patients returned. As a result, two collapsed and died and five more died that night. The examination proved that we had in our ward about a dozen cholera carriers.

On about the second day after the medical inspection, at 1 a.m., after we were settled down for the night and all was quiet except for the groaning of the sick and ravings of the cerebral malaria cases, and the drumming of the pouring rain outside, I was disturbed by a commotion outside the ward. I got up and saw a party of Nips jabbering away about something and appearing very excited. Some of our MOs came along and we soon learned that the Nips had brought the names of the cholera carriers and wanted them moved out immediately. We checked the names and found that some of them were the names of very sick men – one had a temperature of 104.4 degrees and had no clothes or blankets. The Nips insisted that they be removed. Men who had worked hard all day on the bridge were dragged out to put up tents near the isolation hut, where the underbrush was at least 4 feet high and thick, and tangled. The rain was teeming down and it was very dark, but the Nip order had to be carried out. Tents were put up on the thick undergrowth and the sick were placed in the tents. I don't quite know how they managed, but I am sure that very few survived.

Our malaria cases increased at an alarming rate and the dreadful cerebral malaria took its toll – after delirium, death. The Nips, having a few spare mosquito nets, sent them to our ward. The nets were big enough to cover a complete bay so at least a dozen men were covered at night and had a little protection from the mosquitoes. It made things very awkward for us to get at the patients, as we found in the case of the man who shouted.

I had been disturbed for several nights by a patient who shouted in a very authoritative voice for a bedpan or bottle. We had only a few of these which, it will be remembered, we had made from bamboo, so they weren't always available, and this loud voiced patient would curse and abuse the night orderly, disturbing the patients all around him. Each night I resolved to see the man on the following day and ask him to be quieter, but as each day came I was always too busy and let it pass. He was in a bay opposite where some of my ulcer cases lay, with a mosquito net keeping him from view day and night. We didn't pay much attention to the patients in his bay as they were mainly suffering from malaria and resting while taking their quinine course, unless of course they became seriously ill or requested attention for some particular ailment.

Then came the night when I was awakened by a patient in a nearby bay calling to the night orderly 'Orderly, I am dying'. The orderly answered 'What of it, so am I'. Then the patient cried out again asking the orderly if he would take a diary out of his kit and send it to his mother when he died. The orderly told him that he would but to cut out the sob stuff, as he wouldn't die for a long time yet. The cross talk between these two was then interrupted by the strong voiced patient calling 'Pan, orderly, please, and be damn quick'. The already overworked and tired orderly took it to him. I then heard him giving the patient a lecture on how to ask for things and I decided it was about time I had a word with the fellow. When I went on duty next morning, I told the orderly that I had heard the conversation in the night, and he said 'Then I expect you heard him ask about his diary.' He explained that the man had died in the early hours, and added 'I'll have a kitbag full of diaries to send home at this rate'. He then went on to say that the noisy patient had great difficulty in raising himself to use the bedpan owing to a bad leg. He had reported it to the Staff Sergeant of the ward, who came to me later in the day and asked me if I could spare a minute. Would I take a look at the noisy patient and find out what his trouble was? So when I stopped for my midday meal, I lifted the net of his bay and peered into the gloom, immediately recognizing the smell of putrefying flesh. I shouted, 'Who has an ulcer?' A patient answered, 'Him in the corner'. I went in, picking my way between the sick men, and there laid the man I had been wanting a word with for days. But he seemed very ill and when I tried to rouse him he mumbled a lot of jumbled words. His pulse was racing and I could feel his high temperature. I saw that his leg was bound with a saturated puttee from a suppurating ulcer. I unwound the puttee and unveiled an ulcer on the calf of his right leg. It was at least 4 inches across and gangrenous. I realized that the man was past all earthly help, so I called the Staff Sergeant to report my findings. We then lifted him to the front where we could attend him, but he died next day.

Then there was the case of Private James, suffering from fever, ulcers and malnutrition. He refused his food, and kept messing himself. He was reported to the MO who told him that he would die very soon if he didn't eat. The MO got no answer so he tried another line, calling him a coward for letting himself die when there were people at home who loved him and were waiting for him, adding that he was letting them down. This moved James to retort 'What have I to live for? My mother is dead, my wife and little daughter were killed in the Blitz, so why should I try to recover to be worked to death by the Nips? Let me die. I've nothing to live for.' He was a hopeless case and we failed to persuade him to take treatment or food. He lingered for over a fortnight and then died. He was almost a skeleton.

A Sergeant of the Singapore Volunteers had very bad ulcers on both legs and though able to look after himself, he wouldn't keep himself clean. His puttees, used to bandage his legs, were in such an awful state that I refused to re-use them. But later I had to wash them for him. One ulcer covered the whole of the calf of his right leg. One day I found that a black skin had formed over the ulcer which proved to be gangrene. I informed the MO when he came around, who said 'It ought to be cut away, but as there is no anaesthetic and the patient is too weak to stand an operation, it will have to take its course'. The only treatment we could render was to keep heating his water bottle and place it over the ulcer on the chance that it might restore the circulation. The next day the ulcer became worse. The gangrene had hardened and the thick black coating was like leather. When I examined the ulcers on his other leg, I discovered that a fly had got at them and that maggots were moving about on them. I was astonished to find that where the maggots were, the ulcers were clean, so I thought that if they could clean there, they might be useful in cleaning up the gangrene. It couldn't do any harm, as the man was a hopeless case and would die in a few days, if only from dysentery. I picked up some maggots with my forceps and placed them on the gangrenous ulcer, and the next day I was delighted with the result. The experiment had proved a great success. In three days the gangrenous skin had been completely cleared. I removed the maggots and had the pleasure of seeing the ulcers improve a little, but the patient died a few weeks later from dysentery.

Then there was the man with a whitlow. One day when I was doing my dressings, a man who had recently been admitted with malaria came to me for advice about the forefinger of his right hand. He showed me the painful spot and I told him that he had a whitlow and instructed him to bathe it in hot water as often as he could, there being no other treatment available. This the man did conscientiously and came to me each morning to show me the results. The whitlow opened up and was soon looking quite clean. I then sent the patient to the MO who told him to use Eusol to help heal it up. But as the days passed, the whitlow seemed to get worse. I told the MO but there was nothing we could do but to advise the man to keep it clean. Later, a fly got to it and maggots appeared, which were very difficult to get at as they had become embedded well down under the nail. I often felt like nipping off the top of that finger – if I had I might have saved the man's life. It wasn't long before the top of the finger, up to the first joint, fell off on its own accord, but not before the remainder was infected and contained maggots. Each day I probed and removed maggots but still they seemed to breed and soon the second part up to the second joint fell off leaving a very inflamed finger stump and hand. The gland under the shoulder then became swollen and inflamed as septicaemia set in, which proved to be fatal.

While I was on duty one night, many patients arrived who had been sent in off late working parties. The condition of these men was really pitiful as each man was covered with mud and soaking wet from the rain, and was cold, miserable and ill. The first case was brought in at about 10 p.m., groaning with the pain caused by two cracked ribs and utter exhaustion. He had dysentery and had collapsed at work, only to be kicked savagely by the Nip guard. He was also whimpering and finding it difficult to breath, as each breath stretched the bruised muscles around the cracked ribs. All we could do for him that night was to make him as comfortable as possible.

Another night, Waple, one of my Company, was brought in at about 9 p.m. He had gone out on work parties day after day without boots. He had bound his feet up with puttees, and through getting his feet wet and tramping in the mud, foot rot had started, aggravated by the sharp stones at the quarry, which had started them bleeding. Each foot was now one large septic sore covered in dirty mud. He was in such pain and so exhausted that he too was whimpering. It would have been better if he was crying, but it seemed that he was too exhausted even to cry. To make room for him, we had to move two men tight close to each other, and after washing his feet, and giving him a drink of hot water to warm him up, we left him for the night. He never left the hospital, and died at another camp a few months later.

Corporal Bird, one of our little party of Changi days, was carried in one day with a nasty wound on the shin caused by a thrown axe. Apparently he had been in charge of a working party, and one man being ill, wasn't able to do his work fast enough for the Nip, who set about beating him with a stick. Corporal Bird intervened and took the stick away from the Nip, who then became frantic, picked up an axe and chased Corporal Bird. When the Nip failed to catch him, he flung the axe just as the Corporal was turning. Seeing the axe in mid-air and realizing it was too late to dodge it, he raised his foot to try to deflect it, but the axe slid up his boot and cut him severely on the shin. Despite all our efforts, the wound turned septic and was soon a large ulcer. However, when it seemed that we would never stop it growing, medical supplies arrived in the camp by a special party, which I will explain later, and with those supplies came a small amount of yellow powder called hyodrophome (sic). A little of this was applied on a dressing and left for forty-eight hours. When the dressing was removed, the ulcer was left quite clean and pink, and it seemed that he was saved. Later, when he was recovering, he was moved into another overcrowded ward, where a patient had fallen on his ulcerated leg one night while attempting to get off the bay. This left the ulcer badly bruised. Bird never got over it, and died at Tanaybaya.

One evening, another man of my Company came in after being sent by the MO. Later a message came from Tara that this man was lazy and wouldn't do his share of the work. Though seemingly fit he had messed the floor near his bed space. As far as Tara was concerned, he was a malingerer. A few hours after his arrival, he asked the orderly if he could sit by the fire as he felt cold. Fifteen minutes later, he collapsed and died from heart failure.

Though I could hardly spare the time, I always managed to find a few minutes in which to visit my pals in the other wards (which were all in the same hut). In the dysentery ward there were many men of my Company as well as some who had become very close friends of mine – Howell Griffiths, Ken Scovell, Dick Richards, Darky Ross and Jock Hunter. The dysentery ward was a dreadful place where men lay and died in their own excreta. The smell was almost unbearable, and men who had lived quiet, reserved, clean lives were now suffering not only from their varied afflictions, but from the humiliation of their condition. Although so ill and weak, they would attempt to cover themselves in an effort to hide the filth and seemed embarrassed when I called to see them.

In this ward the ridiculously small staff worked day and night to ease the suffering of the patients who, having dysentery, lay helpless to do for themselves. An attempt had been made to separate the more serious cases from the others, who were placed in a bay together, which became known as the 'Death Bay'. I heard many hoarse voiced men give resistence, however weak, to being moved into it. That was where I found Dick Reynolds. After looking for him in his usual place and finding that he was missing, I learned that he had been taken there as he had taken a turn for the worse and had messed all over himself and the others around him, with the danger of spreading infection. I found him in a coma, looking like a skeleton and in an awful mess. In an effort to keep himself and the place clean, he had used his mess tin as a bedpan but it had tipped over and hundreds of flies were buzzing around him. I must have had a catch in my voice when I spoke to the MO about him, because he told me to pull myself together as he had done his best for Dick, and there was nothing more he could do.

Poor old Dick, he had been in charge of the canteen at Changi and was such a clean fellow, always smart and well known for his honesty. I had made for him, in a very amateurish way, some jam (from waste fruit) which he had sold in the canteen. He had made labels for Marmite jars and sold the jam in the jars. He had spent many hours planning ways and means of giving the customers good service, and many schemes turned out quite successfully, the jam being one of them. All this went through my mind as I looked down on that wasted form. He had been good and kind in his life and now he laid dying in the vilest of filth. My faith in a merciful God was put to a test when I saw things like that. I decided he would die clean at least. So I got warm water and washed him down. As I was finishing the job, he roused from his coma and said 'I knew you'd come, Taff, to take me from here. I told them that you wouldn't let me stay here. I looked for you and hoped you'd come in time to stop them putting me here.

You'll take me away from here won't you?' I had to turn away, I couldn't answer him as I was too full up for a few minutes. To think that he had such faith in me and I could do nothing for him. After a while I recovered sufficiently to tell him that I would get him some medicine and see the MO about getting him moved. As I moved away, being glad of any excuse to get away for a few minutes, Staff Sergeant Gordon Davies came along. He had an egg, (purloined from the Nips) which he had cooked and brought in for Dick. Men would have risked their lives for an egg, and here was Gordon giving one to Dick, but it was just the kind of thing Gordon would do, anyway. I moved off with the promise to return soon.

When I returned to my bay I found that Jim had purloined some tea which he was about to brew. I waited until it was ready and got half a mug of it for Dick. On my way back with it I met the Padre. I told him where I was going so he accompanied me and when I gave Dick the tea he sipped it with great appreciation, no doubt feeling the warmth of it comforting. The Padre whispered words of comfort and hope to Dick, then Dick laid back and stretched himself as if he seemed comforted. He closed his eyes, murmured something and half smiled. We left him then, and two hours later I returned to find the smile still there, but Dick was dead.

Howell Griffiths, my pal who had taken me to church at Changi, who had helped me with the affairs of the Welsh Society and who had met his schoolmate from Australia at Changi, was also very ill and seemed to be wandering in his mind. He talked of fancy food and of titbits he would like. Poor fellow, the dysentery germ was rotting his bowels and he was dying but he spoke of the future and of what he intended to do when he returned home. One of the first things would be to have a good feed. He told me that the MO had told him that he must get strong quickly for all the sick men would soon be moving to a new camp where there would be many facilities for dealing with the various illnesses. So Howell said he was going to make a great effort as he knew he would be all right.

I checked up on what Howell had said about the new camp and found it to be true. The result of this news gave much hope and encouragement to the patients and gave them something to talk about. Sadly, as the weeks went by, and no further news came in about the new camp, the men's spirits fell and many more died having lost hope. Howell was one of those.

Darky Ross had served with me in France, in Dunkirk, in England, and had lain by my side when I had my bout of cholera. He had remained in the hospital when I left and now his complaint, aggravated by the starvation diet, had developed into beriberi. His legs were swollen and he had lost the use of them. He got worse and worse and eventually died.

Ken Scovell, another very dear friend and confidant was also ill and had come to me asking that in the event that something happened to him, would I see to it that his book of musical arrangements be taken home safely to his mother. I spoke rather sharply to him and told him that he wasn't to think of such a thing, that I was quite likely to be gone before him, and I hoped he wouldn't talk about it again. He turned away and seemed very crestfallen. I felt very sorry that I had spoken so sharply to him, but I had hoped that it would shake him out of his melancholy thoughts. But he must have felt very ill and guessed he was dying because he called the Padre to him a few days later and had the last prayers and sacraments said for him while he kneeled before the Padre in the ward. He died shortly afterwards. I had much trouble to gain possession of his music book after that but later, in Tanaybaya camp, Padre Duckworth managed to get it and, knowing that I had been enquiring about it, gave it to me and I managed, eventually, to get it safely to his mother.

Towards the end of my stay at Sonkurai, the ulcer cases had increased to such an extent that part of the hospital was cleared for them and became known as the Ulcer Ward. My more serious cases were transferred to this ward and I was able to pay more attention to the minor cases. My old patients asked that I might be transferred with them but the Staff Sergeant wouldn't hear of it, instead he allowed me to go to the Ulcer Ward every other morning. One of these patients had very bad ulcers in the crotch and, though weakened by his ailments and starvation, he always insisted that he would get out alive. His words were 'Here's one fellow who is going to make the grade'. He really tried hard, but one morning, when I was dressing his legs, he told me that his throat was worrying him as it was sore. I examined it and knew

175

by what I saw that he had diphtheria. That afternoon, he was moved to the diphtheria bay. This was a dreadful place as few patients left it alive. It is true that about six men stayed there for about six weeks and survived, but all the others that entered died in a short time.

It was my job to attend to those diphtheria patients who also had ulcers and I had the unpleasant experience of having to withhold dressings and treatment owing to the fact that they would soon be dead and the dressings would be of more use to someone with a reasonable chance of recovery. Things had got to the stage at which we had to make this serious consideration – if there was no hope for a patient, then medicine would not be wasted on him.

It was while the ward was at its worst that an officer was brought in with diphtheria. He lay in the front of the bay and at the extreme end, which was next to the partition of the end of No. 2 hut. The first thing he objected to was the smell of the primitively made bed bottles and pans which were kept outside. Twice a day, Tara sent him his compliments and bottles of boiled water and so forth. Tara had managed all this time to keep a man doing for him as I had been, boiling water and the like. He now showed how much he cared for his officer by keeping him supplied with boiled water. However, Tara would not come near the hospital himself. He had a healthy respect for the ward where contagious cases lay, so he just sent his compliments night and morning.

During the day the officer would shout 'Orderly, bring me a light,' and the orderly would have to leave his job and take a light for the officer's cheroot, which was smoked in sight of men who hadn't had a decent smoke in ages. I was disgusted, but the officer was a patient and had to be attended to. The patient next to the officer was in a bad way, having diphtheritic ulcers, and large black blisters which he kept demanding me to burst. I had had instructions not to touch them and, as they grew in number and size, the patient became particularly repulsive, his tongue hung loose over his lower lip and saliva dribbled down his chin. I dreaded attending to him because of the nauseating smell and the splashes he made when he made his incoherent demands for treatment. The officer strongly objected to being near him, but we couldn't help him as we were so overcrowded. When the man lay dying, I sat by his side and comforted him all I could. The officer

176

looked on and chatted away, saying that he never dreamed that conditions were so bad, adding that we orderlies were doing a fine job. I thanked him for his kind observations and then raised the bit of old blanket to cover the patient who was now dead. The officer wanted to know why I did this. I told him that the patient was dead. He looked quite startled and said in a subdued voice that he had never been so close to death. He was very alarmed and I rather pitied him.

The other diphtheria case that I had brought from the ulcer ward lasted about ten days. With all his pluck and determination to live, it wasn't enough. He failed in the fight against impossible odds.

As I handled so many contagious cases, I had to be extremely careful about myself. The only disinfectants available were ordinary lime, PP and WSP but only a little of each. I kept a tin of lime and rubbed my hands with it whenever I could, but I had many frights about infection, and many times awoke in the morning with a very sore throat. Being very alarmed, I would snatch up my mirror but failed to find what I was looking for. I would always report to the MO and what a relief it was when he said 'Inflamed a little but otherwise OK'. He considered that the sore throat was due to the long hours I worked over the ulcer cases and he advised me to wear a pad over my mouth and nostrils.

We were now all desperate for want of sufficient good food. We were always on the lookout for anything to supplement our meagre rations and had by now eaten snake, fungi (found on old rotting tree stumps), the soft centre of banana tree stalks, bamboo shoots, frogs legs and leaves of peanut plants. A favourite was leaves from wild marrow plants. Those leaves were the only greens we had had since our arrival and it was discovered that they helped beriberi cases considerably.

Padre Duckworth visited our ward regularly. One day, after giving a lecture to the patients about using their Bibles for cigarette paper, he told them about the food value of these marrow leaves and advised everyone who could walk to go out and gather the leaves, boil them, eat the leaves and drink the water. Many patients struggled out to gather them and one fellow named North, who had swelled up very badly in the last few weeks, was given about four pint mugs full of leaves to eat. He drank two pints of the green water. That night he called for the bedpan and had to remain on it most of the night with the orderly at his side. The next morning, North was almost normal again, but the reducing process had apparently been too rapid and the strain too much for his heart, for he died later that day.

Our little store of medicines and drugs was almost exhausted. Now we relied chiefly on many old fashioned home remedies. Much charcoal was taken for stomach derangements, banana leaves were used as dressings, shirt sleeves and trouser bottoms were collected from the men to make bandages, and salt and WSP were used as antiseptics for ulcers and skin complaints. But conditions got desperate as men died by the dozen from the many diseases, known and unknown, that prevailed in our camp. Beriberi, malaria, smallpox, dysentery, cholera, diphtheria, fits, jaundice, ulcers, tuberculosis, insanity, starvation, pneumonia, corneal ulcers, food poisoning, septic scabies and worms. All took their toll and each morning we removed the dead to be carried away to the fires.

Permission was granted for a party of men to try to get through to Nieke for supplies. They left one afternoon to return three days later with the few necessities they had managed to get. There was also a great shortage of necessities at Nieke, but the MO in charge gave our men a share of what he had. The party had a terrible time getting through. They had to ford swollen streams, holding the precious supplies above their heads, and, at one point, it almost ended in disaster. They were crossing a stream when one of the men stumbled in a particularly deep part. As he struggled, the others rushed to his assistance only to find themselves in danger as well. After a very unpleasant few minutes, they managed to get to safety and, by extra good luck, they had managed to keep the supplies dry. They completed the journey back to camp safely, bringing back a small amount of hyodrophome (sic) which, when applied, worked wonders on some of the very bad ulcer cases.

During the first three months at Sonkurai the rain hardly ever ceased. Our camp became a quagmire. We weren't able to step outside the huts without sinking into deep mud. Patients visiting the latrines got drenched and covered with mud, their bare feet and legs becoming caked with mud of the foulest kind, and they returned to their bed space on the bamboo slats in that filthy state.

178

The streams which ran through the huts had been only small trickles of water when we arrived at the camp, but had swollen with the rains and became little raging torrents. The latrines had also filled with water, overflowed and polluted the area all around. The men being ill and weak had little inclination to go out into the noxious contaminated mud to get chilled, wet and dirty. In many cases, they just defiled their bed spaces. The streams carried the mud and germs into the huts, causing contagion. The infection spread and we were helpless to stop it. We tried kindness, and we tried frightening the men in an effort to persuade them to stop defiling the inside of the hut, but each morning we had to clear the gangway before we could move anywhere and the smell was sickening. These were the circumstances under which the men ate, slept, and lived during that awful period. While living in those conditions, many became like beasts. Some would rob the sick and dying. Some would neglect themselves to conditions beyond human understanding, with long beards and matted dishevelled hair; hollow eyed and gaunt sharp featured, they looked like wild men. When some became mentally unbalanced, they were frightful to look upon.

I had many surprises when such men as these died and their effects were examined. I sometimes saw photographs of their home life and they could not be recognized as the same person. On one occasion I had to help carry a sick man to the isolation hut. I had handed the patient over and was returning down the centre of the hut when a hollow cracked voice from behind me called, 'Hey Taff', I looked around but I could see no one I knew, then a hideously deformed man struggled to a sitting position and said 'I thought you were going to pass me by'. I looked hard, but failed to recognize him. He apparently noticed my embarrassment for he said, 'God, I must look bloody awful for you not to know me,' then, with an awful sickening sensation in my insides, I recognized him by his blonde hair and accent; they were the only clues. It was Sid Ford, a close friend and a member of our Company. I had got to know him during the fight for Singapore and, later, when he had come to me for first aid. Then at Changi he had come to me for advice on how to start a county society and later he had founded the Lancastrian Society. I made some silly excuse for not recognizing him but he said, 'It's all right, I know how I look, but

I'll soon be all right, I'm much better today'. I stayed with him for a few minutes. I felt stunned and tongue-tied. To look at him made me feel like screaming. His face was oblong, bloated with beriberi and coloured with jaundice. He was in an awful state and would need hours of hard work to clean. I thought I was hardened but when I left the hut, I vomited. He died the following day, 2 July 1943.

On my way back from the isolation hut I passed the native quarters. Coming from the place where the yaks were tethered was a babble of excited native jabbering. I could see the natives who were causing all the commotion. They were seemingly all talking together and gesticulating in an excited way to a Nip guard, who looked blankly at them as if he didn't understand a word of what was being said. I found out, when I returned, that the natives had lost a yak. This news didn't worry me a lot as I had a large hunk of it in my bag which Jim had hidden away for me. Some of the patients who were able to move about had gone to the stream (No. 2) to wash. At the junction of Nos. 2 and 3 streams, they saw a yak which had strayed. They got behind him in the bush and gradually manoeuvred him nearer to the hut and eventually into the stream. While they were doing this, others were fetching knives and an old axe which they had purloined from the Nips. At the right moment, the yak was felled with the axe and rolled over into the shallow stream. The gang then set to work and, in a short space of time, had the beast dissected, casting the unwanted parts into the deep part of the fast flowing stream. The remainder was then hacked into chunks and distributed among the patients.

With their hunger appeased, many went to sleep on a full tummy for the first time in months. This was only the beginning, as several yaks disappeared in the following weeks! Angry Nips searched the huts for pieces of meat which, fortunately for us, were never found.

During the whole of the time I was at Sonkurai a continuous stream of Nips passed through on their way to Burma. Night and day they could be heard chanting their queer marching song as they climbed the hills along the track near our camp. I looked for their weapons and saw only the small mountain guns, rifles, machine guns and the NCOs with their swords. The difference in the condition of the Nips and of ourselves after doing the long march, as we had done, was very noticeable. They were spattered with mud and looked weary, but were sturdy, well fed and fit. They passed in parties of about fifty and pulled their little carts loaded with kit.

One night I had been awakened by one of these passing parties and the noise they made was dying away in the distance when I heard a terrible scream. The scream was repeated and seemed to come from a man who was terrified almost to death and struggling for life; it seemed to contain horror, hopelessness, loathing and agony. I lay there almost transfixed with fright at the terrible cry from the otherwise silent jungle. The scream ended suddenly with a choking gurgle and there was dead silence again. I sat up and asked Jim if he had heard it. He said he had, but there was nothing we could do about it. The night orderly peered out into the darkness in an effort to see something of the terrible tragedy that had taken place, but he could see nothing.

Next morning, I took a few minutes off to search in the jungle in the area where I thought the scream had come from, but found nothing. The screams will no doubt remain a mystery forever. Many men had wandered away into the jungle and, as there were so many dying, they weren't missed by the Nips, so a fair explanation would be that one of those men, either going or returning, must have been the victim of an attack by some wild jungle animal. Although the happening remains a mystery, that awful scream still remains with me and I often wake in the night with the horror of it ringing in my ears.

Soon after that incident, lorries managed to get through to our camp. The rains were easing off and we had a few short spells of sunshine. The road was taking shape, despite the deterioration of our men. Previously, lorries attempting to get to us had broken down or had sunk in the mud. One lorry stopped at our camp and unloaded food. The driver, being one of our men, came in with news from outside camps. Every camp had had a hard time and the death roll was very heavy. He told us of many rumours and we gathered that the war was not turning our way, though later much of what he said proved to be wrong. We were hungry for news and so were prepared to believe even that the war was over. He said that another lorry, driven by a man from my old

181

Company and loaded with food for the Nips, fish, peanuts and rice, had broken down outside No. 3 Camp. The driver and the Nip with him had gone back to No. 3 Camp for the night.

That night two of the malaria patients were missing but turned up again at about 6 a.m. with packs on their backs. They had sneaked quietly into camp and one of them came to me, wanting to leave his pack in my care. It contained fish, peanuts and rice. He told me that he and his mate had heard about the broken down lorry and decided to take a chance in an attempt to get to the lorry and get some food. Their journey through the jungle had been a frightful experience but they had kept close to the road and had eventually found the lorry. They took as much of the food as they could carry and made the return journey over the road. When nearing a bend in the roadway, they heard someone approach. They prepared to kill him if he was a Nip but, luckily, it was a native who took little or no notice of them. So they got back to camp safely. It must have been an extremely hazardous task for men so weak. That night I joined them in a feed of boiled rice, baked salted fish and toasted peanuts.

About the middle of July, when conditions were at their worst, some of our patients complained that they had lice. Soon we knew all about it, for in a few days every man was being tormented by this new menace. The lice got under the bandages, where the patients couldn't get at them, and men couldn't sleep at night for the maddening irritation caused by lice bites. Soon the scratching caused raw places which turned septic and the lice spread infection from patient to patient. Scabies started and spread and before many weeks there was hardly a man in camp that didn't have septic scabies. A small watery pimple with a maddening itch turned into a yellow blister. When it burst, it turned into a small sore, later forming an ulcer. Men lay for weeks on end writhing in an agony of torment from the pain and irritation caused by the ever increasing lice and skin diseases.

Each morning I noticed a flight of very large birds with very long necks and hooked beaks. They flew over in groups of five in a 'V' formation. Their wings spread out were six to seven feet from tip to tip and caused a swishing sound as they beat up and down, while the long neck and head stretched out straight in front. They flew over the camp, and returned later, seeming to give us a good look over as they passed overhead. I wondered about them and longed to possess their freedom.

Both Padres in our camp did fine work. They helped with the grave digging and with the burials and in the few moments they could spare from their gruesome tasks, they came into the wards to cheer up the patients, holding short services, and occasionally celebrating Holy Communion, using a small piece of burned rice, dipped into water, in place of bread and wine. They gave us what news they had and, when Padre Foster Haig came to see us, he would sing to us. His voice could be heard all over the camp. He came to me many times to have his legs dressed, as he had a few small ulcers and he liked to sit and chat. He told me one day that he had a pain in his chest and that, at the least exertion, it became increasingly difficult to breathe. He asked my advice and I told him that it was very similar to what most men complained of, but I told him to see the MO. He continued to work hard and I think he overtaxed himself for he died shortly after I had left the camp. I was told he died from cardiac beriberi.

Padre Duckworth almost worked himself into a similar condition. After his hard day at the cemetery, he came into the wards and lectured to the patients. He followed his lectures by getting the men to join him in prayers and singing hymns. It was a delight to see either of the Padres, as we were sure of a little break in the day's monotony when they were about. These tireless men were a constant source of comfort and hope, and they never failed to speak of God's mercy. They encouraged the men to more effort in their fight against death by setting an example in their faith in our God.

In early August, we were again told that the Nips had promised us a hospital camp and that all the sick would soon be moved there and would receive proper attention. Although the men had been told this before, they took new courage from this renewed promise.

When Colonel Dillon and Colonel Harris arrived from Nieke they brought with them a Nip, Lieutenant Wakabayashi, who was a more reasonable being than the Nip Lieutenant Abe, previously in charge of our camp, had been. Things improved, sick men were allowed to rest and Australians from other camps were brought in to assist in clearing up the camp. The sun came out more often and the rain eased off. At this brighter aspect the awful depression seemed to rise from the camp like a heavy cloud rolling away to let the sun slowly through. We began to breathe freely again and it seemed that everybody had a brighter outlook for the future. I was able to think more clearly and the sunshine seemed to give us a new lease on life. Men were still dying at the rate of ten or more each night but it seemed as though we had survived a horrible nightmare.

Great excitement reigned over the camp as lists were prepared of those who were to leave for the hospital camp in the first lorries. Parties of sick men started coming through from Nieke and No. 1 Camp, the fittest of them staying on at our camp. Hundreds of natives came from the north to work on the railway. All were dressed in gaudy colours, some with elephants, some yaks and carts, but most of them were walking. As they walked along, they talked and babbled, shouted and sang. They travelled with their families and, above all, could be heard the children, some laughing, some crying. I thought 'God help them if they have the same treatment as we have had,' but the rough work had been done and now all they had to do was to lay the rails and place some foundations. They soon set to work stretching along the track for miles in either direction and although they did very little work individually, the railway soon took shape.

Aubrey King, who had remained working with me in the ward, gradually weakened and in the end had to give in and become a bed patient himself. He had stayed on his feet as long as he could in the hope that he could remain with Jim and me as we were on the list to go to the hospital camp with the last party. He almost cried when we parted. We helped him on the lorry and told him that we would see him soon, as we would follow on with the next party. He only shook his head, he was almost too weak to do anything else. Many patients died. The exertion caused by the walk or by the effort made while being carried from the ward to the lorry proved too much for them, but they went, as the Nips had insisted that only fit men were to be left in the camp. My party was left until last; we were fit to walk a short distance.

We were to leave on 5 September, so on the eve of our departure we packed our few things together, then Jim and I lay down in the empty ward. All was now quiet and I couldn't help thinking back over the past three and a half months, to the horror and pain, anguish and fear suffered by the poor fellows who had passed on from this camp, whose remains now lay in the little cemetery across the road. About 650 lay there in their last long rest, all having died during that short period. This left approximately 1,000 men alive of which about 800 were booked for the hospital camp. The other 200, deemed fit enough, were to remain at the camp to carry on working on the railway until it was completed. I felt rather bucked when I learned that I was to leave this jungle 'hellhole.' But it left me depressed when I thought of all the splendid fellows, and particularly of my pals, who had died here. On the morrow I was to say goodbye to many more with whom I had become very close friends. They would remain while I went on, although their future was as uncertain as mine.

During the few months we were at the camp we had managed to get a little official news and many authentic rumours. I discovered that a wireless set, concealed in the false bottom of a water bottle, was the source of the official news. A little water was always kept in the top of the bottle in case the Nips made a search. I was told that the set was almost discovered on one occasion when a Nip tipped the bottle up and practically emptied all the water out. The batteries came from a lorry which was kept at the riverside, and as the engine was used to drive a pump, our driver had a grand opportunity to charge the battery, though he had a difficult task in getting the heavy battery to the set and back to the lorry in one night as it had to be done under cover of darkness. It was a very dangerous and difficult job, but he managed it occasionally and we got news through a few times.

As soon as Colonels Dillon and Harris arrived at our camp the Nips were persuaded to allow the construction of a separate cookhouse for the sick at the back of the officers' hut. A little oil was allowed by the Nips and so, during the last few weeks, some of the very sick were given rissoles or rice balls fried in oil. They were tasty and very appetizing and just what was needed to tempt the sick men to eat.

Fat and oil had been as scarce as good food, and the only oil I had seen since my arrival at Sonkurai was after a peculiar incident. One evening I was standing near the entrance to the hut and one of the patients stood near me. I had spoken to him, when he drew my attention to a dog that was sniffing around. He said 'Whose dog is that?' and I told him that I thought it belonged to one of the officers and expressed my surprise that the dog had lived so long among so many starving men. The patient said that it was a shame that the dog was allowed to roam about while so many men were hungry, and fat and oil was so urgently needed. He mentioned that some of the most expensive oil came from dog. I laughed, but seeing the look on his face I realized he meant it. A few nights later I noticed the patient with some of his friends very busy cooking at the big fire. They were using their mess tins and a grand smell of fried meat came from their direction. This wasn't a strange sight as it often happened that men cooked at the fire having perhaps killed a snake or another yak that had been lured into camp. I had to attend to this patient's ulcers a few days later and he, like most of us, was suffering from skin derangements. Our skin was dry and sometimes scaled, and if we pressed the back of a knife along our arms or legs skin would fall away like dust. The lack of fats or oil over such a long period probably had something to do with it. I told this patient that a little fat or oil would be just the thing for his dry skin and to moisten the caked edges of the ulcers. To my surprise he produced a bottle from under his blanket almost full of clear oil. I was about to ask him where he got it when I remembered the dog, so I asked him if he had killed the dog and he answered 'Yes, but this is all that is left'. That was the only oil I had seen since arriving at the camp and the officers saw to it that any oil issued by the Nips went to the sick men's cookhouse. The only snag as far as we were concerned was that the cookhouse was handy to the officers' hut, and they decided 'in their wisdom' to have their food cooked there also.

A certain amount of oil was allowed for the workers and they received a fried rissole at night. About eight patients in my ward also received a rissole at night, all other patients and medical staff having to do without. But the officers had rissoles, I know, because I saw their meals. When I enquired about where they got the oil, I was told that they had bought it. Then I remembered overhearing an officer tell some of his men (who had complained while on the march) that it was now every man for himself. So I understood the convenient cookhouses only too well and my blood boiled at the thought of it. Even at a time like this, they didn't believe in sharing.

The morning broke on 5 September. I had been awake most of the night, chiefly because all the men moving out with my party had been crowded in among the men who were remaining, who were already overcrowded, which made the conditions impossible for sleep. We were literally on top of one another. I was as excited as a schoolboy over the fact that I was going away from this awful place.

I was up early and, after a rough wash in the stream, collected my breakfast and got ready to move off. My little party was to march to No. 5 camp and from there we would proceed by lorry. We had been told that plenty of time would be taken on this march and there would be consideration for our condition, so we said our farewells and got into some kind of order so that we could be checked and counted.

Tara came out looking in rather a bad mood as though he was annoyed at having to see us instead of returning to bed, as he usually did after seeing the working parties off. I had expected him to see us off and wish us luck, but he started off by counting us and said that we were one too many. At this he began to rage and said in a loud voice that he had had to send out one of his Sergeant Majors that morning because one of the work parties was short and he said that if he found any 'scrim shankers' (his name for anyone who dodged the work party) in our party, he would flay them. However, he had made a mistake and our numbers were correct after all.

Chapter Fourteen

We Move to Tanaybaya

When our officers and the Nips who were to escort us arrived, we moved off. I heaved a sigh of relief – we were going away from that dreadful little man and the horrible camp. As we started off, I thought it rather a coincidence that a year ago today, 5 September 1943, I was moving out of that other 'hell-hole' (Selarang). Two years ago, I was preparing to leave 55 Company after receiving posting orders to Divisional Troops Company. Three years ago, I had been called up on 1 September, war was declared on the 3rd, and on the 5th my Company was feverishly preparing for the crossing to France. September, especially the 5th, was becoming a month when I could expect great moves. I was almost in rags, my boots were nearly falling off, and I was certainly far from being clean, but I was full of hope for the future.

On the March Again

As I plodded along with the others on the first stage of the march to the hospital camp, I didn't give one glance back at that place of horror which already seemed like a very bad dream, and the memory of it made me shiver.

We waded across No. 2 stream and reached the road north of camp. There we rounded a bend and came upon one of our working parties. The Sergeant Major that Tara had spoken of was with them and many of our party took the opportunity to get at him by advising him not to work too hard and asking him how it felt to be on a working party. He must have been thick skinned because he just laughed as though it was a huge joke.

At midday we stopped to eat the rice we had brought with us and we noticed that the two officers moved to a place where they could eat unobserved in order to conceal their meal of rissoles from us.

After a short spell, we continued our march and soon came in sight of No. 3 camp. Gangs of our men were labouring on the railway only a few hundred yards away and we were able to recognize many of them as men of our Company. One was Pilgrim, our Company office boy, who had been so weak and anaemic. He recognized us, and waved and shouted. I heard later that he died a few weeks after we passed through, from a mysterious tropical disease.

We passed through No. 4 camp, which consisted of only a few small huts on the roadside. There again we recognized some of our men. They shouted and waved but got beaten up by the Nips when they attempted to move near to us.

We arrived at No. 5 camp at about 3 p.m., and had to wait there until about 5:30, when lorries arrived for us. Once loaded, we were off again and arrived at a big camp at about 7:30 p.m. We were given a meal and then shown our quarters for the night. These were at the end of a hut occupied by natives with enough room for about twenty men to lie and stretch out, but there were 160 of us. We were told that we would have to get in somehow, as no one would be allowed to sleep outside.

Before being allowed to go in, we were sprayed with some kind of disinfectant by a Nip who stood at the entrance. He turned the spray full on us so that we were soaked and dripping with disinfectant when we got inside. We started the almost impossible task of finding a place we could stretch out. Gordon Davies and Jim Payne grabbed three medical hampers and put them together side by side, and this made an area on top of them about 5 feet by 3 feet and the three of us lay, very restless and cramped, on them all night. The place was packed and there wasn't a spare inch anywhere. Most men were sitting or standing, very few were able to lie down and all were sick. (The Nips had promised no hardships this time.) Next morning I learned that many of our sick men who had previously come this far had died and were buried in this place. I could well understand it as they had been in a serious condition when they left Sonkurai.

We received our issue of rice for breakfast and rice to take with us, together with a piece of uncooked dried meat which was like a piece of black leather. We could eat almost anything but that meat beat us and most of it was thrown away.

We waited in the sun from 8 a.m. until 12:30 p.m. Then the lorries arrived and we loaded up and started off. As we left the camp, I noticed that the railway had been completed this far and that light diesel cars were running over it. Soon all my attention was taken by the awful jumpy, jerky ride that we were having. The road wasn't completed and was a track just wide enough for lorries. The mud had been baked by the sun and become hard like lumps of rock. Furthermore, the road sometimes dipped to the left or right, with deep potholes. Rough bridges had been made over streams. Our driver must have thought he was on a track like Brooklands, as he kept going at such a speed that we were thrown about from side to side. We grabbed the framework of the body cover, but with us all holding on to it and being thrown about as the lorry hit a pothole or bump, the framework gave way and collapsed on us. I have never had a ride like it. Two of our men had fainted and were being tossed about helplessly. We did what we could for them but the torture continued for three hours. How the lorry stood up to it I can never guess. Even more miraculous was how we ever came out of it alive. We were all bruised and bleeding and when the Nip driver saw us off at the rail head he just grinned and said 'No goodiga uh!'

I thought about the ulcer cases – what hell they must have suffered. Some had ulcers so numerous that they were unable to sit down. They had had a ride like ours and it would have been worse than being beaten to death. It seemed as though the Nips were out to kill as many of us as they could, and they were succeeding. Men were dying and many died later, thanks to that awful journey.

Torture by Rail

We were kept waiting at the railway junction until dark, then a train pulled in and we crowded into the trucks. They were of the

190

same type as those that we had travelled in on our journey from Singapore to Bampong. However, whereas we had been twenty-six to a truck then, we now had to pack in forty, so we had to stand. We placed boards across the doorways so that men could stand and lean on them without danger of falling out.

We started off at about 7:30 p.m. The engine seemed to open up suddenly and we started forward with such a terrific jerk that we were all thrown on top of one another. As we tried to sort ourselves out, so we were jerked down into a struggling bunch again. We were getting worn out by this continuous jerking and bumping. Sometimes the train stopped for long periods, but we had to remain in the truck in a state of sheer exhaustion. The journey from Singapore now seemed like a pleasure outing compared with this.

We next pulled up at a wayside camp in the jungle. I could see hundreds of torches and large fires all along the line. The natives there were making a terrible din, yelling and screaming and jabbering. They tried to board the train and the Nips were running in among them, beating them with sticks in a mad frenzy. After a while, the Nips quieted them down and they formed up in a queue. Some were allowed to clamber on top of the loaded trucks, then the men in one of our trucks were ordered out. Our four trucks had held forty men in each and it seemed that we were already loaded to capacity. However, the Nips ordered the men from the now emptied truck to sort themselves into three parties and get into the three remaining trucks so thirteen men went to each of the other two trucks and fourteen came to ours. How we squeezed them in I do not know but they got in and we stood packed tightly together – fifty-four of us. The doorway was blocked up by the tightly packed men with little air getting to the inside of the truck and soon we were gasping for breath. The train started off again with a terrific jerk, but this time we were solid and hardly moved. After a little while, men cried out to be allowed to get to the doorway for air, but no one could move to allow the fainting men passage, so men fainted and remained standing, tightly jammed in an upright position. Two men, unable to control themselves, fouled themselves and those nearest them. Then they became hysterical and tried to fight their way to the door. Men swore, cursed, prayed, screamed and groaned. Some shouted orders and instructions, while others answered with abuse. We choked and gasped, strained and struggled against the pressure that threatened to crush us any minute as the train rattled and banged, jerked and bumped on its journey. It was utter hell.

Tanaybaya

At about 1 a.m. the train stopped and we were told to get out. It was raining heavily but we piled out, falling over each other in our endeavours to get out into the air. Over the side of the truck and on to the rail track we jumped, falling on one another in the dark and propelled forward by the crush behind. I fell into the ditch at the side of the track and picked myself up as others splashed in behind me. I noticed lights moving towards us and voices shouting for us to wait until they could help us, but they were too late. We were all out of the truck in a matter of minutes, except for the still bodies left behind, either dead or unconscious. We had arrived at the hospital camp and the staff turned out to meet us with primitive stretchers which they had made at the camp. Most of our party were carried in and placed on the bays in the huts. We were simply past caring. All we wanted was to lie down. If we never woke up, it didn't matter to us any more; everything seemed to be going from bad to worse.

I awoke next morning to find the sun streaming in through the gaps in the atap roof. Was this the start of another period of horror? I dared not think of it. Others were rousing by this time so Jim and I very reluctantly got up.

We were able to get a wash in the little stream that ran behind the cookhouse. Three places had been fenced off – the place where the cooks drew water for the cookhouse, an area for the staff to wash and an area for patients. Most noticeable here was the feeling of freedom from depression. The place seemed lighter, instead of the tall trees and creepers that darkened the camp at Sonkurai, the jungle here was of low growing shrubs and bushes and all so different. Also Sonkurai had been on a hillside and had seemed shut in. The monsoons had made it damp, dull and depressing. Now the sun shone brilliantly and gave us a feeling bordering on exhilaration. It seemed as though a great load had been lifted from us and that we were having a new lease on life.

The hardship of the previous night had left its mark on many of us but the thought of it was soon discarded as we splashed about in the cool stream and warmed in the morning sun. It was good to be alive. Gone was that hopelessness of yesterday. We were now interested; we now cared.

As Jim and I walked back to our hut, we looked about. Everything seemed to be tidy, no filth about, roofs were covered, the latrines were situated in convenient places, and the huts seemed to be orderly and clean. At the back of the camp towered a high rock, much like the many I had seen on my journey up through Thailand. I had seen them rising sheer out of the ground as though they had been placed there like large tombstones. Jim remarked that he hoped this one didn't prove to be our tombstone.

When we arrived back at our hut, breakfast was being served – plain boiled rice. This didn't seem to be a very good start, but our officer came and explained that he was sorry that breakfast was so poor, but rations hadn't arrived yet, so we had to manage the best we could until the train turned up. This officer was our hut officer. Two officers had been placed in charge of each hut and they lived in the hut with the men, maintained order and were responsible for the welfare of all in the hut, being always within call and in contact with the men all day. I thought it was a splendid arrangement, and thought to myself 'There's an organizer here somewhere; somebody who has the right ideas at last'. I met him sooner than I expected for we were called out to parade before our Camp CO, Major Hunt, of the Australian Army Medical Corps.

Major Hunt told us that we were welcome at the camp but our coming had somewhat crowded the place and rations had not yet arrived for our party. So, for a while, we would have to put up with short rations, and then he started a lecture I shall never forget. He said something like this:

I am in charge here and I want you all to remember it. My word is law, and I will not stand for any disobeyance of my orders. While being considerate, I shall be severe. You people have arrived from a hell. You have come here to rest and recover from your various ailments. My job is to do all I can to get you that rest, to help you recover and get you back home to those who are waiting for you. My aim is to do that, and I will not tolerate any obstruction or anything that might endanger fulfilment of that aim. You have lived the lives of pigs. When you came into this camp you weren't men but beasts. You have sunk to the lowest. Some of you found it too far to walk to the latrines. You fouled your beds, your huts and the area around the latrines. I consider any man who does that as a menace to the lives of us all, so I will flog any man caught doing this. I have instructed my staff to knock down a man, regardless of his condition, if he is caught endangering the lives of his comrades.

Some of you have stolen from the dying, some have eaten the food of sick men with the excuse that it would waste owing to the sick men being too ill to eat. I will not take that as an excuse. The patients must be made to eat their food, and if a man is brought before me for eating another man's food, I shall knock him down without compunction. From today you are men and you have got to live as men. We need every man's help and any man that doesn't pull his weight here is not wanted. Our lives are at stake, so there will be no slackness, nor carelessness, and all will live decently or take my punishments. I will not hesitate to introduce corporal punishment if the crime merits it.

Major Hunt had spoken frankly, just as I had found in most Aussies. What they had to say, they said, and no beating about the bush. I resented his outspoken accusations at first but finally admired him for his guts. He meant to do his best in the insurmountable task before him. He had made himself clear and we understood him. I felt that we were in for a fair deal.

The task he had was to save as many as he could of the 2,000 men now in the camp and when it is considered that the 2,000 had been drawn from the three horror camps as the worst cases there, the enormity of his task becomes plain. Already men were dying. His job was to check the death rate and, once checked, to keep the remainder alive as long as possible, despite being without the essentials to do so – food, medicines and surgical instruments. If any good could be done by care, attention and hard work, then Major Hunt meant it to be done. One advantage was that no working parties were expected from this camp. The only work necessary was for medical and camp maintenance.

My party was paraded before an MO, and those considered fit to do a little work were graded by types. I volunteered for ward work and was delighted to find that Doc Emery was the MO. I was detailed for night duty with Jim in Ward 5 where there was a mixture of cases – dysentery, beriberi, malaria and ulcers. I was given instructions before going on duty and told that I could punish as I thought fit any patients that fouled the floors or bed spaces. Night latrines were prepared during the day, holes being dug in the ground spaces between the huts, so men didn't have far to walk.

I found that most of the patients were bed patients. Some were unable to walk because of their ulcers; others were too weak or too ill.

Men who had two mess tins were asked to give up one and these were used as bedpans, for use in bathing ulcers and to wash in. We found that we weren't so overcrowded as at Sonkurai and, as men were dying at the rate of ten or more each night, there was soon plenty of room for all.

Hours of duty were twelve a day. I worked for seven nights a week from 9 p.m. to 9 a.m. We had to take turns at chopping wood for the night fires and this meant turning up at 8 p.m. to cut and stack the wood for the night.

Our duties were to care for the patients during the night – a full-time job as bedpans were always in demand – keeping the fires going, washing helpless patients before handing over to the day orderlies, and removing the dead before daylight if possible, then carrying the bodies to the crematorium before 9 a.m.

It was no easy job and I was always glad to get to my bed space in the staff hut where I managed to get a few hours disturbed sleep. After finishing duty, we would walk to the stream for a bath. Then we had breakfast. By the time we lay down to sleep, it was always after 10 a.m. The midday meal was at 12:30, so we had to get up for it or miss it. Then back to bed again until the evening meal at 6 p.m. Roll call was at 7 p.m., and duty again at 8 or 9 p.m. Many of us were still ill and weak, so many cracked up. Jim and I went down with malaria at about the same time and were given a week off to get over it.

I found that the name of this camp was Tanaybaya and that we were only about fifty miles from Moulmein with Thanbyuzat about ten miles away. Trains passed through the camp two or three times a day, our only contact with the outside world. When a train stopped, we knew that rations had arrived for us, and often a cheer would go up from the huts from men who couldn't see but only heard the train as it pulled in. Then every able-bodied man would rush out to collect the rations. On the next day we would all feed on vegetables, rice and sometimes meat stew. The feelings of the sick can be well imagined when on short rations and knowing that food meant life to them. They waited and listened for the trains to come, only to hear them rattle straight on. When a train was heard a shout would go up 'Train coming', then deadly silence. As everyone glanced at each other they were afraid to breathe and when it chugged on, the men's faces changed to expressions of despondency. Perhaps it was the last train for the day and still no rations for the morrow.

When a train was approaching and intended stopping to deliver rations, the men knew by the screeching of brakes. That is why they kept silent so that they could hear any sound that might give a clue that it was going to stop. Then they would cheer and I am sure that the engine driver, when he heard the cheering, would deliberately ease up and then open up again to pass through the camp – his idea of a joke.

My pal, Staff Sergeant Gordon Davies, was given the job of keeping records in the camp. Owing to the shortage of paper, bamboo was split and trimmed off, and writing was done on the plain wood. Each day when I met him I enquired about things in general in the camp. Gordon told me that he had been instructed that death figures were not to be divulged as it had a demoralizing effect on the men, but I knew that the death roll was heavy as I had assisted in carrying out the dead from my ward to the crematorium and there I had seen the dead in heaps.

One morning, a few days after my arrival, I met Gordon and he said that he would break the rule this once to tell me that one of my workmates of Sonkurai, Aubrey King, had died that morning from cardiac beriberi. This was indeed a blow. It reminded me of how upset he had been about having to part from Jim and I when he had been taken away so ill. It was very sad. He had done so much for other sick men and his efforts and good work had no doubt accelerated his end. His death was the first of those of many friends and pals of mine that died at Tanaybaya.

When we settled down to our different jobs we found that, with men being discharged from the wards, more were becoming available to work in them. So we were given a night off once a week. This gave me an opportunity to visit the other wards and look up my friends. I decided to visit the ulcer ward first to see how my old patients of Sonkurai were faring.

The ulcer ward was situated on the other side of the railway and to get there I had to pass the elevated sentry box. I saluted the sentry, this being a Nip order. Anyone who didn't satisfy the sentry took the chance of being beaten or punished by any of many unpleasant forms of punishment. Major Hodginson was one day passing this particular sentry box when he failed to satisfy the sentry and was made to return and salute correctly. He had to remain for many hours in the sun standing to attention, and, when released, he had to salute and march away correctly. It must have been very humiliating for him because all the time he stood there our men passed to and fro. Many of our men had their faces slapped or were kicked for not saluting correctly but that was quite common.

My salute was returned, the sentry dropping his head forward a little after a pretence of coming to attention, and I passed on along in front of No. 4 hut, turned left and then passed the Nip guard room, where the Nips sat. The sentries who weren't on point duty always remained this way and were to be found sitting like glass mummies facing the roadway. As I passed I gave 'Eyes right' and saluted. All the Nips there grinned and the NCO in charge, while keeping his seat, acknowledged my salute by saluting in British fashion.

I then passed on over the railway to the ulcer ward, known as 'K' Ward. It was crowded with men lying very close to one another and many were in a pretty bad way. Though very ill, some of my old patients smiled a welcome to me when they recognized me. They had had a rough time of it. The journey here had almost finished them, but they seemed to be getting over it and were cleaner and brighter in this new atmosphere. The ulcers of many were now dressed in clean white bandages.

There seemed to be plenty of orderlies to attend to them and a number of men were kept employed on boiling water night and day for the needs of the ward. Three or more MOs were on duty. One of them was a surgeon and had more time to care for the patients, yet the death rate in this ward was very high. Patients were given the titbits of our meagre supply of food, special dishes being made up for the worst cases.

Some of the very bad ulcer patients were to undergo operations. I spoke to one of the patients. On his left shin he had a large ulcer which was to be cut out. By doing this, treatment could be applied to the clean flesh, creating a much better chance of healing. He smiled bravely for he had great faith in the surgeon. There were many like him who just gave themselves wholeheartedly to the care and skill of their doctors.

Weeks later, I was informed that things weren't going just right in the ulcer ward. Limbs were being amputated almost daily and cases that were considered almost hopeless were operated on as a chance that they might pull through.

The surgeon must have been one of the bravest on earth as I am sure he knew the chances were so slender. The patient's condition would surely worsen and very soon he would die; an operation might save him or have the reverse effect and shorten his life. So the surgeon had to make the decisions but he would never operate unless the patient expressed his willingness to take the chance.

Operating instruments were, in some cases, very primitive. The saw, for instance, necessary for amputations for sawing through bone, was an ordinary carpenter's saw – the Nips had used it for sawing firewood. One day there were four patients to be operated on. The surgeon borrowed the saw from the Nips but they grew so impatient waiting outside for the amputations to be completed that the saw had to be returned and some of the patients had to return to the ward without having had their operation. Catgut used for absorbable ligatures was scarce and, as far as I know, what little they had was not dependable as it was old. I was told that cotton was used to tie up arteries in some amputation cases, though I cannot vouch for this as I didn't see it myself. The evidence taken from results proves that whatever was used as ligatures was very poor.

Amputation cases were cared for meticulously. They were the surgeons' special care, with orderlies standing by to do all in their power for the patients. Days passed and the patients, looking fine, said they felt grand; they were having the best attention possible. Then, when recovery seemed certain, the ligatures gave way, followed by serious haemorrhages. I have known the surgeons and orderlies to work on a patient for hours to stem the blood, but haemorrhages continued until the final collapse of the patient. When those patients died, they were sickly white.

No word of praise can ever be high enough for the people who fought so hard for these men's lives. It was heartbreaking work. I actually heard the surgeon sob after one particularly bad case, when a patient had four haemorrhages in one night. The surgeon had been there in a moment to fight through the night for the patient who remained conscious and talking, thanking everyone for what they were doing for him and saying that he knew he was going to die. The strain on the surgeon must have been terrific. His devotion deserved the highest honour.

There were some horrible ulcer cases in the ward. One of the worst I ever saw was a patient who was suffering from dysentery. He had grazed his right buttock on the bedpan; the graze turned septic and formed an ulcer which rapidly increased in size, eating deep into the flesh and spreading to the left buttock. The patient was kept on his stomach and bedsores formed on his chest and knees. His cries were pitiful when he used the bedpan; his motions appeared as discharge through the ulcer. The man died, and no one will ever comprehend the unbearable agony he endured.

Martin, one of the patients from my Company (the shell-shock patient of Chancery Lane) when at Sonkurai had aggravated a small ulcer in an attempt to be passed unfit for road work. When I treated him, he told me that he didn't want to go out on road work so meant to stay in by preventing the ulcer from healing. The ulcer had deteriorated rapidly, getting entirely out of hand. It had enlarged to about the size of an ordinary saucer and he was frantically trying his best now to arrest the deterioration. He nursed it patiently, then the surgeon told him one day that it had gone too far and that the only hope for him was amputation. He was now really frightened, so agreed to allow them to take off his leg. I went over to see him the morning before he went into the partitioned-off section called the theatre and he told me that he had every confidence that he would pull through and had great confidence in the ability of the surgeon. He went the way of the others, improving daily for a few days, then haemorrhage and death.

Corporal Bird of the Changi Concert party and my patient of Sonkurai who had an ulcer after a blow from a Nip with an axe, had his leg amputated and got on so well after the operation that a few days later he sang two songs in a sing-song in the ward. But, although a good fighter, he succumbed to haemorrhages on 17 September 1943. This kind of thing went on continuously and if the surgeon said 'Operation,' it sounded like a death sentence.

No. 2 ulcer ward, known as 'L' Ward, was for minor ulcer cases, such as men who had septic scabies which had turned into small ulcers. Some were covered from head to foot with blisters, white with pus; the pitiful part of it being that most of these men had other ailments, such as dysentery, malaria, beriberi, and sometimes all those afflictions together.

Jim and I had got over our bouts of malaria and reported back for duty. Jim got a day job in No. 4 ward and I was sent to the officers' ward as special orderly to a Colonel Pastor of, I believe, the Provost Company. He was very ill with amoebic dysentery. Dysentery is of two kinds, Bacilliary and Amoebic. The former is due to a bacillus and causes inflammation of the large intestine with mucus and bloody evacuations. The latter was the most dangerous in my estimation, owing to it being so highly contagious, and is due to the *antomoeba histolytica*, which I understand means that the amoeba parasite attacks the minute structure of the tissues of the body. Sometimes it leaves the patient without appetite, he gets weak and languid and eventually collapses and dies, if not treated in time. I understand the only real cure known is that of the use of Emetine, of which it is necessary for the patient to take a long course of injections (we didn't have Emetine). It was my job to care for the Colonel and watch him die. He was very weak and had to be assisted in everything. I had to collect his meals, which were always special, and feed him, raise him on to the bedpan and hold him there like a baby. I was very sorry for the old boy and did what I could to comfort him, but I couldn't help comparing the treatment of officers and men. The food brought in for the Colonel was what I had thought unobtainable, yet it came for him.

When the Nips allowed us a canteen, fruit and eggs came in for sale and, naturally, the officers, having money, were able to buy.

A system of sharing the supplies was adopted and each ward was allowed so much according to the number of men in it. My allotment was one banana and a small square of gula malacca, if I could pay for it. The canteen foods to us at that time were a very important thing and a banana was a wonderful treat. When there is hunger, it makes the hungry ones very keen, and so we watched the distribution – so much to a man, if he could afford to pay for it. We wanted to know what happened to the issue that had been allotted if the man could not pay. It didn't take a keen observer to see where it went. At least the officers were well blessed with canteen food and my Colonel received more than he could eat. At the same time, helpless sick men looked long and longingly at such things as fruit and eggs, which they couldn't buy.

Major Hunt made two free issues to the very sick patients, but what I'd have liked was that, since food meant life, money ought to have been pooled and each man receive an equal share. It was known that some officers had brought canteen funds with them from Changi, money with which they were to start a canteen. This money really belonged to the men, as it represented the profits and monies of the canteen at Changi, which in some cases had been financed by the men.

I know of a case where an officer holding the money admitted that he had it and was willing to pay for the canteen issue of fruit, gula malacca or eggs to each man of his unit, who didn't have money. I know that some men got as much as three dollars' worth of goods, which wasn't much, as eggs were over fifty cents each, bananas ten cents, and gula malacca four dollars a pound. He would not give any money for tobacco. I saw the record he kept of such payments and there were about thirty names and a total of about sixty dollars paid out from the hundreds of dollars which he held. What happened to the remainder of the money? All I know is that when, later on, at another camp, the men requested more money be paid out, they were told that the wallet containing all the money had been lost.

Men were always bitter about the way the officers lived, with plenty of everything, comparatively speaking. Compare the treatment of my patient with the treatment of hundreds of our men whose condition was as bad or worse. Special meals, one orderly to himself to tend to his every want and, when canteen supplies came in, he was allowed to purchase more than he required. A special bed was made for him. Two sacks with the bottom corners pierced and six foot bamboo poles pushed through, then kept apart by another piece of bamboo, making the sacks taut, this frame being placed on blocks, one at each end, which made a reasonably good camp type bed.

The rest of the men lay on bamboo slats (bamboo poles split and tied to supports), many were without blankets and they lay with the sharp edges and knots of the bamboo pressing into their emaciated bodies. If they couldn't eat the general issue of food, they went without. For attention they had one orderly between fifty or 100 patients. If they wanted the bedpan or a bottle, they took their turn, many having to wait until one became available, which perhaps was then too late. Regarding canteen supplies, they got what they could pay for apart from the two free issues and there was no one with time to spare to do their washing, while the officer patients got most things done for them.

I remained a few weeks caring for the Colonel. I was warned by the MO, Major Hanbury, to be very careful and to take every precaution against infection from amoebic dysentery. Although I took every care, I soon had reason to be concerned about my condition as I was having intestinal pains and it soon became evident that I had another dose of dysentery. I was detailed to report to the OC of No. 3 hut which was one of our dysentery wards. I left the Colonel in the hands of another orderly and off I went, to pick up my little bag of kit.

I reported to the ward master at No. 3 hut and found him to be my old wardmaster of Sonkurai. The MO was one with whom I had worked at Changi and Sonkurai. I remained as a patient for about a week. There was nothing they could do for dysentery but allow the patient complete rest. All I received was six doses of Tanic acid and daily doses of charcoal. I felt I couldn't lie there among men who were so ill, who were messing themselves unable to hold on until a pan could be brought. I felt that if I remained there I would soon be like them so, when the MO came on his round one morning, I asked him if I could get up and do a light job. He agreed and told me I could help with the ulcer cases. I started doing a few hours a day and, as I recovered, so I put in more hours and was given more patients to care for.

I used to like the bedside manner of the MO. He walked along the bays looking down on each patient as he passed along and greeted each man with 'Good morning, are you eating your food, how are your bowels, how many motions?' – all these questions were asked in a broad north country accent, and he usually finished up by saying 'You must eat your food. You know that if you don't, you'll die. If you die you'll burn: so be sure to eat your food.' He was always laughing and joking with the patients even when he was asking the most personal questions. Many said he would be ideal for a women's ward, as it seemed that he greeted the men in the morning as though he was addressing women patients. It was rather funny that later we were informed that he had come into the RAMC from a maternity hospital, so when patients heard this they had much fun at the expense of the MO through joking about their different ailments. For instance, a bad beriberi case with a badly swollen abdomen asked the MO one morning if he thought it would be long now. The MO looked quite surprised, and the patient said 'You won't let me suffer will you Doc, you could give me twilight sleep you know.' At this the MO, realizing what the man meant and the joke being on him, roared with laughter and from then on played up to the men with their jokes about his maternity occupation.

Another patient with a swollen abdomen on being asked, 'And how are you this morning?' said 'All right Doc, but there's signs of movement, I'm so excited.' The Doc laughed and said 'What over – worms?' Another patient told the MO that he couldn't eat his food. He said that the rice made him sick to which the Doc jokingly remarked 'Being sick is a sure sign, but you must eat your food. We haven't steak and chips you know and you must eat what we've got for you'. The patient said 'Well, I'm surprised at you saying that Doc, as I thought that everyone in my condition should have what they fancy.' And so the ragging and raillery went on, making the MO's visits an occasion for much fun.

I told him one morning that I felt fit enough to be discharged. He answered by saying that he wasn't going to discharge me but, as I was feeling fit again, I could do a full time orderly's job in the ward. So I started off by caring for the worst skin cases. My first was a case of pellagra. I think it was one of the most dreaded of skin complaints and was the first of its kind I had seen. It started with recurring purplish redness and exfoliation, large blotches appearing on the patient's arms and legs. I was keenly interested and watched its development day by day.

That patient suffered from dysentery as well as pellagra and, from the first, I didn't think he had a chance. It wasn't long before mental symptoms developed and one morning, when he was babbling away and in a high fever, the MO said he wouldn't last long. Poor man, on top of the dysentery and pellagra, he now had malaria. He died that night.

Pellagra, I understand, occurs through lack of vitamin B and, in the following months, there was a steady increase in the number of men suffering from this horrible disease, brought about through the absence of necessary vitamins in the food they ate.

Some of the patients I handled were in an awful mess. They were all virtually rotting away. One patient, an Australian, Hunter by name, and about twenty years of age, had septic scabies all over his body. They were in his hair and all over his face. There was hardly an inch of him that didn't bear some evidence of scabies. Each morning I had to burst each blister with my sharp pointed forceps and, by pinching each one of the hundreds of blisters, I let out the puss and wiped it away with a pad wet with WSP Eusol. I had nothing suitable to cover such a large area. I first tried a weak solution of permanganate of potash. Then I thought that if I had something to dry up the blisters it might be of some use. I realized it was necessary to kill the germ before there could be any hope of healing up the exposed flesh after puncturing the blisters, but we didn't have any sulphur which was the known antidote. I asked the MO if he had any of the maclurochrome left which I had given him at Sonkurai. He said he had handed it in to the dispensary, but I could get some from there. He gave me a chit and I duly collected a small bottle of it.

I told the MO what I wanted it for, and he said that I could try it but it was sulphur that we needed. I made a liberal application of the maclurochrome, completely covering the patient from head to foot leaving him brilliantly red. As he walked about almost naked he looked rather odd and had his leg pulled unmercifully by the other patients. But he put up with that and decided it was worth it when after a few days of this treatment there were fewer blisters in the mornings. Many had dried leaving a dry scale which, when removed, left a clean spot. Maclurochrome was applied again and again until only a few patches were left. We were all very pleased with the progress he was making. He was a good patient and did a lot towards bringing about his own cure. Then the heartbreak – he had a relapse of dysentery and went off his food. I tried hard to get him to eat and he responded by making a great effort, but as he masticated he immediately vomited, and he would then rest and later try again. I don't think I ever saw a young chap put up such a heroic battle for his life. It was a wonderful effort, and he must have suffered terribly, trying so hard to eat such unappetizing food. Each mouthful caused him uncontrollable retching. After days like this, it was discovered that he had worms. He must have been full of them, eight being in evidence before he died. He had fought hard for his life, but the odds were too great.

One morning the MO told me that he had a patient he wished me to take over. Then, after giving me full instructions and details regarding the patient's condition, he told me that he wanted me to spend quite a lot of my time in caring for this particular patient, the reason being his helpless, hopeless and pitiful condition. I was to look after him, feed him, keep him clean and care for him in every way.

Another orderly took over several of my other patients so that I could find time to do this and I was taken along to see the patient. The MO stopped by a heap of rags under which was the most grotesque man I've ever seen. He was lying on his back with his head nearest to me. I got up onto the bay and looked down at him – his face was bloated and dirty and there were marks left by saliva, as it had run from his mouth, making a dirty white trail, also where tears had run down over his temples and over his ears. His hair at one time had been fair and curly. There were still a few curls but the rest was matted and dirty. I moved the rags to expose his barrel shaped body, bloated arms and legs and his hands filthy with his own excreta. I disturbed him as I moved the rags. He groaned and two slits appeared in the puffy swollen flesh where his eyes were. I saw his eyes through the slits looking at me as though weighing me up, then he smiled and said 'Wotcha old cock, 'ell of a mess ain't I?' This took me somewhat by surprise, but I managed to smile back at him, and told him that I had come to look after him. He said 'Blimey, what have I done to deserve this, anyhow, good luck to you mate. You've got some job, and I don't envy you.' I saw the funny side of his remarks and laughed. He joined me and I pretended I didn't notice, but his face was ghastly, his mouth seemed like a horrible gash and when he laughed his cheeks shook like a jelly. I turned away – there was a man almost certain to die and he knew it, yet he could laugh and pass wisecracks.

Before I finished with him I decided that he was undoubtedly the most plucky fellow I had ever known. His cockney accent and humorous sayings kept me and all the men around laughing.

I decided that my first job was to wash him. This was no easy job, so I got Jim, my pal, to give me a hand and we gave him a blanket bath without the blanket. It nearly made me vomit. When turning him over my hands sunk into his puffy flesh and when I removed them there were the indentations, ugly looking hollows where I had gripped him. He must have suffered agony while we were washing him, but he kept ragging us all the while telling us we were tickling him, or wouldn't he make a beautiful baby, when were we going to put on his napkin and so on.

While washing his back, I noticed that his neck was raw, caused through lying in one position for a long period. A small bedsore had formed and when I examined it closely I found that a fly had got into it and maggots were just visible, bubbling in the watery flesh. He also had a small bedsore on the base of his spine, so I told him that he would have to lie on his stomach until the bedsores were better. He said 'OK,' as though it made no difference to him.

After dressing the sores, I got Jim to help me make a frame to which I fixed two sacks, making a bed like the Colonel's. When we returned with it he became quite excited over it, but stopped short while thanking us to say 'But surely there are worse cases than me'. I told him it was because of his bedsores so there was no more argument. He was able to lie on his back once more and every time I treated his sores or when I took his meals and he had to be lifted up to a sitting position he always insisted on helping by grabbing his hair with his right hand and pulling himself up. All I had to do was to place both my hands under his shoulders and lift, he did the rest.

206

Each morning I spent at least half an hour probing for maggots. I took out forty-eight on the first day and sixteen and more on the following days. The MO suggested that I use Mag. Sulf crystals so I made a pack of crystals and placed them over the opening. It had a little effect and I cleared twenty or more that morning, but they were spreading down and around his neck and little inflamed punctures appeared to show the advance of the maggots. In the punctures appeared a bubble and if I was quick enough with a well directed jab of my forceps I'd catch a maggot in the pointed jaws, but they seemed to be advancing very rapidly and dangerously. Often, while searching for a sign of them, blood appeared, giving proof that they were gnawing through small capillaries and eating his life away.

I told the MO that the maggots had got beyond control and he brought out his syringe, which he used for local anaesthetic. Where he had got it from I don't know – it was just another of those little mysteries. The syringe contained a chemical for freezing. He pointed it at the small hole in the patient's neck and sprayed it with the chemical. A frosty film appeared over the small hole and remained there for a few minutes. I then replaced the pad and waited for half an hour, and when I removed the pad I found about forty dead maggots of all sizes. I thought it had cleared them but next morning there were as many as ever again. It seemed hopeless, yet the patient always joked about it all. He was getting weaker, failing fast and suffering acutely. A supply of morphia had come in and he was given enough to allow him to sleep each night.

The day before he died, I was washing him. He had made a mess of himself during the night. While apologizing for his state he said 'Of course I did tell you to put a napkin on me'. Then for the first time he gave way to the awful suffering he was enduring. He looked up at me with tearful eyes and, with a catch in his voice, he said, 'Oh, Taff, it hurts'. It must have been agony for he was completely raw in the crotch and scrotum, and although I was careful I knew he was going through hell.

He had lain on his stomach the night before to ease the pressure on the bedsores and, being drugged with morphia, he was sleeping when he had made the mess. When I started to wash him, he was caked in bloody faeces which had made him raw. The sob came from deep down. It contained all the weariness that must have been his after the torment of such long suffering, but even as he said, 'It hurts,' he checked himself and said in a very weak voice, looking from side to side, 'Now didn't I ought to be ashamed of myself saying it hurts when all these men around me are suffering so much'. At that point I very nearly broke down. Those words will forever be in my mind when I think I have something to complain about and whenever I hear of heroes, I think of him.

The next morning I took him his breakfast and shook him to rouse him from his drugged sleep. He roused and raised his hand, grabbed his hair and tried to raise himself, only to fall back slowly – he was dead. He had tried to help himself to the last and had shown throughout that he could take it. Every cockney and every Britisher could well be proud of that man.

That cockney was such an example that one could not help feeling his influence. I felt small and, compared with him, I felt mean, but thinking of him kept me going many times when I felt I could not go on a minute longer. His courage was an inspiration, and I know of many whom I would have liked to have seen his bravery and the example he set.

A patient named Beak, suffering from septic scabies, said one morning when I was attending to him, that he felt queer and asked me if I would postpone his treatment until the next day as he didn't feel up to it. I didn't like leaving the blisters unpunctured but I couldn't resist his appeal. Though he looked all right and his temperature was normal, he refused his meals that day, so in the morning I spoke rather sharply to him and threatened to report him to Major Hunt if he didn't eat his food. He told me that he would eat if he could, but later he tried and couldn't saying that he felt he was going to die. I told him that I was disgusted with him, but as I was worried I told the MO who, after finding a normal temperature and pulse, told him he would have to pull himself together.

That night I was awakened by someone shaking me. It was Beak. He apologized for waking me and said he was frightened and wanted to lie by my side. I made him comfortable. He was trembling, but I was still unable to find anything really wrong with him and he couldn't give any explanation for his fear. I lay down beside him and talked a while with him. Then when I heard him snoring I dropped off to sleep again. I awoke a few hours later as day was dawning and thought Beak looked strange as his arm was crooked in the same position as when he had gone off to sleep hours before. I moved back his blanket to expose a deathly white face with eyes glaring into space and mouth wide open. He was stone cold, stiff and dead. He was yet another victim to some strange tropical germ and just another mysterious death. The strange thing about it was that he was so sure that he was going to die. Before dropping off to sleep, he had requested me to see his photographs home safely to his wife in the event of him dying and had thanked me for the little services I had rendered him.

When I examined the snaps, I found that they were of a family group, he, his wife and little boy sitting among the flowers of their garden somewhere in England. I took charge of the photographs so that I could send them to his people if ever I got out all right, but that picture of a happy family scene in a little corner of dear old England upset me for weeks. I showed them to Jim, who said 'Let me once get back there and it will take all hell to get me away again'.

While I was having my midday meal one day, I overheard two orderlies talking. They were discussing an incident in their ward of the previous night. One said 'I showed that Sergeant Major what was what, just because he is an SM he thinks he can do as he likes, but I quieted him,' and the other said 'Yes, you did quite right'. I then butted in by asking the name of the Sergeant Major and when told, I became more interested because I knew him, so I asked for details. Apparently the SM was a patient in their ward and had been behaving very oddly of late. On the night in question, he had been shouting deliriously and babbling to the general annoyance of the other patients in the ward, who wanted to get off to sleep. The orderly had coaxed and threatened him in turn to keep quiet and, having no effect, promptly hit him on the jaw, hoping to put him out. He failed, so struck several blows before finally silencing the Sergeant Major. I was amazed that a man could brag about such brutality, and I told him so, only to be told to mind my own business as I wasn't there when it happened so I couldn't be a judge. The tragedy of it was that the Sergeant Major died the next day. My feelings are too strong about this incident to dwell on it. I only know that when I enquired about it, I was told that an enquiry was being held, but I never heard anything more.

Food in the camp continued to be very poor though with more variety than at Sonkurai. We were getting some vegetables, though not enough food containing vitamin B, so beriberi was on the increase. Major Hunt was continually pestering the Nips for supplies, and finally succeeded in getting a few sacks of rice polishings in for us, though at first there was only sufficient for the worst beriberi cases to have two ounces a day. Later, there was plenty for all. I remember Major Hunt jumping in his excitement when he received the news that bags of rice polishings had arrived, and saying that it would save many lives.

Rice polishings are from the brown husks of the rice, taken away when the rice is polished and it contains vitamin B. We were compelled to take four ounces a day. It was horrid stuff but it did us a lot of good.

Major Hunt rather favoured keeping the men informed about their physical and mental condition, their chances of survival and how their various diseases would affect them when they returned home. He lectured nightly in the wards, taking each ward in its turn. After the lecture, he gave a week for the patients and staff to prepare questions, then he returned to answer them.

.It was really entertaining to listen to the questions and answers. The men asked a great deal of questions and were very anxious about our present condition and chances of survival. In each case, the Major told the questioner the hard facts about his complaint and explained how the patient could help the doctor in his recovery.

I was surprised at the large number of enquiries about the future. Sex easily topped the list. The chief concern was 'What effect would the years of starvation and disease have on a man? Would his power to procreate be affected? Would the fact that having not been in the company of the opposite sex for so long, with the system having been weakened by the rigors of prisoner of war life in the tropics, have a lessening effect on the sex desire or shorten puberty?' Answers to these difficult questions were anxiously awaited by the men who were of mixed ages and stations in life. Some were mere boys, some elderly men, but all were keen to know what to expect regarding sex in the years ahead. The Major said that, except in serious cases, there would be hardly any effect at all. When the men had had a month or more of good food, they would be as good as ever, and when they returned home and found themselves being caressed by their wives or sweethearts, they would think back and laugh at their past fears. But what was most curious was that the patients always seemed to be so concerned about their health after they returned home, forgetting for the moment that they were so ill and so far from home.

Padre Duckworth, our tireless Padre, also kept the men entertained at night. He talked about his experiences while cox for the Cambridge Boat Race crew. I think he said he had been cox for three years running. Although he gave talks on the subject hundreds of times, it never failed to draw a crowd. I always thought he would make an excellent political speaker. He often stomped his feet or banged his hands together when warmed up. He was a great critic of officers and their hypocritical ways. I remember on one occasion he was talking on the Olympic Games in Germany. He was there as cox to the British crew. He said that a special demonstration of the military was put on and, after watching tanks, guns, armoured cars and motorcyclists drive past in formation for an hour or more, he and his pals got fed up and went up to their room at the hotel where they were staying. His room was on about the third floor and some of his pals were on the floors above. He opened his window to look down into the street at the noisy passing of the military motorcyclists, adding that they were very pompous, bumping and roaring by, each man stiff and helmeted. Just then something whizzed past his head. It was a 'Jerry' from the room above and landed on a passing steel helmet. He had popped in before seeing the result. As he said, 'Jerries from heaven crashing on Jerries on earth'.

Another incident of which he told us, was when all competitors at the games had to march past Hitler. One man was detailed to give the order of salute and as they marched past, the man got very excited and gave 'eyes right' instead of 'eyes left' getting everyone mixed up: half were turned one way and half the other.

Our Padre hated the Nips and didn't attempt to hide his hatred of them. They had been the cause of him losing some of his best friends, and he had seen them at their worst. He had been at Sonkurai with us and had every cause to hate them. His lectures often ended with uncomplimentary words about the Japs, such as 'These little yellow scum', or when giving the Olympic Games talk, he usually said that 'Instead of fighting against Germany, Britain and Germany ought to be allies in an effort to wipe out these little yellow murderers – our hosts'.

The men called him the 'Mighty Atom'. He was very short, dynamic and sincere, and one of the most genuine men I have ever known. His place, he said, was with the men and he spent most of his time with us in the wards, always doing little things that endeared him to us. His church was in the open with logs for seats and bamboo for an altar. The men gathered there daily for communion and short services, and the hymns we sung brought back memories of other services at home. When we sang 'Holy Father in Thy Mercy' and 'Abide With Me', the voices resounded through the jungle and echoed back from the big mountainous rock which towered menacingly at the back of the camp. Often during the service we would have to put up with the smell of burning bodies, as the smoke from the crematorium's large fires was wafted our way by the wind.

The crematorium was only about 100 yards away in the jungle and the men were working so busily that often their meals of rice were left to get cold. I have seen them warm their rice on the large fires where parts of bodies still smouldered. These men, who a few months before had looked the other way in dread when a body was carried past them, were now hardened and callous. The fires were a means for heating their meals, so what difference did it make if there were a few smouldering bodies? That was how men had become. What changed characters they would be when they returned home. I often thought that in some cases the change would be tragic.

I was informed that the Colonel I had cared for had died about a fortnight after I had left him. It struck me that if he, with the best treatment possible in our camp, could not hold out against amoebic dysentery then the many other sufferers could have little hope.

About the middle of October, we were threatened with a water shortage. The stream running near the cookhouse was drying up and becoming muddy. This gave the men an opportunity to catch the small fish (or tiddlers as we called them) in the little pools that were left as the stream receded. They proved very tasty when cooked. Soon we were unable to wash in the stream. The cookhouse was moved to another stream, outside the camp, which also dried up after a week or so and so the cookhouse was moved a third time about a mile away from camp and almost under the mountainous rock at our back. There was a fast moving narrow stream, cool and clear which ran along in the shadow of the rock. In this stream teemed thousands of little fish, ranging from an inch to about four inches long.

A clearing was made in the jungle on the side of the stream for the cookhouse and a place made also for bathing. An area was roped off for officers and what was left was for the men. Though it was such a long way, many of the staff and patients did the walk each day for the great pleasure of being able to lie in the clear, refreshing, cool water.

The men who were covered with septic scabies and sores found that the little fish swarmed around them and nibbled at the pimples, blisters and sores. Many men lay there for hours while the fish nibbled and cleared the blisters away. One patient informed me that he had found that some of his sores were healing since he had been bathing in the stream. I made further enquiries and found that many others were the same. There was a noticeable improvement in the sores, so I encouraged my patients to go to the stream as it helped, if only to keep them clean. I think that there must have been a mineral content in the water which had some healing effect; perhaps the stream ran over or through rock that held a sulphurous deposit. However, whatever was in the water was doing good.

One day, while I was assisting some of my patients to wash and clean themselves, I saw a termite army on the march. An old branch had fallen from an overhanging tree and lay across the stream. The termites were marching eighty or ninety abreast in unceasing rows. They came from the undergrowth in the jungle, marched up the trunk of an old tree that leaned down over the bank, then along the branch that led them to the water's edge and the fallen branch across the stream. The termite, or bull ant, is a ferocious looking little creature, much like the ordinary ant but thicker set and about a quarter to half an inch long with two small crab like pincers at the front. When used, they can be very painful, just like two sharp needles being pushed in together. However, the ants kept in formation and seemed to be too concerned with getting to their destination to take notice of us. I was really fascinated by their behaviour. Their formation was much like infantry when on the march. There were about 200 or 300 such rows following close up to one another, then a small gap in which there were two or three odd ones who kept running about in all directions contacting the outriders. These outriders were running ahead and well out to the sides of the column as if they were the scouts, dodging to and fro and always in a terrible hurry.

I dropped a piece of earth in front of one of the columns to see what would happen. There was a sudden panic. The column stopped their advance about six inches away from the obstacle and all bunched together as if talking excitedly. The scouts came forward and examined the pile of earth and quickly returned to the column leaders. Then with their heads together, they shook and nodded, just as though they were conversing. They all formed up again and advanced, making a circuit of the earth pile. I was amazed. I'll swear that there was some kind of language or understanding movements, and the organization of the formation marching was wonderful.

I wanted to see more, so I moved the branch that lay across the water just out of their reach. The scouts came up to the water's edge, seemed to confer again and then set out back along the column. As they met other squad leaders they paused long enough to shake and nod then passed on down the column. The column slowed up but moved to the water's edge where they crowded in a large moving mass. I then put the branch back and was astonished to see that there were some on the branch seemingly waiting to guide the others. There was no rush and the waiting termites slowly formed up into rows again and continued the march. It seemed endless and they were still marching the next day, though thinning out a bit. It was a fascinating spectacle and conclusive proof to me of the intelligence and organizing powers of the ant.

One day a large snake, about eight feet long, moved over the floor in our hut, causing much excitement and disturbance. It hadn't moved very far when it received a sharp blow, breaking its neck. One of the men picked it up on the end of a pole, carried it outside and on being told that it was not edible, he deposited it in the rubbish pit. The rubbish pit was sunk in the ground at the end of our hut. It was about 6 feet deep and the sides were sheer, having been cut straight down. The snake wriggled at the bottom for many hours but there was no chance of it recovering as its head was almost severed, and even had it recovered I doubt if it could have climbed the sheer sides of the pit.

Next morning I was amazed when I approached the pit to see the snake halfway up the side. I went closer and noticed that, tail first, it was moving so slowly as to be hardly discernable. On closer inspection I found that the snake was quite dead but was being dragged up the pit-side by thousands of ants. During the night they had moved it about 3 feet – more than half the snake was still on the bottom. The ants were doing the almost impossible and the peculiar thing about it was that the ants had joined forces which I had never seen them do before. There were little ants and large ants of different colours all busy in one common cause. Obviously so busy and the cause so important, they had chosen to ignore their different families and work together. If I could have spared the time, I would have stopped to see them work. As it was I visited the spot three times that day and three times the next. On each occasion the snake was noticeably nearer the top and the ants were hurrying about as busy as ever.

On the evening of the second day, the tail of the snake was over the top by about a foot. I noticed that a hole was being made to receive the prize. Ants were dashing about with small grains of earth or sand and the hole gradually opened up and went in deeper and deeper.

By the morning of the fourth day, the snake had completely disappeared into the hole. It was a brilliant feat, and if I hadn't seen it I would never have believed it. I wondered how the ants finished up – did they fight over possession or did they share by letting all the other ants draw from the well-stocked larder? That is one thing I shall never know, though the achievement left me with a great admiration for this wonderful little insect. After that, I spent many an interesting hour watching the ants at work.

There were many incidents that I would have liked to write about but, owing to the similarity of the cases and morbid and tragic endings, it is perhaps as well if I describe the remainder of my stay at Tanaybaya as briefly as possible.

During the whole time I was at Tanaybaya (from 7 September to 24 November 1943) the food was of poor quality, lacking in vitamin values. It was not good enough to live on indefinitely and was of no use for the sick to build upon. It consisted mainly of rice, mixed vegetables, occasionally a little meat and, once or twice, dried fish. We had an exceptional treat when, on three or four occasions, we were issued with five prawns each and, at another time, about six small English potatoes. Beans we had often, though owing to the scarcity of salt the meals remained tasteless. Twice we had artichokes. No tea was issued though we some times substituted it by burning rice black then adding it to water and boiling for a while. We kidded ourselves that it tasted like coffee. Milk, of course, we never saw. Sugar was also very rare, but we used gula malacca when we could buy it (which wasn't often). Eggs arrived toward the end of my stay at the camp but were only for those who could buy them and the very sick who were given a few, paid for out of the general fund. A few bananas came in but only enough for a small distribution, chiefly to the sick. Medical supplies and equipment were hopeless, as I explained in the incident of the saw, though we were much better off than we had been at Sonkurai.

We were still very poorly off for clothing and footwear. As men died, so their clothes were put into a store and issued later to the most needy. It was becoming very cold at night and clothes were required for warmth. The terrific heat of the day and the bitter cold at night were elements that required much consideration, especially for the sick.

Some of our men contacted the natives and started a black market. They exchanged their clothes for cheroots or anything they could obtain to eat. This became a serious offence as the natives would not sell to our local purchasing officer when they could get fancy prices and clothes for their goods, and men who parted with clothes were endangering their own lives and encouraging theft. When the men obtained cheroots, they usually broke them up and made cigarettes by using newspaper or Bible pages.

Soap was almost unheard of and washing was done by using plenty of elbow grease and water.

Discipline was very strictly enforced and punishments were awarded. Major Hunt carried out this threat and awarded corporal punishment to all whose offences he considered to merit it. The ward master had to mete out this punishment, so when one of the staff committed an offence and was awarded corporal punishment our ward master had the unpleasant duty to carry it out. We were all called out on parade, the charge and judgement was read out, and the offender was ordered to step out in front, drop his trousers and bend forward placing his hands on his knees. He then received fifteen lashes with a stick. He was allowed to dress after this and return to his place on parade.

Many arguments arose regarding this form of punishment. Many held that corporal punishment had been abolished in the British Army years ago, and questioned the right of Major Hunt to revive it. Others said that there was no other effective punishment as men were not in a condition for the ordinary punishments, therefore the shame and humiliation of corporal punishment would have the desired effect and would not injure their health as many other punishments would have done.

I only know of one attempt to escape from Tanaybaya. A fellow was reported missing and a search was made but he couldn't be found. The following day the Nips brought him into camp having caught him at Thanbyuzat. One of our officers was sent for and the Nips explained that the punishment for escaping was death. The officer whispered to the man to act silly and then told the Nips that he had always wandered off, that he was mentally unbalanced and not responsible for his actions and that wandering off was one of his weaknesses. The Nips were impressed by the argument but punished the man by making him stand to attention all day outside the guard-room. He became the cause for much amusement to the Nips and some of them gave him fruit to eat while they enjoyed a laugh, or grinned knowingly.

In October a few of our officers from Sonkurai arrived. They came with Nip sentries to escort Colonel Hinkson back to Sonkurai. He had been in charge at Sonkurai when the eight officers had made the attempted escape and now he was wanted to give evidence. It was rumoured that he might receive punishment if he couldn't prove that he knew nothing about the escape beforehand, and it was hinted that he might be shot for allowing the escape. However, he could only hope for the best.

The officers brought the news of the death of Padre John Foster Haig. This was indeed a blow to us all and he was mourned by all who knew him. The concert party which he had run at Changi was now almost completely wiped out:

Kenneth Scovell (musician and composer) - dead
George Wall (baritone) – dead
Reginald Renison (brilliant pianist) – dead
Aubrey King (tenor) – dead
Dennis East (brilliant violinist) – very ill and his fingers covered with large ulcers.
Cyril Wytchely (pianist) – left at one of the roadside camps while on the march.

And now our Padre, the leader of that little party that had given so much musical entertainment to our men at Changi, was dead. Where would it all end?

The officers brought good news also about the progress of the war. Things were turning our way and reconnaissance planes had been sighted near our camp. They also said that soon we would all be returning to Singapore and many of us thought that it was probably because our troops were advancing into Burma. Rumours to this effect were soon circulating and the excitement radiated throughout the wards. Everyone knew a little more than someone else and in the end, if the tales of some of the patients were taken seriously, we would have believed that we were surrounded by our own troops!

A few days later, a party of Nips started digging in the jungle at the back of our camp and when they had finished we saw that they had made large underground rooms which soon were filled with stores brought to the camp by train. Some even suggested ammunition was being stored in our camp in preparation for the coming battle with our advancing troops and excitement ran high. When bombs were dropped at Thanbyuzat, some of our patients considered we were as good as free.

The bombing of the sidings at Thanbyuzat caused much damage and resulted in a great delay in rail transport. No trains passed through our camp for four or five days with the result that our rations were cut and a party had to go out with the Nips to carry as much food as they could from Thanbyuzat.

The bombing also caused concern for our safety. Our planes were quite likely to attack our camp, not knowing we were imprisoned there, so permission was obtained from the Nips for a large red cross, made of blankets, to be laid out in a clearing in the centre of the camp. If our airmen came over we hoped that they would see the cross and understand that we were here.

One afternoon in early November, Major Hunt announced that he had received a small amount of rock sulphur from the Nips (he had pestered them daily and at last they had got some for him). The sulphur was crushed, mixed with coconut oil and the men in each ward were marched down to the stream where they filed past medical orderlies who scrubbed them raw and smeared them from head to foot with the sulphur and oil. They certainly looked a queer sight covered all over in a yellowish oil, but what a wonderful difference it made in just a short time. Men who hadn't had a complete night's rest for months due to irritation and pain of septic scabies now had peace and were able to sleep. The scabies cleared as if by magic. It was wonderful to be free of that vile infection. During the evenings we were pestered by the noise of a flute or some similar musical instrument played by one of the Nips. He played for hours without stopping. The tune was something like the ones played by Indian snake charmers. It was enough to drive one crazy.

First thing in the morning, the Nips turned out for PT. All their exercise movements were done by number, each man droning out the numbers with emphasis. It sounded like this, '*Oz-yh-oh-uh, oz-yh-yh-huh*' and so on. After exercise, they turned to the east and chanted a prayer to their God and, when that was finished, they ran off parade shouting, laughing and playing like a bunch of small schoolboys.

About the second week in November, we received definite information about the move. The railway was completed and all the men of 'F' Force were to be moved back to Singapore. There were now only a few out of the original 7,000 that were of any use to the Nips for work, and they were needed to care for the sick. The figures that were given was that approximately 2,500 had died. Over 3,000 of the remainder were too ill to do any work, and most of them were expected to die. As we were of no further use, the camps that were occupied by the personnel of 'F' Force were to be cleared.

I was also told that Major Hunt had asked the Nips to allow some of our men to remain at Tanaybaya as they were too ill to be moved. This was granted. So, for a few days, ward masters were busy with the MOs making out lists of those that would move and those who were to remain.

There was one case of two pals, whom the move threatened to separate. One was an Australian and the other an Englishman. They had become mates in the ward and had shared everything and helped each other. The Englishman had very bad skin trouble, which had developed due to lack of proper food. He had become raw all over and was covered with a continuous discharge, seemingly through the very thin skin and raw places. Each morning I had to take away his blanket, which had stuck to him during the night. During his helplessness, his pal, the Australian, cared for him though being ill himself. When lists were made known, it was found that the Australian was to go and his mate to remain. They were very distressed over this and told me of their trouble. They wanted to remain together if possible. I told them that the only way I knew for them to remain together was if the one who was to go on the move was to become worse the night before leaving; he would then be crossed off the list and left behind.

The night before his party was due to leave, the Australian started talking in his sleep. He rolled and turned and appeared to be in a bad way, so the night orderly attended to him and reported the situation to the ward master, who duly crossed him off the list. The Australian was informed that he couldn't leave as now he was too ill. Nevertheless, he kept babbling away with quotations from the Bible and telling God that he was coming. I was rather puzzled over this as I thought that if he was playing a part it was time he packed it up, so I went along to see him and found that it was no pretence at all. He really was in a bad way. He died that night. Fate had played against him and separated him from his pal by death.

The first party moved off on or about 20 November. There was to be no overcrowding in the trucks. Twenty was to be the most to a truck. The trucks were to be of the open, non-roof type this time, so there wouldn't be the suffocating heat as before. Major Hunt went ahead to prepare the camp where it was rumoured we would stop for a short rest before carrying on to Singapore. The camp was at Kamburi, near the camp where I had spent a few days while ill on the second stage of the march.

As the train pulled out, the men sent up a cheer. No doubt they felt good at least to be alive and leaving Tanaybaya. Every remaining fit man had to turn to and help move the remaining patients to wards 4, 5, 6 and 7. From my ward ninety patients were to remain. Five were so ill that it was useless moving them into ward 6, so they were placed together in a row, where they were left to die. One of them, I discovered, was Waple, the man of my Company that had come into the ward at Sonkurai at night off a working party with his feet raw from foot rot. He was now hideously bloated with beriberi and breathing his last.

As I carried my kit out of the hut I gave one glance at the five grotesque forms, and I thought that there lay five men each of whom was loved by someone, and there they lay dying, left in that lonely ward to breathe their last with no one to care about them. In the morning, men would return to the ward to take them to the crematorium. Can anyone imagine a worse or more lonely end?

Jim and I were moving off with the last party. Before we left to go to the railway, we strolled around the wards to bid farewell to some of our old friends whom it was unlikely we would ever see again. We said farewell to one, and he answered 'It's goodbye as I shall soon be dead'. I didn't attempt to disillusion him. Why try to bluff a man who knew he was near the end. He had been one of our best players in the football team at Changi. Not many months ago, we had been cheering him as he scored the goals which won a high position for us in the Changi Prisoner of War League. Now he lay there telling me he would soon be dead. I could only pretend I hadn't heard him. I waved and passed on. Many others we spoke to for the last time. All fine fellows, but now they were almost too weak to shake our hands. I was glad when the ordeal was over and, as we left the last ward, I heaved a sigh of relief. As I moved away, a voice said 'Cheerio, you two, look after yourselves'. It was Johnny Kinch and he was terribly emaciated. Johnny had been the comedian in our little concert party at Changi. It was he who had thrown eggs at the audience. He looked at us and grinned 'Hope you'll have a good journey lads'. He said 'Get a stage rigged up by the time I catch up with you, I'll be thinking up a few gags'. I told him that we would do our best about that. I felt a cold shiver as I passed by.

Next we called on Doc Emery, who was remaining in charge. He shook our hands warmly and wished us luck. Then our Padre Duckworth, who had a grin that hardly ever left his face, and was always to be found where he was needed most, with the sick and ailing. I was told that he had been captured before the fall of Singapore. He had remained with the wounded when the Nips advanced in Malaya and so was captured early in the campaign. He beamed at us, 'So you boys are leaving us'. He took my hand in his and said 'May God's blessings go with you'. And when I took away my hand, I found a dollar note in my palm. I opened my mouth to object, but he stopped me with a gesture and said 'You may need it on your long journey'. He asked me to give his regards to Padre Cordingly who was at Kamburi. He had remained there when we had moved on during the march. Having completed our farewells, we found it was time to parade so we picked up our kit and fell in with the others. We were issued with a meal of rice and stew and also given rice to take with us, as we didn't know where our next meal would come from, or when we would get it.

We then marched up to the side of the railway where we were ordered by the Nips to open our kits and spread them out to be searched. They examined every article minutely. The tin which contained the sealed film in the false bottom was picked up, the lid taken off and examined. I tried not to appear concerned, but inside I was shaking, as I thought that the Nip would be curious about the palm oil of which we hadn't received any since Changi. Fortunately, as there was only a little of it, it had melted a little by the heat, and when the tin was tipped up some oil ran out, the Nip gave a grunt and handed it to me to replace the lid. I was immensely relieved.

We moved to the railway at 7 p.m., expecting a long wait. At 9 p.m. Doc Wolfe, an Anglo-Indian MO, who had assisted Doc Sillman in one of the dysentery wards, came up to have a chat with us. I enquired about the five patients that had been left to die and he told me that two had already died, and an orderly was going to remain in the hut with the other three until they passed away.

The moon came out and I could see the outline of the large rock rising majestically and somewhat menacingly. It seemed to over-shadow the camp. This was indeed a tombstone for the many who had died, their ashes being buried in the jungle cemetery over which the rock loomed so ominously.

Approximately 712 had died in the two and a half months we had been there, ten more dying each night. When I checked the list of dead for men I knew, I found many little parties to which I had belonged were now almost wiped out. Six months ago we had set out full of hope, looking to the future like those who had set out for the promised land centuries before. Our outlook had been bright then, our spirits high. We had laughed and joked. We were leaving Changi and what we considered a miserable time, behind us. But now, with sadly depleted numbers, we were about to start the journey back. God only knows how we that were left had longed for the security and comfort of Changi. We had a long journey ahead of us. Though we were getting used to being dis-illusioned, to tragedy and suffering, we looked longingly for the start. Unable to see into the future, we could only think of the good that we hoped would surely be the outcome of this journey. When the train eventually pulled in at about 1 a.m., we were all ready to forget our dread of the past by thinking and planning for the good times ahead.

We were left with approximately 1,250 men. Of these, 352 were to remain at the camp (staff 102 and patients 250), the remainder travelled on either of the three trains. Our train was the last and when it pulled in, we clambered aboard the trucks excitedly. There were a few of the closed-in type trucks, but the one that my little party was allotted was an open one. We were to be twenty-six to a truck until we arrived at a station further on where more trucks would be added to the train. We were then to be given more room. The train started off with a terrific jerk and we were on our way.

Part Three

Back to Changi and Peace at Last

Chapter Fifteen

By Rail to Kamburi

We were rather cramped but we didn't mind much. We were leaving the jungle at last and returning to Singapore. That was the most important thing. We decided to stretch out and sleep in turns. The men opposite were to sleep first so all on my side drew up their knees and sat hunched up for three hours. Then it was our turn to stretch out, so the others were awakened and we got down to it.

When we awoke the sun was shining down on us. The night had been very cold so the sun was welcome. The train had stopped in a siding at the railhead where we had entrained after the awful lorry ride on the way up. We remained there for twenty-eight hours and were given a meal. We weren't allowed to leave the train so we were not very happy about the journey after a day in that open truck in the blazing sun.

During the day we were confined to the area of the railway siding. The railway became the place used as a convenience with the usual stink and millions of flies. As we were in the open truck the sun which had been so welcome in the morning, became unbearable during the day. Many crawled under the trucks to get away from the rays of the sun, only to find that many of our men had already found that spot had offered a little privacy as a convenience.

When evening came, an engine was heard puffing and clanking in the distance. As it shunted back and coupled up to our train with a clatter and a bang, we scrambled aboard and were off again with a terrific jerk. As we travelled slowly along the jungle track, I leaned over the side to catch what little breeze there was and gazed into the thick, impenetrable jungle on either side of the track. Very tall trees with creepers as thick as the trunk of an English birch hanging from the topmost branches, welded into a profusion of undergrowth which was matted with bamboo and creeping plants of all kinds. I thought of the men who had escaped into that terrible place, and I shivered as I thought of their fate. Just then I noticed two little animals running in the thick grass by the side of the track, making for the cover offered by the jungle. As I got closer I could see that they were tiger cubs. They disappeared into the thick undergrowth, and although I kept my eye on the spot until it passed from sight, in the hope that the mother would show up, nothing happened.

As the sun went down, it began to grow colder and colder and we started to shiver. It was as if the train was on a switchback and we were jerked unmercifully – sleep was out of the question. I noticed that the lad beside me was growing deathly pale. Jim and I had to hold him frequently as he relieved himself over the side of the truck.

It was a relief when daybreak came and the sun came out and began to warm us. Jim and I leaned out of the truck to have a last glimpse of camps 5, 3 and the awful Sonkurai No. 2. We missed a sight of Camp 5 but as we approached Camp 3, we could hear men shouting. As we drew slowly closer we could see a crowd beside the track. Those who could stand rose to shout us a welcome and we were able to hold a short shouted conversation with them. They told us that they had been waiting for a train all night.

We now strained our necks for a sight of that terrible camp, so full of tragic memories for us. We all fell silent as it came into view. Each man was lost in his own thoughts, recalling those months of unremitting toil, acute suffering and sadness at the loss of so many of the best men and friends that one could ever wish for.

As we passed the camp cemetery on the edge of the jungle, our feelings of bitter hatred for our captors and tormentors rose to fever pitch. We all swore silently that one day they would suffer for their evil misdeeds.

We passed through the camp and I looked for the hut in which

I had spent so much time. It was still there but was now a wreck. It looked as dejected and crippled as if it were now suffering as had all those who it had sheltered over the past few months. I turned away, feeling sad and depressed.

We were nearing the bridge and I wondered what the completed structure, that had cost so much in human life was like. Our engine stopped for water before going over it, so the train stretched through the camp. Out of the hut that had been occupied by our officers came a number of Aussies. They were yelling all kinds of good humoured banter, and brought with them a bucket of thick stew, which they passed from truck to truck. We ladled ourselves out a helping and gulped it down, as we were starving. It was over-salted but it was good. The Aussies then brought us buckets of water and we filled our bottles. We had probably eaten their midday and evening meals, but they were the kind of fellows who I am sure were feeling good at being able to live.

Those Aussies were really great guys. They were being kept there to do maintenance on the railway. We did not have long with them as we were on the move again within minutes. As we crossed slowly over the bridge, it creaked and groaned as though it was giving forth the sounds of the torment, sorrow and misery of the men who had died to build it. Within a few hours we had arrived at the big junction at Neiki. Our train backed into a siding and we were told that we were staying for the night.

We were given a meal during the evening. Only our second meal in two days. It was rice and weak pumpkin stew. Jim and I wandered off and found water and soaked ourselves as we were smelling and covered in grime, in addition to much evidence on our clothes and bodies of crushed bugs, the smell of which was always with us. We then made ourselves as comfortable as we could in the tangled undergrowth at the side of the track and near our truck, as we didn't know when the Nips might decide to move off. When the time came, we knew that the noise of the engine would wake us, and that we could scramble quickly onto our truck. So we stretched out and lay down. It was heaven compared with the truck, as here we had as much room to stretch as we liked. It is true that mosquitoes buzzed and made themselves a nuisance, while ants and other insects crawled over us. Hard lumps and fallen branches found tender spots as we put our weight on them or rolled over. However, I was able to stretch out and I was dead tired, so I soon slept. I dimly remember that during the night there was a commotion when one of our men, while walking to a convenient spot, trod on a snake. Then again, when an engine clanked up close to us, we roused and prepared to rush for the trucks, but it passed on and we settled back to sleep, though the crickets with their peculiar creaky noise, coupled with other jungle noises, seemed to do their utmost to keep us awake.

It was barely daylight when Jim shook me and said that a train had pulled into the junction loaded with POWs. I was shivering with cold and decided to get up and walk about to warm up. Jim suggested that we take a look at the other train. So we manoeuvred our way wearily along to where the other train was stopped at the small station. We got there without being seen by the Nip guard and found that the men on the train were all up and about and busy. Sick men were lying about all over the platform, some were dying, some were dead. Others were lying helplessly watching what was going on around them. I saw a man I thought I recognized, so I told him who we were and asked him about his train. He told me that they had come from No. 3 Camp (they were the men who were waiting at the rail side when we passed through). He said that the Nips had ordered complete evacuation of their camp, regardless of the many sick men for whom it would be fatal to move. This, their first stop, had given them the opportunity to check the trucks and see how the sick had stood up to the first stage of the journey. I could see them getting out all the very sick patients, of whom many were amputation cases. They looked deathly white and some were raving in delirium with cerebral malaria. All looked starved, dirty and cold. I saw a man take a blanket off an unconscious stretcher case and put it over one of the amputation cases. I asked him what he was doing, and he brusquely answered that the unconscious man would soon be dead, and would not know that his blanket was taken away. The amputation patient, who now had the blanket, had a chance to pull through if he was kept warm. I passed on speechless, with a last glance at the unconscious man who lay breathing his last, whose nude body was dirty and covered with sores on a crude stretcher which was stinking. I was shivering in the cold, sharp morning air. Thank God that poor fellow could not feel any more.

I was then hailed by a voice I knew quite well – a man of my Company, whose brother had died as a result of tropical ulcers in one of our camps. I was so pleased to see him. He was able to give Jim and me news of many of our old friends who had been at No. 3. He informed us that Old Bob had died there from malaria and beriberi. Though bloated and hideous, he had joked up to the last, telling everyone that he had a marvellous constitution, as he got fat while others got thin. I think that the news of Old Bob's death affected me more than any other. He had always said that when he went it would be his fate, so why worry. 'When my turn comes,' he would say, 'there's nothing to stop it'. His turn had come and I can imagine how he must have been. Full of spirits up to the end and joking all the time. This world is really much emptier for his going.

We were told of many other deaths of men we knew, including that of the little lad who waved to us as we passed through his camp when we were on our way to Tanaybaya, young Pilgrim, our Company office boy. Some men were carrying bodies away for burial and others were getting back into their trucks, so we decided it was time to return to our train. As we passed one of the trucks we heard one man say 'Well, we'll miss them but at least we have more room!'

Jim and I got back to the train just in time to collect our ration of rice and stew for breakfast. By then the sun was up and getting unbearably hot. As there was no sign of any move being made before midday, our OC asked the Nip in charge of the train if he could march us through the camp to the river and this was agreed. We lingered in the cool water for as long as we could but the Nip got tired of waiting for us all too soon and ordered us back to the train.

At about 4 p.m., having been given more rice and stew, we were off again. The line now crossed a series of wooden bridges, each creaking alarmingly as the train crossed it, even though we were moving very slowly. Looking over the side of our truck I could see flowing streams many hundreds of feet below us and numerous trucks which had become derailed and had gone down the ravines to be dashed to pieces upon the rocks below. It all made me feel most uncomfortable.

The following night we pulled into a large junction. It was nearly midnight and we were told that we would stay there for about an hour so permission was obtained for us to send parties for drinking water. It was most noticeable that the Nips were jittery and that air raid precautions were being enforced. We had to keep lights shaded and this made our task of finding the water become very dangerous and difficult. However, after many falls and tumbles, we eventually found the river and filled our containers. The water was brown and muddy but would be boiled at the first opportunity, so we trudged back to the train. On nearing the train, I noticed a procession coming towards us in single file. Their torches of oil-soaked rushes, which were also kept shaded as much as possible, were casting shadows and giving very little illumination. I thought it was another party after water, but found that it was a funeral – or rather they were carrying two bodies to a suitable spot for burial. Just as animals would be buried, a hole was quickly dug and the bodies rolled in, the earth being immediately thrown back into the hole. Although there was no time for the usual prayers, I have no doubt that the dirty sweating men closed their eyes for a moment, as I did, and offered a silent prayer, for those seemingly forgotten souls. I was getting used to death and primitive burials, but now and again a particular death or burial brought a lump to my throat as this one had. Two young men who, not many months ago, were fit and looking to the future with hope, had been buried in a hastily dug grave in the jungle, which would be overgrown in a few days and forgotten. The grave diggers hurried to get away and back to the train as soon as they could from that eerie spot. No doubt the death of these men had been a real nuisance to those who had to bury them, because it meant an added strain on their already overstrained, weak and aching bodies. That is no slur upon the men concerned, because all were ill and few had the strength or will to move out of their stinking trucks. But how tragic that those who died had to be in soon-to-be forgotten, unmarked and overgrown graves having spent their last moments of life in pain and loneliness and then been buried carelessly.

By 2 a.m. we were on our way again. I must have dozed off because, suddenly, I was woken by men shouting and realized that the train was slowing down. The noise of shouting became louder as we came to a stop, so I got to my feet and peered over the side of the truck. Dimly, I could see a crowd of mixed Indians – men, women and children. Some of them were wailing and moaning and all seemed to be jabbering at the same time. The children were crying, and I don't think I have ever seen or heard such abject misery. Then I saw a Nip passing through this crowd, shouting at them to get out of his way. He was hitting out right and left with a long bamboo stick and giving an occasional kick, which only increased the crying and wailing. Eventually, he reached the truck next to ours which was a closed-in box type truck. He struggled and shouted as he wrestled with the locked door, which eventually opened. He shouted something to the Indians who immediately came to life, getting painfully to their feet and hobbling towards the truck. Then, a British voice could be heard, yelling foul abuse to hurry them to the truck. As they passed by an awful stench arose, which I immediately recognized to be coming from ulcers. Many were leaning on sticks as they hobbled, each seeming to be in great pain and finding it difficult to walk, but were nevertheless being urged to move at a faster pace by the Nip with cries of '*speedo, speedo*', followed by the smack of a stick on bare flesh and a pitiful cry from the unfortunate one. Then we heard the British voice, 'Get a move on you bastards,' followed by other foul oaths, and, again, the noise of a stick landing on naked bodies. They were being driven like cattle. They reached the truck, which was about three feet above the ground, and were bundled up into it wailing and crying out in pain.

There must have been at least 100 men, women and children crammed into that truck. How it was done was beyond our understanding for on our journey from Tanaybaya to Sonkurai, in a similar wagon, fifty-four of us, standing up, had been unable to move.

The truck was now so full that some of the Indians were hanging out of the door. Even so, there were still a number of them left standing by the track. The Nip clambered onto our truck and shouted at us to make way for the remaining Indians. Our truck was already overloaded. Many of the sick, some sleeping, took little or no notice of him or did not move quickly enough to please him. He yelled out and jumped down from the side of the truck onto the men below. There was hardly a square inch in the truck that was not covered by the body of a man either sitting or lying down, so the Nip landed on top of them. There was an immediate scramble, and frightened shouts of pain as we all tried to get away from the Nip, who now wielded his stick right and left. He cleared his end of the truck and bunched us up in the other end. The Indians came in and occupied the emptied end, though there were now only half a dozen, the others, no doubt, having found some other place. We were smelling, but these poor devils were stinking and each was nursing a foot, leg or arm very tenderly while omitting hissing noises as if in great pain.

The noise from the truck occupied by the Indians was heartrending to hear. When the train started off with its usual clatter and terrific jerk, the wailing in the truck became a scream as they were no doubt thrown on one another, with some being trampled on. God, what a nightmare! The man who was next to me and was now very ill murmured in a delirious way for us to stop the noise. It sounded like bedlam. As we started off, the man with the British voice jumped aboard. I don't think any man in the truck had the will or spirit at that moment to say anything about how they felt over his behaviour to the Indians. However, he became quite friendly and chatty and when he produced a packet of some kind of native biscuits, we were only too glad to forget the awful feeling of disgust we had for this fellow a few moments before. I think the biscuits were musty, but they tasted wonderful. He told us that he was one of a party of British medical orderlies, who had been left at the Indian Camp to care for the sick. This party were very bad ulcer cases, unfit for work, and were being taken to a camp further south, where they would most likely die.

We got very little sleep that night. Our general misery was deepened by a piece of typical Nip brutality. The train had stopped at a small jungle station where a particularly officious Nip seemed determined to keep the vile prisoners off his pristine platform and drove us all back into our trucks when we got out to stretch our aching limbs and backs. One poor lad was subjected to the most terrible beating for dropping a banana skin on the sacred platform. The Nip raved at him, striking him the most cruel blows with his bamboo stick until the man fell, whereupon he was then subjected to a series of ferocious kicks. Two brave men stepped forward and picked up the half-conscious figure and helped him back into the truck. It was one more beating which we swore would be avenged when the time was opportune.

As we sat in that siding, a Nip troop train came through, the soldiers sitting in open trucks like ours. One truck was full of Geisha girls, chatting happily away as if they hadn't a care in the world, although I believe that they had a terrible time from the Nips they had to 'entertain'. It looked as if they had been forbidden to take any notice of us, although we could see a few sly glances coming our way.

At last we moved off, only to halt about a mile down the track for the train to refuel from one of the many woodpiles alongside the track. We were allowed to get out to stretch our legs for a bit, so Jim and I started a fire upon which to boil some water. Very soon, some Indians, who were in a terrible state, came along to beg for water. The Nips also came round with the Indians' daily ration – one biscuit. Goodness knows, we were getting a poor enough deal but theirs was far, far worse.

Suddenly, we heard a Nip voice calling us in good English. A young man and his companion were occupying a truck loaded with medical stores. He came across to our fire and I noticed, to my utter surprise, that he was carrying a copy of the *Oxford Book of English Verse*. The only other copy I had ever seen had belonged to my dear friend Ken Scovell, who would never be parted from it, even on the march, when so much kit was being thrown away to lighten loads. When I remarked on this, the Nip said it was his favourite book and he took it everywhere with him. In our subsequent conversation, I soon realized that he was no better than any of our foul Nip guards – truly oriental, bestial and cruel. How strange that two men who were so utterly different in character, the one a monster and the other English, inoffensive, gentle, kind and wise, should have both loved the same book. The rest of the journey was completed in misery. The Nips wanted still more room so we had to vacate our truck, and were divided into three parties of nine. Each party of nine was crushed into one of the three other trucks occupied by our men. I'll never forget the last stage of that journey. I was now in a closed truck with just enough room to sit down, trying to sleep with knees cramped up under my chin. Men were quarrelling and shouting at each other

235

when they tried to stretch limbs and invariably kicked someone, probably injuring an ulcer or tender spot. Then I developed dysentery again, with all the misery of having to rush to the door more times than I care to think about. I couldn't help trampling on men who shouted abuse about making the door in time so that there wouldn't be a mess in the truck and perhaps on them. This all went on in the dark, with the wailing of the Indians in the trucks behind and me being held hanging over the side of the truck. I couldn't imagine Hell being worse.

During one of the last days, I had one of my bouts and had just been pulled in from hanging over the side of the truck when I heard shouting and looking around I saw a gang of POWs standing at the side of the track, waving and shouting to us. Among them I recognized many of our men who had left Singapore with the early parties, among them Ronny Budd who had been a batman with me in our Company Officers' Mess in England and Singapore.

Of the rest of the journey I remember very little. We had been six days and nights on a journey of about 280 miles with an average of one meal a day. On the last morning, I felt a little stronger. I hadn't had to run during the last few hours and I was sitting up, looking out of the doorway when, in the distance, I saw on the track a crowd of men. I told the others in the truck and they all craned out their necks to see what was going on. The train slowed up and stopped. The men on the track were our men and they had been waiting for our train. This was Kamburi hospital camp and they were shouting a welcome. At the head of them was Padre Cordingly and many others whom I knew. They were there to take off all hospital cases. Fit men were to remain on the train and go further on to the fit camp. I was advised to get off the train and go into the hospital camp, but I declined as it would have meant being separated from many close friends. I decided to take a chance at the fit camp. When the very sick men had been taken off, we proceeded to Kamburi Station, where we were instructed to get off the train and line up in the station yard.

Strutting about the station were many Japanese civilians in the uniform of high-ranking officers. These men held administrative posts under the Nips. What surprised me was that our guards didn't salute them. Soon we were told to pick up our kits and we started marching. At the end of the first mile we were given a rest and at the end of the second mile we were at the fit camp.

The road and the country seemed vaguely familiar to me, but I couldn't think very clearly, being rather distressed. The starvation diet and dysentery had left me very weak and I was now on the point of collapse again.

Chapter Sixteen

Kamburi

We were told to dump our kits and rest. This I did and lay down in the shade of the protruding roofs of a hut. Many of the men already at the camp came out to welcome us. They were the remnants of 'H' Force, and men who had arrived earlier from Tanaybaya and No. 2, Sonkurai. Suddenly, someone grasped my shoulder from behind. I turned around to find Gordon Gleeson's smiling face. We clutched each other and laughed with pleasure at our reunion. He offered Jim and I six hard-boiled eggs. We scoffed these down and agreed that we had never tasted anything like it. It was the first real food we had had in months. Gordon informed us that this was a camp of good food and plenty of it, with a canteen where we could purchase almost anything if we had the money. But very few had money!

Soon we were called to receive our first meal. It was pork stew. We could hardly believe our eyes. There were lumps of fat pork floating at the top of the rich stew. We each received one pint of stew and a pint of rice. It was a feed I shall never forget. It was so tasty. We had been so long without tasty food that I wouldn't have believed that food could taste so good. Then we were shown our sleeping places. These gave us just enough room to allow us to roll over. But we could stretch out and that night I slept, even though the rough ground made bumps into my back through my thin groundsheet and dropped away where I needed support. When the men sleeping above moved, they disturbed bugs, which dropped down on us below. But sleep soon came and I remembered no more until the next morning. The breakfast awaiting us was boiled rice, served out as a wet clammy mess, like porridge, and a mug of tea without milk or sugar. Nevertheless, the meal was good, and I thought that if the food remained like that we would be all right. We had no work to do as yet. The men of 'H' Force were preparing to leave for Singapore, and I was told that we would only be staying for a short time, before we also had to move on. But I felt that I had had enough of trains and was quite prepared to rest in this camp of plenty as long as they wished to keep us here. Jim and I decided to take a look around the camp and we met many old friends. As we walked about we noticed a very healthy smell coming from the direction of the officers' tents, so we decided to walk in that direction.

We found that there were fires outside each tent and men were busy cooking for the officers. One was cooking an omelette made up of ten eggs. When we enquired, we were told that the officer felt hungry so had ordered the omelette with ten eggs. There were many men passing and looking on, many hadn't tasted an egg for months and hadn't had any decent food (apart from the meals at this camp) for ages. Now there was food to be bought and those with money could feed well, so the officers were indeed feeding well, and the starved men passed by looking longingly at ten egg omelettes!

Beyond the officers' tents, about fifty yards away, was the building that I thought I knew when I entered this camp. Now, as I could see it more clearly, I recognized the camp at which I had stopped when on my way up country.

I was told by some 'H' Force lads that the men we had left behind there when we went on marching were still there. That meant that Captain Wadesley, and some men of my old Company must still be there. I determined to find out and crept up to the hedge and through it. I waited for the Nip sentry to turn his back, then scrambled through the fence into the officers' quarters of this other camp. There I found Major Rogers, the MO who had tended me on my short stay there, and Captain Wadesley, who seemed as delighted to see me as I was to see him. He told me that he had heard that I had died months before, and so I was back from the dead. After showing me around the camp, when the Nip wasn't looking, he helped me safely over the fence. As I left him, he put two dollars in my pocket.

I had been in the camp about one week when 'H' Force departed for Singapore. Owing to this departure the staff at the hospital camp was reduced in number, so volunteers were asked for. Jim and I volunteered and prepared to leave, so we made a round of our pals to inform them that we were going to the hospital. The last man I spoke to was Bill Wainwright, one of the men who had made the perilous journey through the jungle to the broken down lorry for food from Sonkurai, and as we said cheerio, he said 'See you at Changi soon,' and away we went on still another move.

It was an hour's march to the hospital camp and when we got there we were all placed in a staff hut and were told that we would be paid for our work, ten cents a day for privates and fifteen cents a day for NCOs.

The food in the camp was good. Meat and vegetable stew with plenty of rice, sometimes sweet rice and sometimes an egg and fried rissoles.

In the camp was an operating theatre and although medical supplies weren't plentiful, there was enough, if used sparingly. There was a canteen where, if one had the money to spend, one could buy fruit, peanut toffee, peanuts, coconuts, eggs, sago and rice flour, sweet potatoes, pig oil, salt, sugar and pepper. This was wonderful and I could hardly believe my good luck. A fortnight earlier we had been starving and now we were having as much as we could eat, with a small wage and a well stocked canteen.

This was a large camp. I would estimate that we had about 200 staff of mixed nationalities; Australians, British, Eurasians, Anglo-Indians and Dutch. We had plenty of freedom to move about the camp and we could do our own private cooking on communal fires situated between the huts. Each person using the fire would contribute a little firewood. Many enterprising men started businesses of their own, making small rissoles and chips or boiling or frying our eggs for 5 cents, or selling mugs of coffee, unsweetened for 5 cents, sweetened 10 cents. These enterprising men carried their wares through the wards and did a good trade. The sick were put on special diets and a special cookhouse catered for them. Tasty dishes were made to tempt them to eat but, regardless of the fact that we had better food, better conditions and better medical service, the death rate remained appallingly high.

Unlike Sonkurai or Tanaybaya, a funeral was held daily in this camp. The Padre started at the far end of the camp and, as he passed each hut, any dead would be brought out, the bearers joining the cortège.

One day, very much to my surprise, I saw a funeral for a single man. Then I noticed that the bearers were all wearing pads over their noses and I realized that the dead man had obviously died of some very dangerous disease. I learned later from the Padre that the funeral had been Bill Wainwright's. On the very day that he had shouted out to me with such confidence that he would see me in Changi, he had gone down with smallpox.

We had plenty of work on the wards but also plenty of staff to handle it. No longer did we have fires in the wards at night to give us light, we now had hurricane lamps.

For entertainment, concerts, lectures and talks were given in the huts and a few Welshmen got together and went round the wards singing Welsh folk songs.

We were still settling in when an order arrived for all the sick who could travel and most of the fit men to move back to Singapore. My great pal, Gordon Gleeson, came up from the fit camp, having chosen to stay with me.

Jim, Gordon and I volunteered to stay and look after the sick who were being left behind. We were told that we too would be returning to Singapore quite soon.

About a week before Christmas, just after the Singapore party had left, I was sent off, at a moment's notice, with a lorry load of RAMC lads to help prepare the fit camp to receive our residual sick, who were to be moved there in a few days time.

The camp had been left in a shocking state and to make matters worse, what was left of the kit that had been left at Bampong by us when we left for the march, had now been dumped in a pile with cases smashed and the contents all over the place. We started off by trying to tidy up the mess. I didn't find any of my kit but found quite a lot belonging to men that I knew. One thing I saw that made me very bitter was a case, with the contents strewn about, containing no less than six jars of Marmite. Marmite which had arrived by Red Cross ship in the early days at Changi and was issued to the very sick and malnutrition cases only. An officer's case containing Marmite could only mean one thing. I thought

241

again of the officer who had said 'Every man for himself'. Clearly, some meant to look after themselves even at the cost of the sick.

The camp was cleaned up and the only hut made ready for the sick. We were issued with tents which we put up ready for the incoming men. While doing this, we worked near the Camp Commandant's hut where someone was trying to get a station on the radio set. We all stopped work when we heard the voice we knew so well. It was Churchill – just a sentence – then it was shut off. We didn't hear what was said but it did us good to hear the voice. It made us feel that home wasn't so far away after all.

We wondered if the patients would be down in our camp by Christmas, which was now getting very near. Then the Nips decided on a quick move and a lorry was kept going all day and well into the night moving the other camp personnel in. We had an almost impossible job to find places for the patients, but managed to cram them in somehow. When the main body of men arrived they set to building huts and in a short time everybody had a roof over them and plenty of room.

An Australian Captain was made Camp Commandant and Lieutenant Wakabayashi was the Japanese officer in charge of the camp. Our officers seemed pleased that this Japanese officer was in charge, as he had been found to be a reasonable man. Our Captain had apparently made an impression on him at sometime or other and was able to get things for us that we would other-wise have had to do without.

Many patients died as a result of the move. I remember having to carry them to their bed spaces and remaining on duty throughout the night. I walked up and down the hut occasionally, raising my lamp to see that the patients were all right. Two men seemed to be in the same awkward position each time I passed by, so I jumped up to take a closer look. Both were dead. One was the man who had travelled in my truck from Tanaybaya and who I noticed was becoming very ill.

How life had changed for us! It was a wonderful surprise when fifty ducks were given to us for Christmas, together with a free issue of fruit and cigars. We felt on top of the world. A few of the men had been left to look after the isolation cases in the hospital camp and looked like getting a meatless Christmas. Luckily, a flock of goats was driven through our camp. By the time they reached the far end, two were missing! Nobody was caught and the lads had their Christmas dinner!

We had a Midnight Service in our little Church on Christmas Eve and a Communion Service on Christmas Day, which was rounded off with an open air concert. Some of the Nips, who were drunk, joined in with an exhibition of wild dancing which we thought would never end!

Very soon after Christmas we started getting visits from the RAF which caused us great excitement. The planes passed over quite low, almost every night. A few ack-ack guns opened up on the first few nights, but when the Nips realized how useless their efforts were, they stopped firing. Bangkok seemed to be the target and there were reports of native riots because of the devastation caused by our bombs.

It was indeed a wonderful sight to see those planes flying over in the moonlight. The Nips were scared stiff, even though our planes always passed us. Little one-man pits were dug in the ground and as soon as the warning sounded, out they dashed from their huts, diving into their little holes in the ground after what seemed like a super-human effort to reach them.

During those raids, they became very panicky and very strict with us. They wouldn't allow a glimmer of light anywhere and it became difficult in the wards when handling very sick patients during a long air raid.

Our greatly improved way of life in Kamburi went on pretty peacefully although there were, inevitably, occasional incidents. How well I remember the Australian who kept asking me for an early call. One day I asked him about this and, to my astonishment, he told me, quite frankly, that he and one of the Nips, whom he had befriended, would slip out of camp to sleep with a couple of native girls! To my surprise, he never got VD!

Screams from the Nip quarters were fairly common. One night, a drunken group had dragged in a wretched native woman, who tried to escape. Her subsequent screams were terrible. God knows what fiendish torture she was being put through.

On another night, we heard similar screams and yells for help in English, together with the sounds of a fearful struggle. We never discovered what had occurred but I felt sure that some prisoner had been caught, either trying to escape or returning from some escapade like the Australian's with the two girls.

Then there was the fearsome scene when a drunken Nip was heard screaming abuse outside the Nip Lieutenant's quarter. He was dragged away by his friends to their hut, closely pursued by the Lieutenant, armed with a heavy stick with which, after a further altercation, he proceeded to beat the daylights out of the offender. I was fifty yards away and the sounds of stick on flesh and the man's cries of pain were blood-curdling. He was on the sick list for over a week.

After 'H' Force had left for Changi, the camp, adjoining the one in which Captain Wadesley had been staying, was used as a rest camp for Nip infantry. Small companies, while marching north to Burma, stopped at the camp either for the night or, perhaps, for two or three nights. During their stay they spent their time rehearsing their war song. Their buglers practised all day and reminded me of boy scout bands. The continuous bugle calls became very irritating.

Other disturbing noises at night were the howling animals in the mountain ranges around us and the drums which were beating regularly every night. I could hear their drumming roll in the hills, as it seemed to be picked up and re-drummed further on. Crickets and frogs and queer night birds all added to those night sounds.

One night, while doing my rounds and answering to the regular demands of my patients, I fancied I saw a glow in the sky so, at the first opportunity, I went outside to investigate. On the hillside, where the bush was very thick, there was a large fire. What seemed very strange, was the fact that the fire took the shape of a large 'E'. Later, when the fire was dying out, our planes came over for another heavy raid on Bangkok.

A few nights later the drums seemed busier than ever and, around midnight, fire started in the hills. This time there were two distinct fires which slowly took the shape of 'SW' and it struck me that it might be a signal for aircraft and might mean 'South-West' and the 'E' might have meant 'East'. That night the planes came again. Thereafter I often noticed that when the fires appeared, so did our planes.

One day the Nips went all jolly. Japanese Red Cross parcels had arrived for them and all that afternoon and evening they played about with their new toys. Each had received tin whistles, rattles, coloured lanterns and many other toys which we would consider suitable for young children. They were delighted with their presents and proceeded to get drunk. The delivery of the Red Cross parcels was an occasion for celebration but it ended up with them fighting over their toys!

One evening some of the younger Nips joined our men in a ball game and this breakthrough quickly developed into quite a degree of fraternization, with Nips even coming into our huts trying to chat with the lads. However, this was soon stamped on by their seniors and all forms of fraternization forbidden. Yet the friendly attitude remained, although they could never be trusted.

I've seen a Nip knock down one of our men for no apparent reason and, hours later, come searching for him to give him a cigarette. They were very temperamental and would rise to a ferocious temper for the least thing. I was surprised to see their cowardice during air raids, after hearing so much about their fanaticism. We came to realize that they didn't want to risk their lives any more than we did.

They always seemed childish and primitive in their behaviour and ready to copy western culture, though they made a pretence of scorn at our ways. They were very cruel, losing no opportunity to torture and seemed to get much amusement out of seeing anyone suffer, while being cowardly about pain themselves. It was quite usual to see them maltreating wild animals which they had captured, presumably just for the pleasure of inflicting pain. The poor creatures would then be left to die.

Towards the end of January we were informed that the men we had left behind at Tanaybaya were on their way down to Kamburi. We had to prepare a place for them and get ready to receive some pretty bad cases. During the short period we had been in the camp our men had been busy and four long huts had been built which made room for all. The electric motor that had been brought up from Changi with us in April was found and brought into camp. Our electrician fixed it up and, with wire and fittings from the Nips, we had electric light in the huts and wards, which was indeed a luxury.

When the Tanaybaya party arrived on 2 February 1944, we were all ready for them. The condition of many of them was shocking though they had come through in pretty good time, taking about two days to do the journey. There were many missing. I looked around in vain for many old friends and acquaintances. When I met my old Staff Sergeant, he gave me the tragic figures. Of the ninety patients that had been left in No. 3 ward, twenty-seven survived. Out of the 250 patients we had left at Tanaybaya, 122 came to Kamburi. The rest had died. Four amputation patients arrived, the only survivors of the forty-four amputation cases. The toll of the railway in deaths was going up and up. The Nips would have a lot to answer for one day. With the Tanaybaya party was Padre Duckworth whom we all welcomed warmly. He was soon in harness and going on his rounds cheering the men. He shared the little church, which had been built out of spare bits of bamboo and atap, with Padre Cordingly. We started a church choir and sang anthems at our services, with the Nip bugler in the next camp doing his best to drown out our singing.

One of the patients from Tanaybaya was an RASC Major. I suggested to him the possibility of organizing a little gathering of the surviving RASC men from 'F' Force, to which he enthusiastically agreed. We managed to assemble twenty-two RASC members, including Doc Emery and the Major himself. That was all we could muster out of a total of 280 who had left Changi in April 1943. A few had already left for Singapore but not many.

We pooled our money and came up with a wonderful meal, after which both Doc and the Major gave little talks before we dispersed. It had been a great success and we all hoped that it would only be the first of many more reunions to come.

At about that time the camp was struck by a violent storm, like a cyclone. Under the terrific winds, the huts groaned and creaked as we hung on grimly to stop them blowing over. The air was full of debris and large pieces of roofing were blowing all over the place, soaring high in the air and then coming to earth with a great crash.

After about an hour, the winds died down only to be followed by torrential rain which soaked all those who were lying under the great gaps in our roofing made by the winds.

Next day, the surrounding countryside looked a real mess with so many things lifted by the wind and blown about. Trees had fallen and tangled up with the wreckage. Men who had lived in this part of the world before, said that it was a common occurrence and was known as a Sumatra.

During February and March the heat became intense; the noonday temperatures reaching about 140 degrees in the sun and 112 in the shade. Our wells began to dry up and water for the cookhouse had to be fetched in a lorry, driven by one of our men, from the river. There he met several other drivers from other camps and through them we were able to exchange news.

During that hot weather we were allowed a daily bathing parade. Every man who was able to walk the two miles to the river went along for a good wash and a swim. The bathing place was the one we had used when we passed through on the terrible death march and the same natives, with their stalls of good things to eat, were still there. The problem was money. As before, the lads began to sell small items to the natives, using the same surreptitious methods and, at first, the Nips failed to spot what was happening. However, they soon realized that there was much more money being spent both there and in the camp canteen than the pittance we received from them would have allowed. A snap check at which we all had to empty our pockets and small packs, revealed all and the items for sale were confiscated with the threat that any further dealings with the natives would lead to the end of our swimming.

We found that we could send letters through the other drivers at the water point to friends in their camps. Another snap check yielded two letters written by Padre Cordingley and Dr Wolfe. These two were handcuffed together and put in an open air raid trench for several days and nights, living on plain rice and water.

The lads were determined to help them. A note was dropped into the trench, when the sentry was not looking, telling them to ask to go to the latrine at a certain time. The sentry duly escorted them there and remained outside. Inside, they found the writers of the note with good things to eat! The sentry apparently failed to notice how much happier his two prisoners were looking when they emerged!

Men who had witnessed corporal punishment strongly resented it though were unable to suggest any alternative in the circumstances. A very unpleasant affair arose out of the only case we had at Kamburi.

247

The crime committed was pretty serious. We were extremely short of quinine and further supplies were very doubtful. The greatest care and economy were being exercised and double signatures were necessary to obtain any quinine from the dispensary. So when a full bottle was missing from one of the wards, a short time after it had been issued, it wasn't difficult to pin down the theft to a particular man. A search was made of his kit. He had been a bit uneasy about things and later admitted throwing the bottle down the latrine.

He was awarded corporal punishment and the men were very resentful. The general feeling was that the man should indeed be given a good hiding, for he had committed an unforgivable and selfish crime. However, to punish him in front of all the men of the camp would mean that the Nips would be there to enjoy the fun, as fun it would be to them. As we had suffered so much from Nip beatings, it was unthinkable to let them see us beating one of our own men. When we had been paraded and formed in a square, all facing towards the centre, the prisoner was led out, the charge was read and the award stated. The two officers detailed to carry out the punishment then stepped forward. As they, very sheepishly, took up positions and picked up the prepared canes, almost every man turned about. The Sergeant Major frantically ordered the men to face their front again. Instead, a general move was made towards the huts. It was mutiny. As the men moved off, they started cat-calling, some Australians shouted, 'If that is English justice, then may the bastard Pommies bust'. A few others took up the cry about British justice, until one of our men pointed out that it was an Australian, Major Hunt, who had introduced corporal punishment at Tanaybaya, and that an Australian Captain was Camp Commandant.

This argument threatened to develop into something ugly, as already Australians and British were taking sides. But their attention was diverted when the whack of the first stroke of the cane was heard. The officers had laid down the canes but another officer had picked one up again and proceeded to carry out the sentence.

Next day each Company apologized while on parade. Even so, the whole camp was punished. The canteen was closed for a week, bathing parties were stopped and several other little punishments were inflicted which were very annoying.

I am convinced that the men would have stuck it out despite their resentment if it hadn't been for the fact that a couple of Nips, one of them being the Nip in charge of the Camp, appeared on the scene with ugly grins which were developing into evil smiles of extreme satisfaction. However, instead of witnessing a painful punishment, they saw the Allied POWs show complete loathing and resentment by turning their backs and walking away.

During the few months we stayed at Kamburi we received the best food and better consideration than at any other time in the whole of the three-and-a-half years we were prisoners of war. We were hardly ever interfered with, we made our own entertainment and hardly a day passed without some form of entertainment being held in the wards – a quiz, concert, sing-song, talk or lecture. Regular bathing parties and swimming and diving competitions were held in the river almost every Sunday afternoon.

The death rate was decreasing and I am sure that the reason was the expert medical attention and food that the patients received. There were eggs – in some cases patients received as many as twelve eggs a day – bananas, ground peanuts, rice polishings and special diets for special cases. Extras for patients were paid for out of canteen profits.

We were at liberty to cook for ourselves on our own fires and the many things we bought from the canteen often made very appetizing dishes. The coffee kings had been kept busy and did a good trade, but they were making rotten coffee. Jim, Jack (a young Ordnance Sergeant we had befriended) and I decided that we would go into business together. This was in the early days at Kamburi and we thought that if we made a good mug of coffee and made a small profit, we had a reasonable chance of re-capturing the market. So we set about it and worked out that to make a four-gallon tin of hot coffee we would spend one dollar on coffee and sugar. By selling it at 5 cents a pint we could make 60 cents profit. If we did this daily we'd make $4.20 a week which would buy a lot of things like sugar, peanuts, fruit and eggs. The opposition sold their coffee at 5 cents unsweetened and 10 cents for sweetened, so we soon found that we could sell five four-gallon tins a day. We had captured the market all right.

We soon realized that there was great scope for expansion into cooking good things to eat. By this time, even the officers had a twice-nightly standing order for Jim's wonderful coffee – the secret of which was that he added a teaspoonful of salt to each 4 gallon tin. When the sugar was then added to that, the result was delicious.

We decided to have a six hour night shift. I would be responsible for the fire and for keeping the water boiling. Jack and I would do the cooking and Jim would be our salesman. We needed an oven. Jim found an old iron box and with this and a few old sheets of zinc, to make a chimney, we set up a reasonably good oven in a little trench.

Jack was an expert rissole maker, so we started with these at 5 cents. They were an immediate success, so we followed up with some special cookies, which included a poached egg, at 15 cents.

From there things really took off. I experimented with bread and a cake, both of which proved very popular. At 5 cents our banana fritters were best-sellers.

An unforgettable highlight was the pig in which we were able to buy a share through the canteen. Gordon, being a butcher by trade, killed and cut it up, making sure that we got a nice piece!

Our oven was heated up and we got to work to make the dinner of our lives.

When the pork started sizzling, we danced with joy and the noise of splashing fat made us feel like attacking the oven. The smell was wonderful. We had to keep pushing the boys away and they laughingly begged to be allowed to remain, if only to keep sniffing, and to hear the crackling and sizzling.

When everything was cooked and the meat ready to carve we had little need to shout 'Come and get it'. Many times, as I shared it out, I had to strike at impatient fingers and all the time listen to a lot of good natured hilarity. There is nothing like knowing dinner is on the stove to make a man content. When I finally poured on the thick-looking gravy they all wanted to marry me. Anyway, they soon became too busy to talk. The dinner was one I shall never forget. We hadn't had a feed like it since leaving home over two years before.

Our little gang also catered for birthdays or celebrations and free gifts of food and coffee to the very sick and those who didn't have any means. Also, when our oven was in use, we invited the patients to put in anything they wished to cook.

Our crowning feed came when Gordon and I, whose birthdays were only two days apart, threw a party. We had a gargantuan meal for which I had made a pie that I called 'Jungle Mystery'. After everyone had eaten to capacity and was almost helpless, cheroots were produced and in clouds of smoke, each one voted the feed as the best ever. Sighing with satisfaction, we laid back and dozed.

It had been a wonderful meal and if we could have done it every day we would most certainly have put on weight rapidly, but as it was, food was pretty good in the camp. For breakfast – boiled rice and crushed peanuts, for dinner – rice and vegetable stew, and in the evening – rice rissoles or tart and stew, so it can be well understood that we put on weight and regained a little of what we had lost in the jungle.

Very soon orders were received that we were to prepare to move back to Singapore, as we were the remnants of 'H' and 'F' Forces. As we had plenty of warning we prepared things for the comfort of the patients on the journey. Double tiered bed frames were made and measured for four to a truck. A lorry was allowed to convey them to the station.

Our gang was kept busy for two days prior to the move, making loaf cakes for the men; twenty-four were made. The oven was kept going well into each night. Then the day came; 24 April 1944, exactly a year after leaving Changi, we were now to return. The tragic happenings that had taken place during those twelve months hardly bear thinking about, but happen they did and one day the Nips will have to show a balance sheet for the Death Railway, with its cost in human life. We must insist then on the account being settled in full.

Before we left, we held a service in our little cemetery. Those who were able attended, and the little cemetery became over-crowded. Our choir led the hymn singing and our Padre, after offering up a prayer for those who lay to rest in this foreign soil, so far away from their homes, asked that the relatives might have God's blessing during the suffering and grief that would follow the news of the death of their dear ones now lying here. His voice echoed hollowly in the surrounding jungle as he recited the words of that very impressive verse from Laurence Binyan's *For the Fallen* to the silent, bowed, bare-headed, half-naked men:

They shall grow not old, as we that are left grow old:
Age shall not weary them, nor the years condemn.
At the going down of the sun and in the morning
We will remember them.

When the little service was over I thought of that last line, 'We will remember them'. I vowed that I would never forget, and I am sure that all who went through the agony on that railway will say that they will remember them. But what about the people at home? How many even know about the railway? How many who know are sufficiently interested to give it even a passing thought and how many are there who will say that they have heard so much about atrocities that they do not wish to hear any more about them, or desire to forget? But I know people who, with broken hearts, will never forget, for whom a day rarely passes without shedding a silent tear for the loss of a loved one who can never be replaced in their hearts. THEY WILL REMEMBER THEM! And for their sakes, perhaps, others more fortunate might spare a kind thought for, and be charitable to, heartbroken mothers, wives and children. Be patient to the demented, soul-seared and disease stricken men when they return to civilization from this hellish experience. They will need all the patience and understanding that can be spared them.

Chapter Seventeen

Singapore Again

Grief grows old
Time plays its gentle part –
Laying healing hands upon the red wounds of the heart,
The secret scars grow fainter with the passing of the years,
Faith returns and Joy comes back to wipe away our tears.
Gleams of sunlight steal in at the windows of the mind.
Hope revives – the future beckons.
Life has something sweet to offer.
Grey skies turn to gold.
Memories remain, but sorrows and grief grows old.

Patience Strong

We left Kamburi for Singapore on 28 April 1944. The train journey was quite a pleasure outing compared with the other train journeys. Fruit stalls lined the track at each stop and we were allowed to buy. Officers in charge of the trucks had been given cash to spend on fruit for the men. We were given fruit to take with us and between the food we prepared for ourselves, the fruit and food issued, and that which we could buy, we felt on top of the world. There was ample room to lie down and the sick had beds of sorts to lie on.

Each day many trains passed us going north, loaded to capacity with troops. At one station we stopped opposite a stationary train with carriages, the nearest of which contained officers of the Free

Indian Air Force. One grinned knowingly at us. They were fighting for the Nips. I felt rather sorry for these people who, in many cases, were being forced to fight. One was reading a magazine and, looking our way, he raised his book so that we could see his fingers behind it, while it was hidden from the others in his compartment. He was giving us the 'V' sign.

The rest of the journey passed off quite uneventfully. We were getting quite excited as we neared Singapore. We felt that to be there again meant security. There would be a hospital and a well administered camp, a place to sleep with a measure of comfort and many other things to which we could look forward after the up-country camps of terrible sickness, primitive hospitals, poor sanitation, little comfort and daily uncertainty. At Kamburi there had always remained with us the fear that if we became fit enough we might be sent back to the jungle camps to maintain the railway, so the further we got away from Thailand the easier we felt.

As we neared Singapore there was many a sigh, mixed feelings and great hope for the future. I stretched my neck in an effort to catch sight of the island as we passed through Jahore Bahru. Some of our bedridden patients had had to give up their bamboo beds for the hard truck floor. The hurriedly made frames of bamboo had stood up to the journey very well but the sacking that had been used for mattresses had given way in many cases. So the patients, now lying on the hard floor, struggled up into a sitting position when the first shout went up that we were nearing the causeway. To get back to Singapore, though very ill, meant a new lease of life to those fellows. The horrors of the jungle and railway, to which they had almost succumbed, were now left well behind and everything seemed bright for the future.

As the train drew up slowly in Singapore station, a convoy of trucks driven by Sikhs of the Indian Free Army arrived outside. They were for us. We soon had our kit stowed and had helped the sick on board before we clambered up and settled down.

As we drove through the city, we wondered where we were being taken. Changi? No, it was Selarang, the place we had dubbed 'The Black Hole of Singapore'. But this was a very different Selarang to the one in which we had suffered such hell for three days.

The first surprise was the immaculate sentry on the gate from the Provost Company. With razor sharp creases in his KD shorts, gleaming brasses and shining boots and, most noticeable of all, a clean skin. Not a sign of sores or ulcers.

What was this? I wondered if the war had ended while we were on the journey. Had we entered an alien world? Soon men came out of clean looking buildings and shouted greetings to us. The houses were surrounded by gardens filled with beautiful tropical flowers and vegetables. The houses in some cases had been owned by very prosperous people but now housed chiefly British and Australian officers. They waved to us and suddenly I realized how we must look to them. I glanced around at our crowd and myself, stinking after having been confined to the hot trucks for so long, clothes dirty through continuous sweat, which the dirt and dust of the truck had adhered to and remained caked in places. Our hair was unkempt and long, our faces dirty and with a good growth of beard. We must have presented a sight that would keep everyone at a distance. These men who looked so clean, soft and smug seemed to be saying, by their look and grin, 'More unlucky devils from the Railway, but more mouths to feed'. I heard later that my guess wasn't far wrong. The officers and men who had never left Changi since the capitulation, and who were considered very lucky, had been moved from the old Camp at Changi to Selarang. There they had a garden, chickens, ducks, and had devised many ways to supplement their rations. They had been here doing routine jobs in and around the camp waiting for release. I didn't envy them their luck, but what I resented was the officers' very superior air, as if they had pulled off something by remaining at Singapore, and were now condescending to have us back.

We were pitied and many watched from a distance as we unloaded in the barrack square, where the latrines had been in the days of the Black Hole. Men came forward to help us. Orderlies came with stretchers for the sick, and others gathered around at a safe distance to see us. I looked for faces I might know and then I saw a man who had been through the campaign in France and Dunkirk with me. We had then spent a few months together in the East, in fact he was Fred Jackson, the man who had driven the lorry that towed me to safety in France during the incident with Jock Campbell. Now he waved in answer to my shout but I could see that he didn't recognize me and I am sure that in our state we must have been very hard to recognize.

We were told that there was no room in the buildings for us and accommodation would have to be found elsewhere. The very sick were taken into the hospital, and we were led into the shade of one of the large buildings, where I was told that a meal would be prepared for us. But, after many hours waiting, an officer told me that of the many cookhouses in the area, none of them wanted the job of cooking for us. One of the difficulties was that that day's rations were already drawn and any food given us would be that much short for the men, so we waited while the people responsible walked about looking very important, clean, smart and cool. Eventually we were given a meal and then we were told that we would have to collect tents from the camp stores and put them up ourselves. It was late that night when we finally settled down. As soon as we had settled in, we made a dash for the showers. There I stayed for a full thirty minutes, scrubbing myself and pummelling my clothes, trying to get the dirt out of them. We were in a new world, there was no sign of death here. Everything was clean. The air was cleaner. We were going to live again.

The following morning, I was up early and under the cold shower straight away. I was up in time to see the sun rising. This was a great day with so much to be done and seen. But I was in for a disappointment for, when we had finished our breakfast, we were told that we were not to leave our little area for a day or so as we were expected to be on call when required. So the day was spent in lolling about. We were brought American Red Cross parcels, one parcel between seven men. One's share was little but very welcome and the contents of tinned butter, milk, chocolate, and other goodies were wonderful. That evening we were given tickets to attend a gangster play given by the men of one of the small areas. It was indeed a tip top performance, as good as many I have seen in theatres at home.

I couldn't help comparing the life in this camp with the one we had recently left. Things seemed very good though food was short and we were to get a cut in our rations. Our rice was to be supplemented with maize (Indian corn). The maize was ground up and made into rissoles, which weren't too bad. After a short period on that diet many had relapses of diarrhoea and some found themselves covered in boils. All RASC personnel were brought to our little area, and other units were made up of their respective personnel. Work parties were detailed to a large aerodrome which was being made over the area where we had been housed before going up country. Southern area, India Lines, and part of the hospital area were already part of the aerodrome and now our men were put to work on making it larger. Shift work was introduced, though our men from up country were not to be used as yet. However, many who had come down in December were being used. I found that I was no longer required for hospital work. It seemed that there were plenty of RAMC men now available, so I remained with my unit. When our period of quarantine was over, we were able to wander about the Selarang area. The blocks of buildings that had housed us during the Black Hole period were now used as a hospital and housing for hospital staff. The Padang, where we had put up our tents was now covered to capacity with tents. When our unit had also moved over it left very little room to walk about. Very nice houses with tropical gardens dotted the whole area of Selarang and when we passed by I saw officers sitting back in easy chairs, smoking and reading. I thought, 'Some of these people are having the time of their lives'. They were probably thinking they had had it rough. Our Colonel, who was living somewhere in the area, in one of the houses, hadn't even found time to visit us. The men remarked that he didn't seem to care if any of our unit had survived, which they resented bitterly.

I met many old friends and told them about the tragedy of 'F' and 'H' Forces. We soon found, from their looks of incredulity, that they could not believe our stories of horror and torture. If they, who knew the Nip for what he was, could not believe us, how could we expect our own people at home to do so?

We heard that Mr Anthony Eden had broadcast a warning to the Nips and threatened reprisals. I also learned that Colonel Dillon had been asked to write a report for the higher level Nips, who claimed to have no knowledge of what had been going on. He was to make recommendations for improvements to the treatment of the POWs. Apparently, although I, for one, did not notice it, the Nips were much better for some time after his report had been received.

*   *   *

We found time hanging pretty heavily on our hands in Selarang. There were many administrative restrictions on us and we longed for something to do. At last our quarantine was up and a medical inspection was held to sort us out in categories for work. The fittest would work on the aerodrome and the rest of us were detailed for gardening or camp duties.

About a week later, orders were issued to evacuate Selarang. We were to move to Changi jail as the Nips wanted Selarang to house their Air Staff and an aircraft maintenance workshop. All our trailers were mustered for the biggest move we had ever made.

Our move, once started, was kept up from early morning until late at night. All available officers and men were used. I, being in rather poor shape, was given the job of steering a trailer. So while a team of officers tugged and pulled, sweated and swore I sat on the trailer and steered. Officers ranging from Colonels to Lieutenants were pulling my trailer which was loaded to capacity with hut partitions. Every hut had been pulled down and moved to the jail area and within a month the whole area was cleared. The engineers received the hut partitions which had been numbered by the demolishers, and put them up as they arrived.

The foundations had been prepared by a special gang and they did a seemingly impossible job. Once the camp had been moved, the population of more than 17,000 men was housed in the jail area in about four weeks, including the hospital and patients. Fit and semi-fit men were housed in the jail itself and the sick, hospital staff and officers were housed in the hastily erected huts in the adjoining area. During the first journeys by trailer from Selarang, I saw the jail occupants peering at us through the bars of the upper floors. They were women internees and were waving excitedly when they saw us. We were as enthusiastic as they were, not having seen English women in years. They had been shut up in this jail since the time the Nips took over. Women occupied one end of the jail and men the other. Some husbands and wives, fathers and daughters, brothers and sisters, separated by a thin concrete wall and rarely, if ever, during the years of imprisonment were they allowed to see each other.

As we waved back vigorously to those brave, starving women, I saw a board being held up to the bars of a cell. On it a message was scrawled in chalk asking if we had news of two named men.

I knew, at once, that they had both been patients of mine in Sonkurai, but I had not the heart to indicate that they had died, so shook my head. Then came another board saying, 'Thanks. May God bless you'. I was deeply touched. A week later the civilians were all moved to an open camp at Sime road.

Chapter Eighteen

In Changi Jail

When we arrived at Changi jail on 10 May 1944, we found many messages scratched on the walls of cells telling us to keep our chins up, wishing us luck and telling us to have courage. Many names were also on the walls of those who had resided there. A large party had arrived from Singapore and settled in before our arrival. To my delight I found that it was the party which had left Kamburi before Christmas. My old pal Gordon Davies, who had assisted me on the march, and John Hawkins, the 'Little Old Man' of Sonkurai were among them and many RASC lads of my old Company. But my spirits were somewhat dampened when I found Tara in charge. However, Tara was a changed man, quiet and morose. He no longer had the life in him that he used to have. I couldn't account for it, unless his up-country experiences had had this effect on him.

We were very overcrowded. Each cell was made for one prisoner. In the centre was a large concrete block with a concrete pillar (large enough for one man to lie on). Each side of the block was a space about 2 feet wide to the wall. So one man occupied the block, one man in the spaces on either side of the block and one man across the bottom at the foot of the three, making four to a cell. The corridors were also used at night for sleeping men who had to lie lengthways along the corridor, leaving enough room for us to pass to and fro. Then, in the centre between the two rows of cells, was a wire mesh, placed there to stop prisoners jumping down between the floors if they were suicide-minded and to allow air circulation. This was also used as bed space and men lay side by side on this wire mesh, obstructing air circulation and making it very stuffy. However, it was the best billet I had had under the Japanese – four strong walls and a non-leaking roof. Once settled in, we were soon organized into some sort of order and units were kept together. The RASC was housed in the north block on the first and second floor C.1 and C.2, and there we lived under Tara for nearly twelve months.

Working parties were soon detailed, chiefly for the aerodrome, where three shifts were being worked. Large new areas were opened up for a big garden and we were warned by the Japanese that we must hurry and grow all we could, as it was getting more and more difficult to get food to us and the garden produce would be required to supplement our rations. So all men able to walk were given a job. Men classed as fit worked on the drome, semi-fit on the garden and unfit did camp maintenance. The jail became like an ants' nest with the men so crowded that when we moved about we rubbed shoulders and jostled each other. All cooking was done at the central cookhouse and no private cooking was allowed. In the cookhouse, they cooked meals for approximately 7,000 men where normally 700 were cooked for. Rice was steamed in such large quantities that bath tubs, taken from war damaged houses, were used as containers. When an ingredient was added to the rice, it was done in the tub and shovels were used to stir it, like mixing cement.

For entertainment, we had concert parties, mock parliaments, plays, pantomimes, housey-housey and the societies flourished again. Our churches held regular services and organized lectures were given by experts on medical, sex and educational subjects. Confirmation and biblical classes were held with choir practice and hymn singing. Days, weeks, and now years had passed as we were wasting away in captivity, and we often thanked God for the people in our midst who had the gift to entertain. They made our lives bearable. When a concert party gave a show it would run for about six weeks so that all could see it. Even with all these diversions offered each evening, men became despondent as time went on and soon gangs began thieving again. There were rackets in food and clothes, both very precious commodities. Stolen clothes were taken out by the men on the working parties and sold to the natives. The money was then used to buy food. So, to

261

combat the thieving, an officer was put in charge of our regimental police and soon became known as 'Desperate Dan'. During the last year of our captivity this man and his sleuths nosed into every corner, listened at doorways and in corridors and became 'Gestapo-like' in their tactics. A small building was allotted for detention and there men were placed in solitary confinement or imprisoned on restricted rations for periods of up to thirty days or more. The innocent were indeed made to suffer for the guilty. What the thieves had started, now became a burden to us all. If we took a little walk around the jail wall we rarely completed it without being stopped and questioned or searched. Morning working parties were searched before departing and on arrival back at the jail. Every new rule or law made by our Camp Commandant was rigidly enforced. We were crowded together and were making the best of a bad situation which was made much worse when we saw some of our friends marched off by Desperate Dan's hirelings to trials that, in many cases, seemed farcical. The accused was very seldom guilty but to the accusers, accusation was the same as guilt and many an innocent man became a victim of Dan's fancy. The sentences awarded seemed ridiculous for the crime: the culprit would perhaps be placed on short rations when we knew that the fellow needed all he could get. Soon the men were seething and muttering and many men committed offences merely to show their indignation.

However, as time went on and discipline stiffened, the men eventually seemed to become apathetic and took whatever came their way, knowing that little could be done about it anyway. Each man did his job by day and spent his evening either resting or at one of the entertainments provided within the jail.

I was delighted to find that the Welsh Society, which we had founded as The Cymrodorians in 1942 in Changi, had gone from strength to strength. Now that letters from home were coming much more frequently, the members of the Society had decided to pool home news and publish a news-sheet from time to time. This was manna from Heaven to us who had, for so long, been starved of news from the outside world though our homes and loved ones were never far from our minds.

I had joined a garden working party when I arrived in Changi and helped to clear all the plants from the garden at Selarang. Everything had to be taken. Everything edible went to the cook-house and the other plants were transported to our new gardens.

Most of the plants for transplanting were being taken to an area given to us by the Nips down by the sea. In the area right on the sea-front was what had been a beautiful house with the surrounding garden now derelict and overgrown. We were going to use this place as our nursery. When we arrived there with trailers loaded we found the gate closed and on the pillar was the name Brighton House. After depositing our load, we were given permission by the Nip guard to have a swim in the sea. This was the beginning of many visits to Brighton House for swimming and whenever there was a swimming parade allowed, the men always referred to it as 'a visit to Brighton'. It was during one of the visits to Brighton that one of our men, known as Andy had a very narrow escape from a horrible death. There were some very good swimmers in our crowd, and many liked to show what they could do. Some challenged others to a race. Five officers and about a dozen men dived into the sea together to see who could swim out to a post just visible above the water about 100 yards out and get back first. Andy was soon in the lead. On arriving at the post, he tried a quick turn around. He grabbed the post with a view to pulling himself around when he let out a scream and disappeared. The officers following behind him, realizing something was wrong, went to his assistance and a great struggle ensued. They brought Andy to the surface, more dead than alive, after they had torn him from the tentacles of a small octopus. It had seized Andy when he placed his hands on the post and had drawn him under. The rescuers were particularly brave as they didn't know what they had to contend with. Andy survived the experience but had a very bad arm for quite a long time.

It was soon after that incident that my garden party was transferred to another area. Rubber trees were being cleared up by our forestry party to make space for extending the gardens. It was our job to follow the forestry party, prepare the ground, and plant tapioca trees. This was a very interesting procedure. The tapioca tree grows to about 4–5 feet high with four or more stalks. The stalks are cut from the root and then cut into 9 inch lengths. Each length is stuck into the ground and in nine months it becomes a full grown tapioca tree with some very good edible roots. When cropped, they are boiled, like potatoes, and used as a vegetable or as a substitute for flour to make pastry.

Our life in the garden was happy. We were doing a useful job, providing food, and it was taking our minds off unpleasant things while learning much about plant life in the tropics. I would say that the seasons here are a gardener's dream, for the weather is the same all the year around. We used to plant a green called biam. In three weeks time it was fit to crop and about 2 feet 6 inches to 3 feet high. We cropped it to about 6 inches and in three weeks it was fit to crop again. We did this four times, then pulled up the roots and put in young plants. This went on throughout the year, except that we occasionally changed the ground, putting sweet potato cuttings in after pulling up the greens. Sweet potatoes are very slow croppers but the stalk and leaves grow along the ground, like marrows at home, so stalk and leaves were cropped as an additional green vegetable. When the greens were cooked not a bit was wasted, every scrap went into the cooking pot including the stalks. This applied to any foods at the cookhouse, even bananas were put in the vegetable stews, skin and all. We couldn't afford to waste a scrap as our rations were so meagre.

During my stay with the garden party I had some very interesting jobs. Being a medical orderly, I had been given a few dressings, antiseptics and so forth to carry with me for first aid treatment in the garden. I carried these in my little bag which I still kept with a few other medical necessities. One day, while I was working on the garden, the Nip guard came to me and told me that he wanted me to go with him to see a sick friend of his. I first saw my officer, Lieutenant Van der Gucht, who said 'Carry on, let me know when you get back'.

During the Nip occupation there were virtually no medical facilities or medicines available for the civilian population of Singapore. The Nips' attitude was that if people fell ill and died, that was just too bad. It didn't take me long to realize that I was going to be passed off as a British doctor and that the Nip was going to make a very good thing out of bringing me to people's aid.

And so it proved to be the case. That first visit, the first of many, was to a Tamil with a very bad leg ulcer caused by a brutal kick from a Nip soldier. The Tamil's Indian wife was overwhelmingly grateful and insisted on my having a drink of Singapore Toddy, a lethal concoction made from fermented coconut milk. After I had seen her husband and done what I could for him, we left. The Nip was staggering under a huge load of fruit and vegetables. I too was staggering, thanks to the Toddy, and carrying the Nip's rifle! After several more visits, the Tamil was well enough to hobble back to work.

That was the first of many cases for all of which the Nip was well paid for my services in kind. I sometimes got a big pack of expensive American cigarettes which I shared with the lads. For my part, I was glad to be able to put all I had learned in the jungle hospitals to good use and to help those poor people, who were pathetically grateful.

During that time, some exciting things began to happen. We learned of the brilliant success of the Allied Forces in North Africa and later of the downfall of Mussolini and the Italian capitulation. We eagerly awaited news of success in Europe, for we felt that without that there would be little hope of a major campaign in our part of the world – we knew very little about the dogged progress of the XIVth Army in Burma. Then, on 5 November, the Americans launched their first air attack on Singapore. As the B29s, the Super Fortresses, passed overhead, we cheered like men possessed. They looked wonderful as they pounded the docks, destroying many important godowns. We returned to jail that night bursting with excitement. This must surely be the beginning of the end and our release not far off. In the event, it would be nine months before that happy day dawned.

Meanwhile, the Nips were getting very jumpy and many restrictions were being rigidly enforced. Concerts and other entertainments were stopped and, worst of all, we went shorter than ever of food, because of the destruction of the Nips' reserve stocks in the bombing. From 5 November never a day went by without us seeing Allied aircraft.

During the evenings we organized quiet talks, quizzes and so on. We were lucky enough to have some world famous sportsmen in our midst – Wilf Wooler, the Welsh rugby and cricket international, Barnett, the Australian Test wicket keeper, our very good friend, Padre Duckworth, cox of the Cambridge and British Olympic rowing eights and Bob Skeene, rated fourth in the world as a polo player. There were many other distinguished men; lawyers, former Members of Parliament and men of learning. All contributed so much to our evenings.

Not long before Christmas, I went into hospital because the left side of my stomach was swelling up after every evening meal. I was put on a diet and placed under observation. My problem was diagnosed as beriberi. The muscles on the right side of my stomach had become paralysed, so my food was being pushed out to the left, producing those swellings, pain and wind around my heart.

I was soon discharged for light duties, and returned to the jail where I found that more and more working parties were being called for by the Nips so that only a very few men were being left behind. However, the usual working party dodgers were there, certain warrant officers and senior NCOs, who had administrative jobs. They detailed sick men for working parties, saying that they couldn't go themselves as someone had to do the administration. I had a certificate stating that I was to do light work only but my floor sergeant, who was of very good physique, decided that I should do drome work. This work was very heavy and under pretty brutal Nips. I pointed out that I wasn't fit for this kind of work and showed the sergeant my certificate. He said he wasn't interested in the certificate. He was a man short for tomorrow's drome party and I would have to go. So I turned out at 6 a.m. next day, drew my three-quarters of a pint of pap for breakfast (pap was watery boiled rice) and joined the party parading outside the jail. As we lined up, my old MO from Sonkurai, Major Handbury, came forward and spoke to me, remarking upon my appearance and enquiring about my health. I told him of my complaint and that I had just been discharged from the hospital. He told me to return to my billet and told the Sergeant that he wanted fit men, or at least not men that would be likely to drop on the march to the drome. I saw many sick men being sent out on working parties and I know that the so-called administrative NCOs could well have taken their places.

The food at this time was very poor and not nearly enough for hard-working men. Half a pint of pap for breakfast, half a pint of water taken from the boiling greens was one's lunch and the evening meal was three-quarters of a pint of boiled rice and a pasty made from sweet potato and tapioca root pastry, with vegetables inside. This pasty was dropped into boiling palm oil until cooked. Sometimes we would have two dessert spoons of fried whitebait, or a small salted fish, followed by a small sweet tart, made of the same pastry as the pasty, and half a pint of tea, unsweetened with no milk. We had a rota of names for men to have a share of what food was left over. There was a different rota for every meal, and the men watched them keenly. They called it the 'Back Up' and talked about it all day. As it was run alphabetically, men were always enquiring about what letter 'Back Up' was now on.

The buzz was now going the rounds that the Allies had invaded Europe and speculation was rife about how much longer we would have to wait for release. In May we heard the wonderful news of the German collapse. The Nips grew more restless and difficult than ever. Through one of our guards, who was learning English, we came to realize that they were all well aware that the end could not be far off for them. Nevertheless, work on the drome was pushed on harder and harder. In addition, various defence works were started and the Nips were demanding nearly 100 per cent attendance for work, sick or fit.

On 1 June, some 2,000 of us were marched to a camp known as No. 12 Camp Changi, to build roads and dig anti-tank ditches and funk holes. A Major Ford was our new Commandant.

I was in the anti-tank ditch digging party and we were marched off about three miles to start work in a swamp. The trench was to be 15 feet wide and 10 feet deep. The work of digging the heavy wet soil was enough to make the strongest of us curl up and we soon began to bring stretchers with us so that we could carry home the men who collapsed at work or on the march back to camp. We looked wearily at our planes as they came over and we wondered if we would last long enough. Would our Forces come in time? Was this toil and anguish ever to end? Our working parties were getting smaller and smaller while our little hospital got fuller each day. I got my lot after only a fortnight's work. We had been slogging at the trench and I felt I could not lift another shovelful. I still had dysentery and was very thin, weighing only 7 stones 10 pounds. We were all losing weight rapidly and everyone seemed done in.

On a day when the Nips in charge were particularly nasty, I had an unfortunate fall. I was trying to dislodge my shovel with its load of wet clay and I was over my knees in filthy sludge, when I slipped on a stone just as the Nip guard was approaching to give me a prod with his bamboo cane. I fell awkwardly while struggling with the shovel and a pain like a red hot needle shot across my chest. The pain was so intense that I was unable to stand up again. The Nip then called two of our men to get me out of the trench. I lay down in the bushes until the work for the day was over. The lads helped me to my feet and I managed to walk back to camp unassisted. I was put on my bed and the Doctor visited me there. He examined me and told me that my work at the camp was at an end and that I was to remain on my bed for a few days. I was then given a camp job as messenger for the Major. I saw the work parties move off each morning and watched them return each night. I looked anxiously for the number carried in on stretchers and reported the particulars to the office. After a gruelling day digging a funk hole or ditch, the men, now emaciated, drawn, ill and hungry, returned to a meal of boiled rice and vegetables. We all knew that it couldn't go on for long.

Some men raided gardens when out on working parties and risked being beaten up by the Nips if caught. Some of the vegetables or coconuts they got by such raids were brought back into camp and boiled or cooked over little fires made in between the huts. I am sure that that stolen food was the means of keeping most of the men going. Walter House, one of my friends, who had worked with me on the ditch party and with whom I had shared the spoils of our raids, now saw to it that I had half of anything he brought back in the way of food. I was very fortunate in my friends. Albert Knight, one of my patients at Kamburi, who had been invited to join in our cooking venture when very frail and weak, and who had recovered sufficiently to go out on the working party, now saw to it that I had a little of any food he managed to scrounge. I'll never forget the wonderful comradeship and kindness. That extra food helped to keep me going during the weeks prior to our release when rations were so very poor. Those left in camp, as I was, were allowed just two thirds of the issue of the workers.

We were cut off from the jail, but had many means of contact. Notes were thrown over the wall and replies received the same way. During July and early August 1945, news seemed to be dead. We had heard that our Forces were moving down through Burma and that the Americans had occupied the Philippines. There were rumours that a large convoy was near Malaya with Lord Louis Mountbatten in command. We were cheered by this news and felt determined to hang on now that we felt so sure that the end was near. When we attended Divine Service, Padre Noel Duckworth led us in praying that our release would come soon, and for the strength to last that long.

Chapter Nineteen

How Peace Came to Changi

August came and I thought of England on Bank Holiday and wondered how everyone at home felt to be free; free from war and its horrors and of the awful flying bombs that we had heard so much about; free to come and go as they pleased, and no blackout. What a wonderful feeling. I was deep in reverie when the siren wailed out its warning, and overhead I saw a grand sight – about a dozen planes, all flying low – the first Lockheed P47s I had seen. One broke away from the formation and swooped low over the camp. I had no fear of it and stood out looking up as if there was no danger. The formation passed over and I knew now for sure that our Forces weren't far away, because these were fighters.

At long last the wonderful news, that we had so long awaited, came to us – in a most extraordinary way. I had got up early on 12 August because I could not sleep and met one of our Regimental policemen who had been on duty during the night. He told me that at about 4 a.m. he had gone to investigate a noise in the barbed wire and had suddenly heard an English voice saying, 'Take this message to your Major. Tell him the war is over. The Japanese Emperor has surrendered.'

I shot off to tell my mates. They were incredulous. They wanted to believe me but were afraid to do so because we had had so many tales and so many disappointments in the past. We knew we'd soon find out whether or not this one was true. Meanwhile the terrible work parties remained.

My heart ached for those men, who were hanging on grimly, working like slaves, starving and now enduring heavy beatings from the Nips as they got weaker and less able to do the work. This went on for five days and each day we were getting more and more confirmation of the surrender. Our Major spoke to the men each morning before they left on working parties. He begged them to be careful and not allow themselves to be provoked in any way, to annoy the Nips. He begged them not to give the Nips any hint that we had had any news, because he was convinced that the guards knew nothing as yet. So I watched those poor lads go out each day, and prayed that when they returned I could meet them and tell them that there would be no more work parties. My prayer was answered on 16 August, when I saw the orders being typed for the following day. The order ended with the information that no more working parties would be required and that the following day would be a camp holiday.

I met our lads when they returned to camp and gave them the good news. They were overjoyed but too weary and tired to indulge in much rejoicing. Late into that night they lay talking and speculating. I have never seen men so elated, trying to keep calm but unable to sleep or even lie still with the excitement that was almost making them ill. Saturday, the 17th, was spent cleaning ourselves up as best we could and taking walks about the camp. To our great delight the Nips brought us extra rations. Then, on the following day, they brought us Red Cross rations. They had been holding and using them for themselves but had now decided that we should have all they could give us. Lorry after lorry arrived with food and comforts. No words can describe our joy. This was proof indeed that, at last, it was all over. We were issued with sugar and we made tea just so that we might taste sweet tea again. That night many of us regretted taking so much of it, because we were terribly sick. In the days that followed, most of us couldn't touch the extra food issued to us. It seemed as though the sugar had poisoned us. We were ill and the food we had longed for for so long was within reach but none of us was well enough to take it. When we started to eat again, we had to take our food in small quantities. Even so, it lay like lead on our stomachs.

On the 19th, we received instructions that the Nips required us to be moved into the jail, so we packed such kit as we still had and moved back, back to our unit and old pals. Some men in the jail were crying with excitement but the Nips had made no official announcement. Nip guards still patrolled outside the jail and among them was Ono, the Nip of my garden days. On our first night in the jail I was roused by a single shot being fired. Next day I learned that Ono had shot himself.

I moved into the jail cookhouse as hygiene orderly. I was then billeted with Gordon Gleeson, my friend from Changi and up country. We decided to try to stick together until the end.

The end wasn't far off. On the 28th a shout went up throughout the jail that a large plane was approaching from the north. There was a mad scramble to get on to the roof, up steps that could only take one at a time. I got up these in time to see a Liberator that was flying very low and was a wonderful sight. Thousands of pamphlets were being dropped, instructing the Nip guards to return to their respective units.

By this time the Japanese had intimated that the war was over and allowed their engineers to fix up a large transmitting and receiving set in the jail. We eagerly awaited its completion to hear news from the outside world again.

On the 30th, in came more Liberators, para-dropping more food and medical supplies. They also dropped six men, two RAF officers, two infantry officers and two RAMC medical orderlies. These were the reconnaissance party from Ceylon who were to provide the information needed by the follow-up force. From then, airdropping was a daily occurrence.

On 2 September the wireless that the Nips had provided boomed forth for the first time and we were able to hear our first radio programme from home, via India of course, since 15 February 1942.

On 3 September, six years after the declaration of war, we held a grand ceremony. All our senior officers gathered on the tower of the jail, the Japanese flag was brought down, and the flags of Great Britain, America and Holland were raised. There was a deathlike silence amongst the crowded men below. I had expected loud and long cheering, but there was only a little clapping and a small cheer.

On the following day we saw something that no man who was there will ever forget. As we crowded onto the roof of the jail, we saw the British Fleet come up over the horizon and enter the Singapore roads.

272

Then began a continuous stream of visitors including many high ranking officers. Lord Louis Mountbatten, accompanied by his wife, was with us, as was General Slim and Admiral Power. Lord Louis gathered us around him and gave us a wonderful talk, telling us of the magnificent achievements of the Allied troops and air forces in Burma. He told us that top priority was being given to getting us home, starting with the sick. There was a shortage of shipping but we would soon be on our way.

On 7 September I attended a Thanksgiving Service at our little church in a courtyard of the jail and the Bishop of Singapore (Bishop Leonard) attended, to confirm some of our men.

When I look back in my mind and think of that period it is with very mixed feelings. The happenings seem to be jumbled up. The excitement and freedom were so strange. We were like children. We couldn't settle down to anything, we didn't know what to do, we couldn't rest. Everything became disorganized and we had to keep to the jail area, with the Nip guards still doing guard duty. Soon the Nips were taken away and placed under guard by the Indian troops who came with the relieving force. Though many of our men wanted to take revenge on them, the Indian guard was there to see that they weren't interfered with. I had expected to see many attacks on them but I didn't hear of one. I, myself, had vowed vengeance but, when the chance came, I found I couldn't inflict injury in cold blood on unarmed, cringing cowards. It is against the nature of the average Briton to kick a man when he is down, so they were left to be brought to trial for their sadistic offences and we hoped that justice would be done.

On 12 September, our Padre, the Reverend Noel Duckworth, was asked to give a brief account of the Death Railway to the people at home, so he broadcast one over the transmitter now installed in the jail. He had written his text and had it typed. He presented me with a copy with a parting message, which I consider the finest compliment ever paid me, and the best reward I could have wished for, for any little thing that I had done for our men as a medical orderly or for the church.

Gordon and I visited Singapore City and went on to the docks and met many of our sailors who wanted to know all about our captivity. They took us aboard their ship, the aircraft carrier HMS *Activity* and gave us our first European meal – bread and butter, pickled onions, cheese, fruit and cream, with cups of tea – a feed I shall never forget. We brought away a loaf of bread and some butter. We were late leaving, so the First Lieutenant gave us a note explaining where we had been. Another night, we stayed on HMS *Nelson*. The crews of both ships couldn't do enough for us. They were grand fellows.

Then came the great day – 26 September 1945. We were told to get our things together as we were moving out of the jail and would embark that evening. We simply jumped and hopped in our jubilation. All our old clothes, boots, tin cans, and so on were piled in the courtyard for a big fire. But the natives, hearing about the move, came in their hundreds and swarmed all over the jail. Piles of rubbish were soon cleared as they scavenged everywhere. I was busy with my last pack when a letter was handed to me. I tore it open feverishly for news from home. All my jubilation faded away as I read that my dear Mother had passed away in 1943. This was a blow indeed – I left my pals to their packing so that I could give vent to my grief in private. However, I wasn't allowed long as we were ordered out to the waiting lorries. The boys quickly found out my trouble and, after sympathizing, set to cheer me up again. Soon they had me laughing as we were being whisked away from Changi jail. One last look around to see it disappear from view and soon we were at the docks.

There, at the dockside, was our ship, the good old MS *Sobieski*. The ship in which we left England was now going to return us there. The Captain was the same man who had wished us luck on our great adventure. Now he would see us through to the end of it. We clambered aboard and were shown our sleeping spaces. From then on we felt on top of the world. The best of food, piles of vitamin tablets, first class medical attention, entertainment and comfort. On 27 September, six years after I had landed at Brest with the BEF, I was looking over the side of the *Sobieski* and Singapore was disappearing in the distance. As we made our way up the Malacca Straits I thought of the future and of my mates around me. What did the future hold for us all? I was thinking this when a dark brown object floated by. It was the body of a man in brown overalls. Many others saw it and shouted the information but our ship didn't stop, and I thought of the tragedy, and the tragedy that would soon be made of some of these men's lives.

When we entered the ports of Colombo, Suez, Port Said and Gibraltar, we took our mail from home and sent off cablegrams. The different information received filled men with joy or sorrow and changed some men from jubilation to misery. There was information about births and deaths, of unfaithful wives and sweethearts. It seemed that these men who had gone through hell and survived might now give way to the misery caused by news they had received.

Fortunately we had plenty of entertainment, and it helped in some cases to take men's thoughts away from whatever was their grief. Finally we came to Liverpool. I will never forget the cheering at the first sight of land, the rugged coast of Land's End. This was home again – the wonderful welcome at Liverpool, the crowds that greeted us, and the Mayor reading out the message from HM the King – then the struggle down the gangway, the meeting of mothers, wives, families and friends and the train journey home after hand clasps and farewells with pals and mates. I arrived at about midnight – a Red Cross van had picked me up in London and brought me to my front door. The joy of being reunited with my wife and grown family is now like a wonderful dream. There followed medical boards and a period at a Civil Resettlement Camp and, though failing to convince the doctor that I was fit for my pre-war job, my employers took me back and gave me light duty.

And so I find myself at Wye, writing the finish to this story, and feeling much better for the telling. It is now past and gone, and has become but a memory. The only time it is likely to become real again is when I meet up with my old pals, John Hawkins (the Little Old Man of Sonkurai), who is now in St Dunstans losing his sight, Sergeant Jack Swales ('Jack' of Kamburi), who is in a military hospital with tuberculosis of the spine and my good friend Gwyn Williams, whom I had last seen in Bampong and who later lost a leg when our planes bombed the Non-Ploduct Camp. That friendship had started in England and picked up again in Changi. And, of course, there are all those who are patients in mental homes, hospitals and sanatoria, who I hope to be able to see once more.

For none of us will the war ever really be over.

Epilogue

Idris James Barwick returned home to Maidstone in Kent and was reunited with his wife Ruby, daughters Isobel and Anne, and son Bob. He wrote *In the Shadow of Death* as he recuperated from the effects of his captivity. Idris was very active in advocating for veterans and helped found FEPOW (Far East Prisoners of War Association). Following the death of Ruby he moved to the United States in the late 1950s. In 1961 he married Barbara Oberdorfer and raised a second family in Ohio – David, Elizabeth and Bill. He died at the age of sixty-eight from heart disease – a direct result of the beriberi and other ailments he contracted while a prisoner of the Japanese.

If he were alive today, he would ask that we:

Remember all the fine young men who died in far off lands and all the veterans who must live with their memories.

Elizabeth Barwick Garland

Appendix

Letter, dated 25 October 1945, from the War Office advising that
Idris Barwick, previously a POW, had been released and was with
Allied forces. Idris had left Singapore in September 1945.

ELECTRA HOUSE,
VICTORIA EMBANKMENT,
LONDON, W.C. 2.

Dear Sir or Madam,

It is a great pleasure to me to be able to send you the enclosed telegram from your relative who is now liberated from the Japanese.

In order to relieve your anxiety at the earliest possible moment this message has been transmitted free of charge by Cable and Wireless Ltd. from the Far East, in co-operation with the War Office.

In the same way we shall be happy to send your reply free, if you will write it - using about 12 words in addition to the address - on the enclosed form and hand it in at your local Cable and Wireless Office or any Post Office where telegrams are normally accepted.

Will you please insert on the reply-paid form the address given in the enclosed telegram and sign it with your surname.

With best wishes,
I remain,
Yours sincerely,

Edward Wilshaw

Chairman.

A letter from the chairman of Cable and Wireless that accompanied the first letter from Idris Barwick to his family after his release.

BUCKINGHAM PALACE

The Queen and I bid you a very warm welcome home.

Through all the great trials and sufferings which you have undergone at the hands of the Japanese, you and your comrades have been constantly in our thoughts. We know from the accounts we have already received how heavy those sufferings have been. We know also that these have been endured by you with the highest courage.

We mourn with you the deaths of so many of your gallant comrades.

With all our hearts, we hope that your return from captivity will bring you and your families a full measure of happiness, which you may long enjoy together.

George R.I

September 1945.

Letter from HM King George VI welcoming Idris Barwick
on his return home.

Index